Winston L. King

A THOUSAND LIVES AWAY

Buddhism in Contemporary Burma

By the same author:

Buddhism and Christianity
In the Hope of Nibbana

Winston L. King

A THOUSAND LIVES AWAY

Buddhism in Contemporary Burma

HARVARD UNIVERSITY PRESS

Cambridge, Massachusetts

1964

©

Winston L. King

1964

Printed in Great Britain

PREFACE

THE THEME OF THIS BOOK IS THE CONTEMPORARY SITUATION of Buddhism in Burma. It has often been observed that Burmese Buddhism is composed of many heterogeneous elements. Dr. King is the first to demonstrate, in a way which strikes me as positively brilliant, that they all form one organic unity, from the quest for Nirvana to the worship of Pagodas and Nats. His further study of the tensions within this organism and the tendencies of its future development break entirely new ground. These tensions are produced partly by the impact of Christianity, modern science and European social ideals. The author discusses, better than anyone before him, the often debated problem of how far the Buddha can be described as a "saviour", and his remarks on Buddhist cosmology are remarkably penetrating. The other source of conflict is the latent struggle between monks, laymen and *gaings* (non-orthodox, magically orientated sects). This involves such problems as the "fundamentalism" of the monks, the nature of the social ideals proffered by the *gaings*, and the new developments in meditational technique initiated by laymen.

A rare combination of talents is necessary to produce something of value on these subjects, and the author has them all. He has a good acquaintance with Buddhist Hinayana literature, an easy familiarity with Western thought, is interested in ideas, has lived in the country, and has no axe to grind. All other publications on Burmese Buddhism I have seen are marred by the absence of one or more of these qualifications. Considering the intricacy of the problems involved, it is astonishing to find that the author never makes a false step, even where this could well be expected, and his exquisite sensitivity, tact and empathy preserve him from the usual crudities and distortions.

The book is not only sound, but will interest many. *Students of Buddhism* have always been concerned about the discrepancies between the Buddhism of European Pali scholars and the actual Buddhism of Burma. *Students of religion* will be glad to learn how one of the religions attempts to adapt itself to the modern world. *Students of Asia* will want to know how the Burmese Buddhists try to assimilate European ideas without losing their own identity. *Christians*, and those brought up in the Christian tradition, may learn how close the Burmese attitude to the Buddha sometimes comes to the Christian attitude to Christ, and yet, at other times, is miles removed from it. There is also a widespread interest in the new Burmese meditation techniques, and much fresh light is thrown on them here. Since the author nowhere offends Eastern susceptibilities there should be considerable interest among Asians as well.

15.8.'62

EDWARD CONZE

From the Author to

FRIENDS AND READERS IN BURMA

IT MAY VERY WELL BE THAT YOU WILL NOT AGREE WITH ALL that I have written about Buddhism in this volume. Indeed we seldom see ourselves as others see us, even when those observing eyes are friendly ones—as they assuredly are in this case.

For I shall never forget the friendliness, the generous helpfulness, and the pervasive gentleness of most Buddhists that I met in Burma in my two years there. Nor can I ever adequately thank all those who so untiringly aided me in my studies of Buddhism—particularly those on the staff of the International Institute for Advanced Buddhistic Studies in Rangoon. If I have failed to understand in any way, it is my failure and not theirs.

But even failures to fully understand—and I am certain that there are some such in what follows—do not represent either ill-will nor the desire to misrepresent. Hence, despite some passages which may be considered by some to be critical of Buddhism, this book is not in any sense anti-Buddhist. Quite the contrary. Herein I am trying to see the Buddhism of Burma clearly, and so to present it to any who may read these pages.

To be sure, no Westerner will perceive Buddhism as does an Easterner who has been born into it. And perhaps these differences of view will be most obvious in Chapters II and IV, where I have recorded some of my experiences and personal views. But even here, as elsewhere in these pages, I have tried to be straightforwardly honest in my descriptions and expositions, setting forth my own perceptions and their interpretations as accurately as I know how. And this, I am sure, is what my Burmese friends in their deepest hearts would wish me to do, even though I may not speak as they would speak about the same matters. I would earnestly solicit their correction of any errors of fact or interpretation which I may have made in what follows.

Winston L. King

Grinnell College
Iowa
April 1964

CONTENTS

I

NEGATIVE STATEMENT AND POSITIVE EXPERIENCE

THE ENDURING ENIGMA THAT FACES ANY WESTERNER IN trying to understand the religious and philosophical mind of the East is its persistence in stating its most profound experiences and doctrines in negative terms. It may be typified by the often-told story of the Christian missionary in China who asked a priest, engaged in temple devotions, "To whom are you praying?" The answer: "No one." To a second question about what he was praying for, the priest answered: "Nothing." And as the missionary retired in some confusion of mind the parting shot came: "And there was no one praying, you know."

And of all the negative Eastern statements, that of Buddhism, on the whole, is the most consistent and emphatic. With some possible exceptions in Mahayana Buddhism, or the more "liberal" variety which predominates in China, Korea, Japan and to some extent in Tibet, this negativity of statement is found in all varieties of Buddhism. But it is especially emphasized in the contemporary Theravada Buddhism of South-East Asia.[1]

Not only is this true with regard to the ultimate realities in particular, but this quality of negativity of concept filters down to lower levels and to the statement of many lesser truths.

---

[1] Mahayana, the "Great Vehicle" or "Superior Way" Buddhism has developed more freely in doctrine and practice than its sister variety which is called, rather epithetically, Hinayana, "Small Vehicle" or "Lesser Way" Buddhism. However, those who have followed the more conservative Hinayana trend and value the "original" scriptural tradition, refer to themselves as Theravada Buddhists, i.e. those who follow the traditional teaching of the Buddha as handed down by the Theras or Elders (monks) through the centuries.

Historical Background

The historical background and process that produced this pervasive negativity, or have at least conditioned its expression, have often been discussed and need only a brief outline here. Buddhism arose in India in the sixth century before Christ. Therefore its basic statements were framed in terms of the then contemporary philosophical and religious doctrines; thus Buddhist teaching represents the restatement of some of these doctrines and the rejection of others. The rejection of various aspects of the current Indian religion was especially noteworthy and to a large extent has been definitive of the continuing Buddhist statement ever since.

There is the specific rejection of the elaborate religious *ritualism* of the day for example. In many of the oldest Buddhist texts the Buddha is consistently portrayed as ignoring, scorning, or gently ridiculing the whole apparatus of sacrifice and ceremonial, so loved and valued by the Brahmin priests of his day. The reason for doing so was simple from the Buddha's point of view: Such rituals belong to the world of unspiritual externals and cannot bring one to that ultimate spiritual liberation which he sought for all men. Further, dependence upon ritual is harmful because it actually hinders the inner work of self-liberation. As a result ritualistic usage in Buddhism grew very slowly, and in Theravada Buddhism it has always remained at a minimum. Dependence upon rites is held to be one of the major hindrances to the higher life.

The actual historical consequence of this rejection of ritualism has been curious, however. Into this vacuum of religious practices created by antiritualism has flowed a veritable tide of popular usages and customs. India contributed its necromancy and astrology, as well as subordinate deities-cum-ritual; and the local pre-Buddhist culture of the various countries into which Buddhism spread in South-East Asia contributed its share of folk festivals, vaguely related to Buddhism or included under its cloak of toleration. (Of these we shall speak more at a later point.) Yet even here the central Buddhist antiritualism has kept extravagances somewhat in check.

Another important rejection was that of *physical asceticism*. The classic story of Gotama's six-year long effort to achieve enlightenment (Buddhahood) by such practices is well known. A possibly embellished version of its extreme physical results has found expression in the scriptures:

> *Because I ate so little all my limbs became like the joints of withered creepers . . . my buttocks became like a bullock's hoof; my protruding backbone like a string of balls; . . . my ribs like the crazy rafters of a tumble-down shed; . . . the pupils of my eyes appeared lying low and deep; . . . my scalp became shrivelled and shrunk as a bitter white gourd cut before it is ripe becomes shrivelled and shrunk by a hot wind. If I thought: "I will touch the skin of my belly" it was my backbone I took hold of. The skin of my belly came to be cleaving to my backbone. If I thought, "I will obey the calls of nature," I fell down on my face then and there . . . If I . . . stroked my limbs with my hand, the hairs, rotted at the roots, fell away from my body.*[1]

Only after the deliberate termination of these ascetic practices and the turning to the 'middle way' of calm insight by a collected mind in a healthy body, did Gotama achieve enlightenment. Since that time the middle way, which is neither ascetic nor indulgent, has been the central ideal of Buddhist practice.

And why was asceticism rejected? Not because of the effort or strenuous discipline involved—for there is much of this in the middle way—but because it was too superficial in its analysis of man's predicament and its cure. It sought to achieve a liberation of the self from the self by means of physical disciplines whose only result was to tie the ascetic ever more firmly to his body in a negative way. Physical states were valued in themselves; austerity for its severity. Buddha did not deny that such asceticism would have an effect upon one's rebirth, but he did deny that it would have the desired effect, i.e. enlightenment. He called rather for a far more radical asceticism—that of the spirit. For though it is relatively easy to abuse the body under guise of its discipline, it is much harder to achieve the full control of both body and mind through the mind. But it is through such self-control one avoids the negative attachment to the body in-

[1] *Majjhima Nikāya*, Sutta 36. PTS, *Middle Length Sayings*, text vol. I, p. 300.

duced by asceticism and also achieves genuine liberation from
the emotional-sensual tyranny of the total body-mind complex; and the Buddha considered it to be the only truly
disciplined way of life.

Another area of rebellion was that against the *soul-doctrine*
of contemporaneous religious belief. While the *Bhagavad-Gītā*
was written much later than the Buddha's time, its central
belief in the soul or atman, as that which is eternal and indestructible in man's soul, as passing on from birth to birth
until it gains freedom by the realization of its oneness with the
World Soul or Brahman, was even then characteristic of India.
Indeed this belief in the imperishable divinity of each man
has been a basic religious tenet of most Indian sects since the
writing of the Upanishads some centuries before the Buddha.

To this central assertion of Brahmanical-Hindu faith Buddhism has always reacted negatively in terms of its *anattā*
(*an-ātman*) doctrine, translated often as "no-self", "no-soul",
"no substantial self-nature". It holds in several scriptures that
it is impossible to identify the "self" with the body, the emotions, consciousness, mind or any other seemingly perceptible
entity in the body-mind complex. Likewise in the famous
analogy of the chariot in the *Questions of King Milinda*
(Meander?) it is held that just as the concept "chariot" applies
only to a collection of items and is "nothing" in itself, so also
is it with the concept "self". It is true that the former passages'
negative interpretation has been disputed by Mahayana,
Hindu, and Western scholars; some of them have held that
the Buddha was only seeking to destroy unworthy concepts of
the soul in the interests of its true understanding. But Theravada Buddhists almost uniformly reject such an interpretation, and strenuously assert that when they say "no-soul"
they mean no soul.

The reasons for such negative vehemence are several. An
eternal immutable soul seems to them to be a static concept,
conducive to moral laziness and spiritual indiscipline. Essentially an immutable soul can be neither bettered nor worsened
by what one does to it. Likewise the soul-concept is the
supreme obstacle to liberation; he who cherishes it in any
form, gross or subtle, is still clinging to self-existence and hence
incapable of deliverance from rebirth. And finally the Bud-

dhist can find no empirical evidence for the existence of a self over and above the elements which compose it and the physical stimuli which call consciousness into activity. He would describe the "soul" as only a temporary unity of passing, changing elements, fully subject to the laws of cause and effect, and capable of radical alteration for better or worse at almost any stage of development. Therefore, Theravada Buddhism seeks always to be on guard lest the ancient Hindu heresy creep back under a new guise.

One final rejection by Buddhism may be mentioned: the rejection of *theism*. It might be said that much of Indian religion and philosophic thought has been obsessed by a hunger for, or a conviction of, the Divine. India has found divinity everywhere and in everything and resultingly created manifold forms for its worship of the divine. In one sense Indian theism, or awareness of divinity, became rampant and promiscuous, greatly debased in some of its forms.

Such theism Buddhism found objectionable both morally and religiously. Yet the Buddha's reaction, though negative, could scarcely be called a simple nihilism or atheistic denial. The gods were not denied, but put in their place—which was one of complete subordination and discipleship to the Buddhas. An Enlightened One, i.e. a human being who has attained Buddhahood, is always superior to any and every god. Thus, though Brahmā, one of the highest of the gods, may think of himself as Eternal, Almighty, Allwise and the Creator of all that he sees, he is actually only an ignorant layman as it were. He is only an ex-human being who arrived first in that particular heaven by virtue of his good deeds in past lives; the other gods, likewise brought there by their past kamma, merely arrived later than their "creator". In the end, their good kamma exhausted, they will all sink like deflated balloons to lower levels of existence. Indeed the wise man pities the gods, for in their billion-year long existences of bliss and splendour they have no real opportunity to gain liberating insight into the impermanence, emptiness, and suffering of selves and existent phenomena, which is open to a human being.

So it is that Buddhism from the beginning devalued "theism", whether multiple or single. "Gods" may be useful friends for those who aspire to wordly success, and sometimes be of minor assistance on the way to salvation. But essentially a man must depend upon himself for ultimate liberation; gods can neither materially help nor hinder him. And far above them all in wisdom and knowledge, like Everest above pasture-land hillocks, towers the Buddha. He is not a god, but a Man, who by the resources open to each man himself, achieved his god-transcending, liberating insight into the nature of reality.

One further negative reaction to the Indian heritage may be noted here: the Buddhist reaction against metaphysical speculation which was rampant in the Buddha's time, and later. This is most explicitly set forth in Sutta 63 of the *Majjhima-Nikāya* (*Middle Length Sayings*) in which are listed the indeterminables or "questions which tend not to edification". They are as follows:

> *These theories which The Blessed One has left unelucidated, has set aside and rejected—that the world is eternal, that the world is not eternal, that the world is finite, that the world is infinite, that the soul and body are identical, that the soul is one thing and the body another, that the saint exists after death, that the saint both exists and does not exist after death, that the saint neither exists nor does not exist after death—these The Blessed One does not elucidate to me.*[1]

Despite the earnest entreaty of Malunkyaputta, his disciple, the Buddha refuses to answer such questions and likens their asking to the petulant and foolish questions of a man wounded by an arrow who insists on knowing the name, caste, dwelling place, personal appearance of the man who shot the arrow, the kind of bow he used, the materials of which the arrow is made—all before he will consent to have the arrow drawn and the wound treated. He will die before all this can be learned, the Buddha sensibly observes. So will human beings who seek answers to all such metaphysical questions before they begin the disciplines of religious living perish before aught is done.

Professor Warren in the introductory note to the above passage is of the opinion that the refusal of the Buddha to

[1] Warren, *Buddhism in Translations*, H. C. Warren, Harvard University Press, 1953, p. 117.

answer these questions has a twofold basis: First, the very framing of the questions presupposes views he considered false; hence they cannot be answered in those terms. Secondly, as so strongly suggested in the parable of the arrow, he looked upon religion as a practical matter not a speculative one. In any case an initial and fundamental emphasis in Buddhism was its turning from metaphysical speculation to a moral-psychological discipline. This is a basic quality of that middle way which avoids contradictory theories about the nature of the world and personal existence, and turns rather to the immediate business of freeing the self from un-spiritual attachments.

The Negative Statement

Such then is the general historical matrix of the negations of Buddhism; its subsequent history as a religion has seen the extension and reiteration of those negations, particularly in the Theravada tradition.[1] Today these negations comprise its staple doctrinal fare, especially when expounded to non-Buddhists. The major items are impressive in their range and depth of denial. We may further describe them in their contemporary assertion as follows:

1. *The three-fold negative character of the space-time order of "reality":*

a) *Anicca,* meaning *not-* or *non-*permanent. Sensible existence in its absolute entirety, including universes, planets, physical entities or "things", gods, men (both "soul" and body), animals, and even atoms are but flux-in-process. There is no permanence, even of the mildest sort in the substantial "realities" of matter and mind, because solid matter and matter-sensing mind are both constantly, even momentarily, changing. Existence is momentary. What exists, exists only in the moment of its appearance and then is gone. Where has it gone? The past is nothing, no longer in being. It has poured its all into the present moment of existence; this in turn will pour its all (past effects plus present modifications) into the next

---

[1] Many Theravada Buddhists believe that Mahayana Buddhism has reintroduced a positive self and made Buddha into a god, though still using "orthodox" Buddhist terms. Even so, there are many conceptually "negative" elements in Mahayana, especially in some of its Madhyamika forms and in modern Zen.

B

moment of existence, when it arrives as a present moment. Hence the moment of existence cannot be said to go anywhere at all: there is no past in existence, nor future, only the present, which is all that there is . . . but which will be different in another flash. In any case, existence and existent entities are transient and in the process of continual change in every aspect. All permanence therein is an illusion; true knowledge of things as they are will reveal their basic quality of anicca.

b) Anattā, usually translated no-self or no-soul. Or it might be better put in such terms as these: The quality of insubstantiality, or of having no true self-nature, or of having no continuing identity. The Buddhist doctrine of "dependent origination" centres around this negation, for every entity, physical or mental, or physical-mental, is a compounded entity, or a "confection" to use one translation. That is to say, there are no identical substances or beings which continue with new qualities added or in new states or conditions. These new qualities and states *are* the substance or being, which is different from, though connected with, the previous condition. And this is true at many levels. Mountains are made up of particles of granite that are made up of elements or molecules that are made up of fields of force. Mind is made up of consciousness that arises because of stimuli; which in turn is made up of moments only a billionth of a second in duration.

Obviously impermanence and insubstantiality are opposite sides of the same coin. That which changes rapidly cannot in truth have a permanent or identical substance; and that which has no true identity of enduring self or substance must change. It is true that Buddhist thought has somewhat equivocated here, ranging all the way from an absolute idealism which holds that only mental states are ultimately real, to a kind of physical realism that considered the basic elements of tangible appearances to be real. Or else it has taken the position that no metaphysical statement of any sort was needed, and the whole matter of the ultimate nature of reality should be left up in the air, as having nothing essential to do with Buddhist salvation.

Echoes of all these viewpoints can be found in modern Theravada Buddhism. But the most persistent form of the statement of anatta doctrine is its application to the human self: a flat denial of any abiding personality, consciousness, self, or soul. At any one moment of life these supposed entities are in constant flux. Nor is there any self or soul which transmigrates to a new life—only a kind of kammic energy impulse, analogous to a sound-wave transmitted from one tuning fork to another. That is, there is continuity here but no continuing identity.[1] And since the delusion of being a permanent self or dealing with permanent things is held to be the root cause of all our grasping or craving, and hence of all human bondage and suffering, the denial of this self-belief is in some respects the central teaching of Buddhism.

c) Dukkha, or suffering, or unsatisfactoriness, is the third characteristic of existence. Usually it is listed as the second of the three, but this order seems more traditional than logical; for suffering is essentially the emotional result or living manifestation of the qualities of impermanence and insubstantiality of all beings. It is a Buddhist axiom that that which changes cannot produce lasting satisfaction. So, whether it be the desired object that changes or the desiring self that changes in its desires or whether both change, as is indeed the case, the result is dissatisfaction. This quality of perpetually unsatisfied desire is the essence of all sentient existence and constitutes its basic and perpetual misery. It may indeed be said of every sentient creature, as of man, that

> *He's a fool.*
> *When it's hot, he wants it cool.*
> *When it's cool, he wants it hot——*
> *Always wanting what is not.'*

Such is the condition of individualized being, *per se.*

2. *There is no supreme creator-God.*

Contemporary Theravada Buddhism is even more certain than original Buddhism that there is no ultimate deity. Indeed

[1] There is a difficulty here, to be sure, which is evaded as the rule. The factors of permanence, unity, and seeming identity are unexplained or under-valued. And the peculiar unity-in-change which is characteristic of mental life is almost completely denied in theory, but accepted in fact. That is: The kammic impulse which goes from life to life is theoretically not a soul or self; but it contains implicitly or potentially, moral and mental character, memory and full self-identification with the past lives. This is a marvellous kind of "mere energy" which can carry the memory of a million lives and their moral quality through rebirths as ghost in hells, animal, god and man of many sorts!

this atheistic note is sounded quite frequently today in the contact of Buddhism with the West. The standard anti-theistic, anti-creationist arguments which have been current in the West for many years appear over and over again in current writings: How can God be both all-good and all-powerful and have created a world like this one? What caused the First Cause, or is the whole conception merely a concession to human weakness of mind? How can one fit the conception of a personal God into an impersonal, mechanical order of nature? How can one prove the existence of God? And so forth. And those who read European languages make much use of such agnostic writers as Schopenhauer, and Bertrand Russell in particular, to sharpen their points.

Theism is seen as an invitation to the irrational, irresponsible, and immoral element to triumph in human life. One is encouraged to believe blindly (without evidence) in a God—whose existence he cannot prove—in order to be saved from the consequences of his own misdeeds, says the Buddhist. Also the effect is to introduce an arbitrary and autocratic element into the world-order of cause and effect, for what theist can explain rationally why God does what he does, i.e. why reality is as it is?[1] For all these reasons the wise, self-reliant man will reject the concept of God as destructive of human effort and sense of moral responsibility. For the net result of theism is to hinder man's achievement of liberation for himself and by himself.

We may notice in passing, however, that Theravada Buddhism affirms the existence of other spiritual beings with almost the same degree of vigour that it denies the existence of a supreme God, with no better kind of evidence for their existence than a theist produces for the existence of God. Practically speaking, for the masses of Buddhists, as we shall note later in more detail, these spirits, even though ex-humans, are much prayed to for help in practical affairs. And sometimes the essentially theistic attitude found in this realm powerfully affects the attitude towards the Buddha himself.

[1] Theoretically the doctrine of kamma solves the problem of evil. I and all other beings are what we are because of past misdeeds. This avoids the defamation of the supposedly wise and good creator of the present world order. But we may ask whether it is any more *rational* to believe in the actuality of that moral ordering of life called kamma, than in God. See also below pages 137–9.

How and in what degree this is done is a matter of the respective level of Buddhist practice; orthodoxly speaking it is wrong.

3. *Corollary Negations*

Such are the great basic negations of Buddhism. From them as resulting attitudes, or as corollaries of a somewhat different sort, we may note three other negations.

a) There is no hope of permanently or importantly modifying the space-time order (saṃsāra) in which we live.

This is implicit rather than explicit in Buddhist thinking, and is to some extent being denied in the newly-activist Buddhism of today.[1] But it is the logical result of the anicca-anatta-dukkha doctrine. This order in which we live had no discernible beginning; that is, desire-motivated cause-effect becoming has always been, and always will be. It is an order of perpetual impermanence, full of suffering, unsatisfying by nature. Because of the infinitude of existing beings it will never come to an end; for only the cessation of all individual beings in Nibbana could end samsara—there is no Will of God or Last Day, to do it. Hence the only sure salvation is for the individual to escape the bounds of the birth-death cycles.

To be sure, the good things of the space-time order of rebirth have their place. Physical health, provision of physical necessities for all men, harmony between individuals and groups, just social orders, stable governments and the like are all desirable, insofar as possible. For many millions of beings will continue to live in the space-time order (samsara) for millions of years to come; and in general, peace, harmony, and well-being are more conducive to spiritual progress than their opposites. Yet the space-time order will always frustrate man's deepest hopes and cannot be fundamentally altered for the better. Hence the spiritually advanced man will not fasten his total hope nor give his full energy to these lesser goods; they should be only instrumental to the higher quest for Nibbana, which is release from the time-space order in its entirety.

[1] See author's *In the Hope of Nibbana.*

b) The summum-bonum, the ultimate and transcendent reality, Nibbana, is never described.

This statement is true in general and in theory rather than in actual practice, but the attitude toward Nibbana that it suggests is fundamental to all Buddhism with few exceptions. The extremes range from the Madhyamika denial that Nibbana exists as a separate state or condition apart from samsara or the rebirth-cycle in time and space, to the Pure Land as something much like the more colourful versions of the Christian Heaven. But the bulk of Buddhists, including Theravadins, would say that though Nibbana is undoubtedly real, the only unchanging and hence only genuinely real dimension in existence, one can essentially do no more than to say: Nibbana is found in *that* direction. Only those who experience something of its quality in this life, as do the saints or arahats, "know" what Nibbana is; and they assert that it is indescribable in ordinary language, indeed in any language. One can only say: Nibbana is the absence of hatred, greed, delusion, suffering, and narrow individualized existence.

c) The quality of the good life is frequently stated in negative or completely generalized terms.

This appears to be corollary to, and also somewhat the result of, the two previous beliefs about the essential frustration of human hope in space-time orders, and the "negative" nature of Nibbana. For if individual existence in space-time is essentially frustrating (dukkha) and cannot be essentially or permanently bettered, how can one positively state the moral goals of this order of existence? This is not to say that Buddhism has no positive moral principles, but rather to say that even these are often stated in negative terms as consisting in restraint and self-control. Though there seems to be an implicit assumption that human nature is good, and will shine through if its tarnish or impurity is removed, yet the usual way of phrasing this is in reverse. Thus, the supreme moral goal of the Buddhist way of life is to achieve *alobha* (non-greed), *adosa* (non-hatred), and *amoha* (non-delusion); presumably with the removal of greed, hatred, and delusion their desirable opposites will appear.

Or if we shall put the good life more positively, as Buddhism often does in its emphasis upon the exercise of *mettā* (loving kindness), *karunā* (compassion), and *muditā* (rejoicing in others' joy and good fortune), their perfection is found in their complete generalization. To be perfect in their exercise is to extend these attitudes to all beings alike, without particularity or specific relationship to any individual. All beings of whatever sort are to be loved, compassionated, and rejoiced with equally and without distinction. And the crown of the exercise of these virtues is *upekkhā* (equanimity) by means of which one persists in that exericse completely undisturbed within himself and unattached emotionally to any of those to whom he radiates his benevolence.

This of course represents the high ideal for the saint and is not held out as a blue-print for the ordinary moral life. Yet its flavour of detachment from earthly concerns, values, and morally determined tasks is pervasive of Buddhist statement and characteristic of the progressive way to the full spiritual development which it recommends. The higher reaches of the meditative life (the jhanic or "trance" states) are increasingly cut off from sense life and have more and more of a spaceless-timeless-objectless quality. And the maximum state, Nibbana, is apparently that state in which all emotions, all consciousness, all existence of individualized nature are completely absent—the perfection of negation.

The Basic Root of Buddhist Negation

Thus far we have sketched the historical matrix of Buddhist negativity and stated its major negative doctrines and positions. But this is not the end of the matter. For important as is the historical background of rejected Brahamanical doctrine in giving Buddhism the specific forms of its negation, the fundamental soil in which its negativism grows is in its basic agreement with Hinduism and most of the East in one very important conviction: Ultimate reality is impossible of description.

This we have already alluded to in noting the Buddhist approach to Nibbana. But it is important to realize that, though differently stated from other Eastern religions, Buddhist doctrine about Nibbana grows from the same deep mystical rootage as the Hindu conception of Brahman and the Taoist feeling for Tao. For of Brahman one can only say "neti, neti", not this concept, not this idea; and if the Tao can be spoken, i.e. conceptualized, it is not the Tao.

Those in the West who wish to conceptualize even their ultimates if possible, and distrust any talk of ultimates which cannot be thus dealt with, must needs realize the depth of this Eastern conviction if they are to appreciate anything of Eastern, and particularly Buddhist, viewpoints. For the denial that conceptual thought can reach ultimate truth represents, or at least implies, not merely a negative mannerism characteristic of the East, but a whole philosophy and methodology of dealing with any kind of truth. This philosophy of truth-seeking may be put into three corollary statements.

1. *Conceptual and logical thinking is of only limited usefulness in truth-seeking.*

Nagarjuna, the Mahayanist logician, and his spiritual heirs in modern Mahayana Buddhism, have carried this anti-conceptualism to the farthest Buddhist extreme and sought to demonstrate by dialectical reasoning that all logical and conceptual thinking destroys itself. For, say Nagarjuna and Zen Buddhism after him, conceptualization makes distinctions about its subject matter that cancel each other out; indeed the very process of distinction-making can be shown to be self-contradictory when used in making such basic distinctions as being and non-being, motion and rest, cause and effect, subject and object and the like. Operating from a middle position, non-conceptual in nature and without presuppositions Nagarjuna believed, Buddhist logic sought to demonstrate that conceptual thought was mere word juggling.

Not all Buddhist thought has followed Nagarjuna to the bitter end, at which point he says that there is in reality no Eight-fold Noble Path, no Samsara, no Buddha, no Nibbana. But all Buddhists share his distrust of conceptual thinking. It may well do, they hold, for making ordinary distinctions in the ordinary world. It is socially and practically quite necessary. But to apprehend religious truth (if there be such) and ultimate realities (if there are such), conceptual thought is powerless and may even lead one astray when he attempts to push its use beyond its proper sphere.

2. *Because conceptual thought is limited, we should speak of "realizing" rather than "knowing" ultimate truths.*

We are here to some extent on ground familiar to the West. Here is a note similar to that struck by Henri Bergson when he made his distinction between "knowledge about" and "knowledge of" something. The former was, of course, conceptual and abstract; it consisted of bare, skeletalized "ideas", severed from the living experience of the knower and apart from the known object itself. Knowledge of, on the contrary, was held to be direct, intuitional, sensible in quality, full of the sap of life, incapable of being put into concepts, at least in all its fullness.

This is what the Buddhist means when he speaks of "realizing" the truth; it is a direct, first-hand knowing of the truth, not an idea about it, nor the report of someone else's experience but his own personal feeling-knowing awareness. It is neither mere sensation, nor feeling (in a more general sense), nor mere idea, as the Buddhist sees it, but a kind of knowing which has elements of both what the West terms feeling and knowing, here combined in realization. It can be thought about abstractly and given some form in words, but this conceptual cage will never contain the fullness of the realization experience itself. Indeed, the two types of knowing are not merely more and less abstract, the Buddhist would hold, but different in kind.

Nevertheless we must not make the distinction between the two types of knowledge too sharp so as to indicate even different "faculties". It is true that sometimes one is led to think that experience-knowledge gained in meditation, for example, is not only different in degree, but in kind, from ordinary knowledge, or at least that the process is quite different in each case. But this is undoubtedly an emphasis made for the purpose of indicating the necessity of the personal experience of truth for one's own salvation. The more balanced emphasis seems to be that realization or experience-knowledge is one direction in which everyman's ordinary intelligence may be turned. Thus Shwe Zan Aung:

. . . the bare intellectual element may be developed by culture into secular knowledge (lokiya-paññā) on the one hand, ranging from the ordinary reasoning power exercised in the most trivial matters, through all phases of logical reason in scientific matters, to the abhiññā's, or supernormal exercise of thought and will; and into higher knowledge (lokuttara-paññā) on the other, ranging from Path-knowledge . . . to omniscience.[1]

3. *Knowledge-experience, or realization, of the truth inevitably produces a change in the knower-experiencer himself.*

This statement is not to be understood in the loose, indirect sense that if a person genuinely believes something to be true, then this belief will affect his conduct; but it is to be taken in the more direct sense that the realization of truth immediately and irresistibly effects a change in the person. This is the case because realization is no mere idea which may lie about unused in one's mental attic, but a living awareness that issues immediately in character modification.

Such realization is therefore no mere matter of book-learning. Even the Theravadins, who so highly prize scriptural memorization, strongly insist that true knowledge is gained by "practice", not mere scholarship. They are fond of telling the scriptural story of the learned scholar who had taught many a saint through the years his vast knowledge of sacred texts, but who in order to "realize" the truth himself had finally to sit at the feet of a very young saint and take instruction in methods of realization.

Is there then any value at all in scholarly learning for the religious life? Considerable. It provides an orthodox framework for experience; for Theravadins distrust such Buddhist developments as Zen where the almost total emphasis is upon immediate experience. Further, the thorough grounding in, one might indeed say the soaking in, the sacred texts that is the core of the education of the devout layman or monk, makes them a part of his subconscious life itself. And for the intellectualist who wishes to be somewhat logically satisfied before he commits himself in faith, the more abstruse reasonings have some value. Thus Francis Story comments about

[1] *Compendium of Philosophy*, Luzac, PTS, 1956, p. 41.

the Abdhidhamma or third and philosophical-psychological portion of the Pali Canon:

> *'This is for the benefit of those who require intellectual conviction of this truth and whose minds have to be gradually freed from every vestige of clinging by destroying the tendency to self-identification with the factors of phenomenal being. . . .'*

But this knowledge, useful as it may be, must never be mistaken for the true and liberating knowledge, for

> *. . . there were Arahants among the Bhikkhus before the Abhi-dhamma was expounded. Some of these Arahants were very young; mention is made in the Texts of boys of seven years who perceived the Truth and attained Arahantship. This supreme attainment, therefore, is independent of intellectualism and of scholarship; the most important factor in it is pārami, which means progress made in previous births towards self-purification.*[1]

Does all this emphasis mean that no speculation has gone on in Buddhism at all? This might seem to be the logical result of the combination of the anti-metaphysical tendency in Buddhism and its emphasis upon the direct feeling-knowing of experience rather than intellection. Yet it is not quite the case. In the long centuries since the Buddha there has been a great deal of intellectualist elaboration of chosen themes. If Theravada Buddhism has largely rejected the philosophical speculations of Mahayana, and ostensibly refuses, to this day, to discuss the questions not tending to edification, nonetheless developments have taken place. The Abhidhamma is a massive monument to intellectuality, even though it moves within the confines of psychology and ethics and supposedly avoids metaphysics; it has an elaboration of structure rivalling the philosophic system of Immanuel Kant. And, as we shall note in the chapter on Buddhist cosmology, there are many in Theravada Buddhism today who believe that a complete theory of world cycles may be worked out, even though absolute origins of the cosmos are not discussed. Nonetheless the general pattern is to keep such elements to a minimum, or retire them to a secondary place.

One might say in summary that Theravada Buddhism has

[1] *Sangīti*, Burma Buddhist World-Mission, 1954, p. 21.

in some sense become a victim of its negations. Negative statement seems to be its obsession, even a type of addiction. It is tenaciously affirmed and reiterated even when it seems to conflict with the positive elements which are also, in other contexts, most emphatically insisted upon or clearly implicit. The result is two-fold: To some extent there arises a dogmatic scholasticism which values the negative orthodox statement of doctrine more than the positive religious experience. And, secondly, the positive and transcendent religious reality or experience is thus even more deeply hidden from outside view or, when affirmed, as is the mode today, seems completely incongruous with the negative vocabulary.

4. *The Positive Experience*

Thus far the negative position of Buddhism, that face which it presents to the outside world, has been set forth almost exclusively. But this is by no means the sum of the matter: indeed it is the lesser part of it. For strange as it always seems to the Westerner, this apparently negative doctrinal apparatus and religious structuring contain within themselves, or are able to inspire, intense devotion and effort on the part of many followers. Allowing for the vast numbers of nominal adherents found in Buddhism, as in every other religion also, there is a vital core of "positive", even luminous, religious experience within the negative framework.

The true positive-negative tension which is the essence of genuine Buddhist orthodoxy is not found on the surface, where only the forms of it are mouthed. Much of popular Buddhism at the level of pagoda worship has little negation about it. It is filled with "positive" devotion to nats, devas, relics of the Buddha, and perhaps even to the Buddha himself; and from these positive devotions—positive benefits of good health, prosperity, long life, and happy rebirth are expected. The central negations of Buddhism remain far off and largely inoperative in experience and practice.

So also the contemporary tide of resurgence in Buddhism has in it a strong mixture of undoubtedly "positive" elements. The East, long suppressed by the West as a part of its colonial dominions, has been made to feel the inferiority of its culture and religion, as well as its political and economic weakness.

But now in the era of nationalistic freedom, national culture after national culture is asserting its worth and even offering itself to the West as a curative for its social political ills. In Theravada countries where culture has been solidly Buddhist for centuries this means presenting Buddhism to the world with a vigour unexampled perhaps since the days of Asoka. (At least such is the fond hope of contemporary Buddhism.) What proportion of this resurgence is genuinely Buddhist and what is national-cultural remains to be seen.

Yet neither of these aspects, the popular devotion and the new resurgence, is the heart of the positive quality of which we speak. For there is, and apparently always has been, a continuing "positive" heart of Buddhist experience which not only continues to express itself in "negative" terminology, but seems to spring from the negative concepts themselves. Or perhaps it would be better to say that the core of Buddhist experience continues to find the negative expression the only fitting one for its inner life.

We may put the situation thus: When Buddhism says that intellection does not reach ultimate truths and that such truths are incommunicable, it implies or else immediately goes on to say, two other things. One is that there is such ultimate truth to be known, no matter how difficult or unusual its perception. And, secondly, such truth can be known. Indeed, how else should we know that there is such truth, or that our ordinary intellections are limited, unless there were somewhere, sometime an apprehension of the ultimate unlimited truth? Otherwise we might think that our limited apprehensions were omniscient.

To put it paradoxically: The greater the negation the more certain that there is something beyond the negation—unless we arrive at an empty agnosticism or a complete nihilism. And Buddhism's history eminently proclaims it to be neither of these. Hence when Buddhism so strongly asserts the negative element, it is only witnessing to the greatness of the truth it believes it has discovered, a truth too great, too radically different, too absolutely certain to be properly handled in ordinary language and thought.[1]

[1] There is an interesting contrast here with Kantian philosophy. Kant held that logical-scientific knowledge could never reach beyond the phenominal realm

With regard to the fact of the "existence" of an ultimate
reality or truth, there are statements in the affirmative which
now and then show themselves through the prevailing negations. Thus, in the twenty-sixth Sutta of the *Majjhima-Nikāya*
(Middle Length Sayings) entitled "The Ariyan Quest" the
Buddha defines that quest as a search for that which is unborn,
unaging, undecaying, undying, unsorrowing, and unstained
—which he calls Nibbana. And in another statement on the
same theme, the assumed presence of this reality in all his
thinking is thus stated:

> *There is, O disciples, an unborn, not become, not compounded, not*
> *constructed. If there were not this unborn, not become, not com-*
> *pounded, not constructed, no escape could be seen from here from that*
> *which is born, become, compounded, constructed. But since there is*
> *an unborn, not become, not compounded, not constructed, so an*
> *escape is possible from what is born, become, compounded, con-*
> *structed.*[1]

The second aspect of the matter is also of great importance.
Not only is there Absolute Reality-Truth in Nibbana, but it
can be known. This accessibility of such Truth, however
difficult, is indeed the heart of the Buddhist faith. This is the
accomplishment of Gotama Buddha, indeed of every Buddha,
that he discovers such truth, and can set forth the way for
other men to find it. The name given to Gotama's realization
of ultimate Truth is of course, Enlightenment; and as the
Enlightened, Omniscient One, who knows the central Truth
of all truths, he is the Buddha. This faith about the Buddha is
fundamental to Buddhism; it is the "rock" upon which the
Buddhist "Church" is built.

The continuing expression of this conviction is to be found
in the meditational discipline. For while the Buddha's experience of Enlightenment is exceptional, it is not unique. There

---

of time-space existence to the noumenal or "thing-in-itself". For him the knowledge of the latter, or at least some sort of contact with it, is either introduced by
inference from the moral life or by a logical *tour de force*. In Buddhism, however,
it is not so much the poverty of human intellection which makes such knowledge
impossible, as that the height and nature of that knowledge, even its grandeur,
make ordinary language and thought processes incapable of receiving it.

[1] *Udāna*, VIII, 1–3, quoted, *The Doctrine of the Awakening*, J. Evola, Luzac,
1951, pp. 76–7.

have been many Buddhas in the world. And further: To be a *universal* Buddha, as Gotama was, is also to have the ability to teach others something of ultimate Truth.

A host of lesser Buddhas (pacceka or non-teaching Buddhas) and arahats (saints who achieved liberating knowledge) bear witness to this ability of Buddhas to teach, and of men to learn, the ultimate, liberating Reality-Truth.

In Buddhism, as in other religions, of course, the old days tend to be the better ones. In the far-off past there were many, perhaps thousands of arahats living at one time. Now they are few in number; and due to the Buddhist tradition that an arahat seldom proclaims himself to be one, such as there are become known only by a kind of grape-vine reputation. Yet it is a firm conviction in Burma that there are some monks now living, even named on occasion, who are most probably arahats. Thus:

> *Let me repeat what I am never weary of proclaiming, for it is the greatest proof of all of the authenticity of our Theravada Doctrine —namely that there are living Arahats in Burma. For this reason we have no doubt whatsoever that the Dhamma has come down to us through the centuries perfect and without adulteration, for our confidence is founded on demonstrable truth.*[1]

We may note in passing that for Buddhism truth and reality are the same, especially in their ultimate natures. This is implied in the teaching that truth is to be realized, not merely known about, and that realization of the truth makes a difference in the realizer. For a truth which cannot be merely thought about or completely comprehended by words, but must be felt-thought, is one which has a kind of perceptible reality about it. And the reason that the realization of truth makes the realizer a different person is that it is not mere idea which is thus known, but reality itself. Hence Truth-Reality is the proper term for Buddhist Truth. Whether this means that all genuine reality presents itself somewhere to some realizer, else it does not exist, or that unknowable reality is meaningless, I am not certain.

[1] Francis Story, op. cit., p. 119.

5. *Buddhist Mysticism*

The basic quality of Buddhist religious life—negativity of statement, but positive luminosity of experience and conviction of attainable ultimate Truth—would mark it in Western thinking as mystical. For the mystic, according to Western thought, is one who proclaims that he has achieved direct knowledge-experience of ultimate realities but cannot communicate the substance of that knowledge to others in meaningful terms, or at best only in negations of ordinary meaning. His affirmations consist in his assertions of the absolute certainty of his knowledge and the completely self-evidencing power of ultimate truth when rightly approached. He can also indicate a technique for achieving such knowledge, but of that knowledge itself he says: You must experience it yourself.

This definition of mysticism seems to fit the Buddha's experience precisely. But the Theravada Buddhist in particular is very loath to describe himself as a mystic. This is due, as nearly as I can make out, to the traditional Buddhist association of the term "mystical" with the occult—mind-reading, telepathy, clairaudience, foretelling the future and the like. Indeed the four Jhanic or trance states represent a Buddhist form of such occultism, but are a purified and restrained form of it, if such a description may be allowed. The successful Jhanic practitioner does indeed gain occult powers even in miraculous degree, but two qualifications are always made with regard to them: (1) They must never be used for personal glory and power, and indeed should be largely suppressed in their outward manifestations, or else they will be lost; (2) their attainment represents a potential danger to the spiritual life. Upon reaching these states one may imagine that he has attained Nibbanic peace, or else be so enamoured of them that he wishes to remain at these levels for ever.

Likewise the designation "mystic" seems to the Theravadin to read into his highest experience an emotional frenzy or those highly visual-auditory experiences which sometimes are reported by "mystics". But the true experience of Enlightenment, says the Buddhist, must be clearly distinguished from these other experiences. There is no sense of being possessed by another spirit; or having an irresistible force overcome one, as

St. Teresa reports of her experiences. Buddhist insight on the contrary is completely self-possessed, calm, clear, cool. The essence of its quality is that its possessor is completely in control of the situation, "trance" and all; the more complete the insight the greater the control.

Likewise the application of the term "mystical" to the Buddhist experience of enlightenment implies that it is one of a class of similar phenomena and suggests the possibility of a comparison with other religious experiences on a somewhat equal footing. But the Buddhist would reject this out of hand. He is willing to allow to other religions their good men, their excellent moral codes, their mystical attainments even up to the high Jhanic levels; the enlightening knowledge, however, which leads finally to Nibbana is absolutely unique with Buddhism. To suggest that it is less would be a denial of Buddhism itself.

Nonetheless, if we adequately safeguard and carefully qualify the term mysticism, it still seems to be the best Western description of the central philosophy of Buddhism. Thus, if we define a mystic as one who claims to achieve direct personal knowledge of ultimate Truth-Reality by his chosen technique, the Buddhist saint fits into the mystic category. Such a use of the term calls for no one particular form which this knowledge shall take, only that it be direct, i.e. personally intuited or realized; and that it be ultimate in nature. Into such a context the Buddhist realization of Nibbana in this life and the techniques of achieving such a realization may be harmoniously fitted.

6. *Positive and Negative: Evaluation*

In conclusion it may be well to examine further the terms "positive" and "negative" in general, and particularly with relation to their proper use with reference to Buddhism. They are, of course, Western in origin and heretofore we have used them in the traditionally and popularly loose sense. But thus to apply them to Buddhist statements and experiences, directly and without proper qualification, is to obstruct rather than to help genuine understanding. We shall first explore the Western use of these terms.

c

We may note that for the West the term "positive" is generally regarded as "good", and "negative" as "bad". But when we seek to determine the exact meanings of the terms, each appears to be a large and confused complex of favourable or unfavourable connotations. For example, positive in the good sense seems to be a mixture of secular and religious meanings. On the secular side, positive often indicates the concrete over-against the abstract, the realism of the senses against the fantasies of the imagination, and the common sense of the practical man as opposed to mere intellectualist theory. This is a very strong tendency which reappears in some new form in almost every generation; witness the positivists, the realists, the common-sense people. The popular prestige of science in the West, considered to be a discipline that takes concrete physical realities seriously and knows how to manage them, is rooted in this love of the positive.

On the other hand, and somewhat at variance with the instinct for concrete, physical realism, the term positive is also considered to indicate the clear and conceptually definite as opposed to vague and indefinite sense-experience. While Descartes would have called himself a rationalist rather than a positivist and equated clarity of concept with reality—and hence he abstracted from concrete physical reality—his ideal of mathematical precision and simplicity of explanation has exerted powerful influence upon both philosphers and scientific-minded positivists, i.e. experimentalists. Despite romanticist reactions against his rationalism, the hope of achieving clarity and precision in thought in whatever realm remains strong in the West.

Thus it is that many find in modern science the eminently successful combination of the desire for concretion and the Cartesian demand for clarity. Mathematics is here applied · directly and practically to physical phenomena; and as a result of the scientific synthesis of high abstraction and concrete realism, a completely new pattern of life has emerged; previously undreamed of powers of accomplishment and truths about the universe have become available to modern man. The name which one contemporary school of philosophical thought gives itself, logical positivism, aptly expresses the conviction that scientific method represents the only truly positive way in which to approach any reality whatsoever to gain any knowledge whatsoever.

In any case the synthesis of thought and effort represented by science would seem to most in the West to be a more "positive" way of approaching reality, than the spiritualistic "negative" methods of the East, as represented by Buddhism for example. Inherent in this reading of the positive, and the Western preference for it, is a preference for that which can be clearly conceived, be put into definite concepts or expressed in precise quantitative relationships, and be tangibly demonstrated. This would be opposed to the mystical temperament, the intuitively discovered truth, and the intangible or "spiritual" result. (Even when psychic phenomena such as fire-walking and trance-states are visibly demonstrated, the Westerner remains sceptical because he cannot fit them into a logical-scientific explanation.) For the West a positive concept, term, or name gives a sense of power over any experience to which it is applied, while unstable "realization" seems to be dubiously and even dangerously uncontrolled and indefinable.

But there are also religious roots and moral qualities in the Western concept of the good "positive". There is no doubt that the basic Christian conviction of the uniqueness and value of the individual being or soul in the eyes of God has contributed importantly to this aspect of the positive. Along with other factors it has produced a strong sense of individualism in the West. A positive conception of personality, both in oneself and in others, is held to consist in enhancing and respecting the sense of individual value, uniqueness, and dignity.

As long as there was a religious interpretation of human uniqueness, some of its distortions might be avoided. True, it might lead to a fanatical religious arrogance at times, and even to an excessive concern with one's own salvation; yet the full Christian doctrine of individualism had safeguards. Man's uniqueness was rooted in the divine order, not sheerly in himself; and every other person was unique as well, therefore to be respected and loved.

Its modern secularized form has become something of a perversion of the original. The individual is encouraged to express, i.e. to assert, himself as an individual. He wishes to "distinguish" himself from others by "outstanding" achievements; or to expand, protect, and intensify his individuality by differences of dress, manner, and taste, and sometimes by the deliberate cultivation of eccentricities. Actually the average Westerner may be as conformist to his culture as any other average person; but he does it under the guise of his own independent effort and ideas. Even while conforming he sees himself as asserting his freedom of action, his power to accept or reject conventions, and to do as he pleases. He likes to achieve a maximum of physical and personal privacy in order to safeguard his individuality. And sometimes he is resentful of community obligations and pressures which call upon him to sacrifice his leisure time and resources for the common good.

But there is another moral-religious strand, also rooted in the Christian view of the world, which both contributes to and yet somewhat checks Western individualism. We may speak of it as the conviction of the improvability of this present world, which comes both from the Christian conviction of a divine purpose for human life in time and space, and from the immense practical success of Western science and economics. The world is seen as an arena for exploration, experimentation, and improvement. It has that within it which is both worth saving and bettering.

Thus one might say that characteristically the Westerner thinks of "doing something about" the undesirable situations which he sees. That is, he is an activist. Unknown geographical places are to be explored; ancient civilizations are to be excavated; sluggish trade is to be stimulated. Disease, poverty, unemployment, and economic development are to be attacked as soluble problems. There may have been a time when he regarded such inequalities as the inscrutable will of God. This time is largely past, however. Falling back on the even more fundamental doctrine that God wills life on earth to be good; or its secular equivalent, that science and technology can cure any human ailment except death—and considerably delay that—the Westerner attacks all human problems with vigour.

There have also been the more specifically moral, religious and humanitarian aspects of this activism. The characteristic Western approach to undesirable social conditions is a reform movement, or social welfare work, or the establishment of an ideal community. Organized philanthropy has probably never been such an immense enterprise as it is in the West today. So also the missionary enterprise has been an expression of this same activist philosophy. One ought to take his faith, his moral standards, and his physical benefits to those in other parts of the world who lack them. And herein the individualism and activism join together in vigorous "positive" action to improve the present world for the sake of the individual who lives in it. Thus, in a very general way, we may describe the Western concept of positive living as that which has clear concepts, can produce tangible results, cherishes individuality, and expresses itself in vigorous social action. Frequently it is called a "life-affirming" attitude and contrasted, unfavourably of course, with the "life-denying" attitude of the East, which is considered to be mystically religious, and socially passive. And the negative religious terminology of the East, especially that of Hinduism and Buddhism, only serves to strengthen this impression.

However, two very important considerations must be borne in mind when we seek to apply the positive and negative, life-affirming and life-denying terminology respectively to West and East, even in religious terms. First, we must become aware of the possibility of a different and quite reverse way of interpreting "positive" and "negative", from that usually adopted in the West. Whether the Westerner agrees with it or not, he must in all honesty consider it seriously before he so casually flings his positive-negative epithets about.

Let us take the matter of human individuality for example. The Western viewpoint, as we have seen, is that it is to be highly valued and jealously guarded. To a person possessed of this general viewpoint, his own wants and desires are positive elements, mainly because they are his personal wants and desires. He tends to fence in his strength, time and possessions from interference; and the most terrible fate of which he can conceive is for his conscious awareness to be blotted out.[1]

---

[1] The influence of Christianity here has been divided. Its emphasis on individual uniqueness has tended to produce a narrow individualism, sometimes fortified by the concept of a sentient life after death. On the other hand it has called for self-sacrifice and has undoubtedly stimulated a vast amount of communal effort and social endeavour. It has indeed been more conscious of the need of human fellowship in the religious life than most of the Eastern religions. Its church life is integral to it.

But there is another view of individuality. "Wants" and "desires" are not positive but negative in nature; even the words themselves, which indicate that which is presently lacking to the wanting, desiring individual, bear witness to this. That mind which is obsessed with its wants and desires, no matter how active it may be in what it calls "positive" action, is essentially limited and negative. It cannot rise from the narrow particulars of its own inherent insufficiencies to seek or contemplate that which is beyond narrow self. Actually these wants and desires are a bondage of the worst kind, in which the individual serves his own unstable emotions, physical needs and is at the beck and call of the external world of the senses.

Or we may put it another way. The empirical self, the body-mind individual with all its inherent appetites, is a fluctuating and passing thing. What it wants today it does not want tomorrow; or if it gets what it wants at one moment, it despises the same thing in the next. How can there be any inner security, any personal mastery, or "inner-directed" living with such a conception of individuality? Thus much of what the West values as positive individuality, is looked upon by the East as positive limitation and insecure weakness.

This is perhaps indicative of the basically different Buddhist conception of what constitutes the highest order of true individuality. The Buddhist ideal of genuine positive individuality is the expansion of all the limited qualities of the ordinary individual to a completely general or universal scope. The highest consciousness is not my narrow self-awareness, but a universal consciousness that can enter into the thoughts and consciousness of other beings. Fullest individuality, fullest "personal" reality, is precisely that which can erase the sharp, tight lines which the natural man seeks to draw between his self-consciousness and that of others, and experience a generalized consciousness which feels the thoughts and joys of others without distinguishing them from its "own". On this level they are its own; there is no mine and thine. To the Buddhist, the Western and to some extent Christian, concept of individuality is a mistaken cherishing of the impurities of human nature, rather than its true, pure essence. It is the impurities which set us off from each other, make us unable to penetrate another's life or share in it; it is these impurities of limited viewpoint and selfish desires which we cherish as a precious self. Once these are cleared away, the true spiritual nature of man is no longer opaque, completely different from others in its "uniqueness", but lucid, pervasive, fully and maturely spiritual, universal in nature and sympathies. This alone is positive individuality.

The other factor which qualifies the easy use of the positive-negative contrast, is the changing Eastern attitude toward the external, historical world. That a considerable degree of hopeless or phlegmatic passivity towards the world without has characterized the East in the past, may be granted. That the Buddhist doctrines of kamma and rebirth have been widely used to solace those suffering present misfortune and have prevented them from attempting to change contemporaneous social conditions may also be granted. Yet even this has not been so absolutely the case as the West often thinks. The East has also had its great kings and empires; its attempts to create good social orders. And some of these have been Buddhist in inspiration, as notably with King Aśoka who ruled in India two centuries after the Buddha. So also, there has always been a healthy respect for the things of this world among the mass of Buddhist laity, who have thought more in terms of a better rebirth in the next human life, than of immediately reaching Nibbana.

Besides all this, however, there is the new and disturbing influence of the outside world upon the East in general and Buddhist countries in particular, which forces them to take account of political, social, and economic factors in a more thoroughgoing way than ever before. No longer is it a question of passively adapting to things as they are, in a general spirit of detachment. But it is a question of relating Buddhist principles directly and meaningfully to this-wordly affairs. For several South-east Asian countries, which are predominantly Buddhist, this requires the evolvement of a specifically Buddhist social ethic and political philosophy not yet clearly defined.

How will this change the meaning of positive and negative? Undoubtedly something of the Western sense of the positive as the concrete, activist pattern of life will enter into Eastern

Buddhist thinking. There are already signs of this. Hence East and West may become somewhat more alike at this point. Yet it is unlikely—unless it turns to a crass, rootless materialism— that the Buddhist East will abandon its will-to-detachment or its negatively-stated but affirmatively-lived ideal of individuality. It will undoubtedly continue to be sceptical of an absolute, fanatical devotion to the improvement of samsara (the social-political-economic conditions of the space-time order) as anything but frustrating and exhausting in the long run.

It may—and there are signs again of an attempt in this direction—seek to combine something of *its* positives with those of the West. It may translate "detachment" into "disinterested", i.e. unselfish, public concern and service. It may achieve a new pattern of relaxed, moment-by-moment attention to matters in hand, be they this-worldly or other worldly, and thereby avoid many of the destroying inner tensions of Western society. It may evolve a dispassionate but not apathetic, and a balanced but not static, mode of action which will provide a clear-headed, unemotional, but not indifferent solution of political and social problem. The widespread modern practice of meditation, discussed in the final chapter, represents a significant contemporary effort to achieve such balance. But whether this in fact *will* take place and whether Buddhism will be able basically to formulate its own terms for such an actionable, positive-negative synthesis of values, is by no means certain. The pace of change may be so rapid that a Western-style positivism will be forced upon it whether or no.

II

BUDDHISM: HIGH, LOW, AND MEDIUM

To parody a famous description of quite another matter: Buddhism is a many-levelled thing. The truth of this is obvious in whatever way we may choose to consider it. Empirically speaking there are the many varieties of Buddhist practice, tradition, custom, and forms throughout the world, often widely divergent from one another; though here the term "many-faceted" might be better, despite the tendency of some forms to call themselves higher than others. There is also the classic Buddhist doctrine of the lower and higher truth. While Mahayana affirms that its scriptures, on the whole of later composition than the Theravada Pali scriptures, are the "secret" teaching of the Buddha reserved for those who could truly understand it, the general proposition that a person can appropriate the truth only in accordance with his own spiritual capacity would be agreed to by all Buddhists without any sectarian differentiation between grades of scriptures. Thus is justified the amazing tolerance for divergent practice which is so characteristic of the Buddhist world.

Now the further question of the actual dynamic relation of each of these varieties or levels to each other, their relative worth, and the intricacies of all the gradations made in Buddhism between differing types of experience, is a complex and difficult one. In the true Buddhist sense every individual is perhaps a level unto himself. But even if we rather crudely lump individuals into groups or types, the matter still remains confusing to the outsider. Hence I do not pretend to plumb the depths of all the many varieties of Buddhist experience, but rather to indicate some of the relationships involved and to call attention to the variety to be found even within a relatively conservative and homogeneous Buddhist culture such as that of Burma.

The account given here is to some extent autobiographical. Its order represents the chronological order of my own personal awareness of the several facets or levels of Buddhist experience and practice. Since a good many in the West are now reading Buddhist literature in one form or another, this account may be of some interest to those who have not visited Buddhist countries in addition to their study.

Literary and Export Buddhism

For the past seventy-five years or more Buddhist scriptures and associated writings have been made increasingly available to the West. One thinks of the monumental series of Max Müller's editing, *The Sacred Books of the East;* of the work of the Rhys Davids; of the continuing work of the Pali Text Society. And there have been besides a large number of other treatments, translations, and selections by notable scholars and by those interested in presenting Buddhist teachings to the West for various purposes.

Perhaps "export Buddhism" is the best name to give these presentations, particularly the selections from Buddhist writings. (Not that Buddhists themselves have been doing much exporting of their own product, particularly from Theravada countries; most of it was done for them by Westerners, until very recently.) And if the adjective "export" seems to cast doubt upon the authenticity of that version of Buddhism which came to the West and which I personally imbibed in my own studies, perhaps it needs some explaining.

By the use of this term I do not intend to get into the tangled question of whether Western translators have done justice to key terms in Buddhist texts. (Many Theravadins feel that they have not.) Nor is it to disparage in any way the efforts of many able scholars who have made it their life work to bring to the West the documents and teachings of the East. No doubt if I had read *all* they had to say and made a balanced judgment of the matter, some of my naive ideas and misapprehensions might have been cleared away, without direct experience itself. But I have spoken with enough Westerners to believe, that for many who have had acquaintance with Buddhism only through current selections from its literature, such a general portrait as I had in mind from my readings is fairly common among them.

For one thing, the great majority of the work done by the scholars concerned itself primarily with texts and doctrinal study. Comparatively little was written about contemporary Buddhist life and practice from the scholarly viewpoint, in English at least. Certainly there are notable exceptions such as J. B. Pratt, K. L. Reichelt, L. A. Waddell, and others. But most of such portraits were done by tourists or popularizers. And such were paid little attention to in the academic circles where I first learned about Buddhism. This in itself, therefore, tended to give an abstracted picture of Buddhism only in terms of bare ideas—just as likely to yield a balanced judgment of Buddhism as the study of Augustine and Aquinas alone might be expected to yield a genuine portrait of contemporary Roman Catholicism.

Likewise it must be noted that during this same period Western scholars have been much concerned to give a "true" or "fair" picture of "essential" Buddhism to the West. This was in reaction to previous missionary portraits of Buddhism as one of the strange and heathen cults of the East with which the servant of the Lord must do battle, or the superficial travelogue document already alluded to. Such scholars were most anxious to let the scriptures of the East speak for themselves in their own words.

T. W. Rhys Davids was one of the most notable of these scholars, and may serve as one example. His many works and translations are well known; and his scholarship and objectivity are highly respected even today, both in West and East, in the field of Pali Buddhism. He did not suppress any of the traditional materials, though naturally he sought to translate what he regarded as the most important texts first and to emphasize the essentials of Buddhist doctrine over the nonessentials. Nor did he refrain from making a historical and literary analysis of the Pali Canon. Such analysis and the consequent judgments as to the age or authenticity of some materials in the Canon were not always agreeable to Buddhist orthodoxy. Nevertheless he did all his work in a spirit of sympathy and attempted understanding. If anything, he leaned over backward to be scrupulously fair in his judgments and interpretations.

But this in itself led to a kind of distortion, or at least an emphasis which might give an imperfect picture of living Buddhism, if it were the only one available. Rhys Davids, in line with his search for the essential Buddhism, was much interested to distinguish the original from added materials, much as Christian scholars have sought to isolate the "actual" words of Jesus from their coloured interpretations. In doing this he built up a portrait of Buddhism as originally and essentially a sober, rational moralism. He viewed Buddha's extension of the concept of strict causality to the moral realm (through kamma) as perhaps his outstanding accomplishment. He characterizes Buddha's own conception of the way of salvation which he proclaimed as

salvation merely by self-control and love without any of the rites, any of the ceremonies, any of the charms, any of the priestly powers, any of the gods, in which men love to trust.[1]

And in another work, the volume entitled *Early Buddhism*, he ends with the following quotation from T. H. Huxley's Romanes Lecture which serves as a fitting valedictory to that Buddhism which he describes in his own writing:

A system which knows no God in the Western sense, which denies a soul to man; which counts the belief in immortality a blunder and the hope of it a sin; which refuses any efficacy to prayer or sacrifices; which bids men look to nothing but their own efforts for salvation; which, in its original purity, knew nothing of the vows of obedience and never sought the aid of the secular arm.[2]

Another writer, an interpreter rather than a translator, who had considerable to do with familiarization of America with Buddhist thought, was Paul Carus. At a time when there was little interest in Buddhism outside academic circles, and in the face of a prevalent denominational Christian prejudice against anything which sounded like religious syncretism, he pioneered in his studies and writing about Buddhism in a

---

[1] *Buddhism*, SPCK, 1893 edition, p. 41.
[2] *Archibald Constable*, 1907, p. 88.

sympathetic vein. His concern was to achieve the unity of all major religious faiths. In particular he wished to formulate a religious philosophy which would combine the best insights of both Christian and Buddhist faiths. In this spirit he compiled his popular *The Gospel of Buddha*, first published in 1894 and comprised of scripture selections from both Mahayana and Theravada canons. In the preface to the 1915 re-edition he writes:

> *Now Buddhism is a religion which knows no supernatural revelation, and proclaims doctrines that require no other argument than the "come and see". The Buddha bases his religion solely upon man's knowledge of the nature of things, upon provable truth.*[1]

He does indeed recognize the presence of extensive supernatural and miraculous elements in some of the literature which he edited. But most of this elaboration on the "original" gospel of the Buddha, he attributes to later Mahayana efforts which, "following the spirit of missionary propaganda . . . popularized the Buddha's doctrines and made them accessible to the multitudes". . . . Some of this material is retained in his selections, if the miraculous element in it enforces a moral lesson. He "cuts out most of the apocryphal adornments", but "only prunes the exuberance of wonder" rather than casting out the marvellous, root and branch.[2]

There is another type of writer of whom Maurice Collis may serve as an example. A long-time resident of Burma (British government service) and a sympathetic writer about the East, he refers thus to early Buddhism:

> *As most people are aware, there is an early and a later Buddhism. The first—it might be called Apostolic Buddhism—derived from the attempt made by the Master and his disciples in the sixth century B.C. to combat the superstitions of popular Hinduism by teaching that a plain, decent, humane and reasonable way of life was wholly sufficient for a man's salvation.*[3]

Thus we may summarize the "original" or "essential" Buddhism as presented by such writers to be a no-nonsense sort of sober, rational moralism of agnostic or atheistic proportions.

---

[1] Open Court edition, p. xii.   [2] Ibid., pp. xiii, viii.
[3] *The Land of the Great Image*, Faber and Faber, 1943, p. 135.

It asked its disciples for no exercise of faith, but beginning with self-evident truths of observation, or facts of immediate experience open to anyone, moved logical step by logical step to its goals of equanimity, serenity, and stable moral character. Metaphysical speculations were avoided, the miraculous was eschewed, and dogmatism was entirely absent. Here at last the West would see a truly scientific morality in operation, and in the Buddhist doctrine of kamma observe the ethical application of the causal principle even to the religious realm. Whether this was indeed the full gospel of Buddha himself and all the esoteric and miraculous elements found even in the "original" scriptures of Theravada Buddhism, let alone Mayahana, are indeed later additions, still remains a matter of dispute among scholars. But for our purpose here it may be more important to inquire whether this portrait of "original Buddhism" presented to the West, is also "essential" or "true" Buddhism even in the modern sense. There are well-known writers who answer in the affirmative. Two of these, both Western converts to Buddhism, may serve as examples.

In his volume *The Doctrine of the Buddha*, George Grimm indicates the nature of his interpretation of Buddhism by the sub-title: *The Religion of Reason*. He is emphatically certain of two points: (1) That there is an infallible criterion for distinguishing the genuine utterances of the Buddha (true Buddhism) from later accretions, namely, by their absolutely self-evidencing quality: (2) corollary to the above, everything that the Buddha said is eminently rational. The following quotation will serve as illustration:

> *Let our mental eyes roam over all the religious and philosophical systems of the present and the past; and where shall we find one which claims to be able, solely of itself, to point out the supreme actuality . . . and show each man his ultimate destiny in an intelligible manner, that is, with compelling logic; and whose founder in his own person had realized this ultimate goal of mankind? We shall find no such system. . . . But by good fortune the giant of mental giants with his giant truth, in his Teaching, already for the last two thousand years has been living among mankind. . . . He called himself the "Buddha, the awakened to actuality out of the dream of life."*[1]

[1] George Allen and Unwin, 1957, p. xiii, xv. Reprint of 1926 edition.

The other instance is that of Dwight Goddard who writes in the preface to his well-known *Buddhist Bible* the following words apropos of Buddhism:

> *Its rationality, its discipline, its emphasis on simplicity and sincerity, its thoughtfulness, its cheerful industry not for profit but for service, its love for all animate life, its restraint of desire in all its subtle forms, its actual foretastes of enlightenment and blissful peace, its patient acceptance of karma and rebirth, all mark it out as being competent to meet the problems of this excitement-loving, materialistic, acquisitive and thoughtless age.*[1]

So it is that Buddhism has been presented to the West by scholars, travellers, and apologists. This "export" variety cannot be called precisely a false or even distorted representation of Buddhism. For all the elements set forth by our authors *are* there in Buddhism. But the portrait is a selective one; and if the reader who takes it to be a comprehensive description of contemporary Buddhism, as many Westerners including myself undoubtedly tend to do, it may become a *false* portrait. For there are many other elements besides these classic simplicities in living and breathing Buddhist practice.

Popular Theravada Buddhism

It was of these other elements in Buddhist practice, largely present in footnotes to the texts or in casual asides of the representatives of Export Buddhism, that I became acutely aware upon encountering popular Theravada Buddhism in Burma. What I there beheld seemed to have slight relation to that Buddhism of high philosophic quality of which I had learned in my previous reading. Proportions were reversed: That which was relegated in the books to footnotes and asides—the ritual, the mythical, the superstitious—seemed to occupy the centre of the stage so far as actual practice was concerned. At least this was the evidence presented to my eyes and ears. A way of life that had been classically portrayed as free from dependence upon tangible symbols of faith and impatient of ritual, seemed not only much addicted to them but to find

[1] George G. Harrap, 1956 edition, p. viii.

them absolutely essential in following the way of the Buddha.

Since many other works deal in detail with the tangibilities of Buddhist worship, here I shall record only those general impressions (a kind of "culture shock") made upon me by my first sights of Buddhism in operation. It was, of course, the pagoda and its ceremonial—semi-equivalent to a church in Christian cultures—that I first saw. In fact within days of my arrival in Burma, I visited the massive Shwe Dagon, a great golden spire rising over 300 feet from its platform atop a hill and surrounded by a village of smaller spires and temples. The impression was overwhelming. Such colour—the shining gold of the central spire, the red and gold of the small spired shrines clustering about its foot; the intense greens, browns, and silvers of the gingerbready decorations on the tiered temple roofs; the glittering coloured-glass mosaic columns; the arresting orange splotches of the monks' robes. Such a multitude of images of the Buddha, big and little, lying and sitting, alabaster and plaster, plain and shining golden, crowded into Buddha halls by the dozen or seated each in a separate shrine building. And multitudinous other images of attendant beings of heavenly nature, of yellow-robed saints, guardian snarling lions (chinthes), and miscellaneous worshipping animals. So many shrines, all with their worshippers; and such devout worship of reverent kneeling, audibly fervent devotions, offerings of flowers, incense-sticks, and smaller paper umbrellas, washing of images, lighting of candles, and resounding gongs. For this neither my non-symbolic Protestant training, which I had naively imagined to be somewhat akin to the Buddhist practice of religion, nor my readings, had quite prepared me.

The Shwe Dagon is, of course, quite the grandest and most important of all the pagodas in Burma, but the quality, if not the scale, of visible Buddhist religion is much the same here as elsewhere. Everywhere one finds the Buddha image, whether in the Shwe Dagon, the small village pagoda, or the table-size glass and gilt shrine which encloses the image in the home. And everywhere the worshipful amenities are the same: removal of the shoes, the bowing reverence, and the offerings of flowers and incense. To the onlooker the Buddhist attitude toward the physical objects of his veneration seems ambiguous. The multiplication of Buddha statues and pagodas suggests a certain indifference to any individual one. Any one may do as well as any other. The physical symbol is not, per se, of any great importance. Indeed there are stories of the multiplication of sacred items, such as the Sacred Tooth of Kandy (Ceylon), in which the duplicate is as valuable as the original. And in apparent accordance with this is the neglect of many pagodas and the careless unprotected storage of images.

Yet there is another side to the matter. Neglect does not indicate disrespect, but far more often in Burma, at least, lack of resources and perhaps a certain presumption in favour of the building rather than the repairing of pagodas. Also the multiplication of sacred objects, and the great reverence shown to the tremendous reclining statues, some more than 100 feet long, may indicate that each additional statue or extra cubic foot of content increases the total religious value.

It is likewise true that certain specific pagodas and images seem to have a special virtue, which does not accord with the principle of the absolutely indifferent replaceability of any statue by any other. Prayers made in front of certain specific images or shrines are considered more valuable than those made elsewhere. The presence of relics, such as ashes, bones, teeth, hair, staff, begging bowl or robe of the Buddha, make any shrine of unusual value. The Shwe Dagon, for example, traditionally contains at least four of the Buddha's hairs. One of the chief prizes of a Burmese raid on Arakan was an ancient bronze image of the Buddha, reputed to be a contemporary likeness of him; it is now enshrined in the Arakan pagoda at Mandalay. Every year five small images, originally sandal-wood but now covered so thickly by gold leaf applied by pilgrims that they appear to be rather shapeless objects of pure gold, are carried up and down the waters of Inle (lake) in the Shan States in a grand procession. Their visit at each of five villages, in simulation of the visit of King Alaungsitha centuries ago with the self-same images, is considered an especially auspicious event for the village.

Nor must one forget to mention the popular religious art which crowds the precinct of most pagodas. Sometimes there are long friezes of carved wooden high relief, almost three dimensional in parts; or else papier-mâché figures in miniature,

D

or even life-size, in special screened cages; or a series of oil paintings, of the religious-calendar variety, around the pagoda rest-houses. For these the many canonical legends of the Buddha and the *Jātaka Tales* of his former births offer endless subjects for treatment. But there is a tendency to emphasize the more lurid aspects of Buddhist teaching: the gaunt-hot-eyed murderer still holding the bloody knife in his hand; the carrion-eating animals hovering about the dying man; the vivid depiction of the damned being pitchforked into burning purgatories for a million years or so.

Thus the popular expression of faith consists usually in a round of periodic visits to pagodas for veneration of the images or the pagoda itself and edification by its pictures or for occasional instruction by a monk. There are also special visits on festival days, and occasional pilgrimages to the more popular shrines. All this is held to produce merit or good kamma, somewhat in relation to the effort made or the size of the offering given while there. And merit, as a kind of stored up virtue and good fortune for future lives, bringing one to happy rebirth or forwarding him on the way to Nibbana, is most highly esteemed.

But pagoda-religion has other non-Buddhist accompaniments which are often almost as prominent as the specifically Buddhist element itself. In particular, I refer to the worship of nats or spirits, so abundant in Burmese Buddhism. At the eight compass points of many a pagoda, for example, including the relatively new Peace Pagoda in Rangoon, one finds small posts or figures before which candles are burnt, prayers said, and to which flowers may be brought. Attached to, or beneath, many a venerable tree is one or more shelves or little "houses" containing one sort of figure or other, none of them Buddhas. Near the rice fields in some areas may be seen small grass houses, two or three feet square and peaked at the top, upon platforms three or four feet high. (These honour an ogress named *Sāvatthi,* whose life history is given in the Dhammapada Commentary and who is considered to be a patroness of the crops.) Likewise in many a house, city or country, one finds the hanging coconut tied with a bit of red cloth, and coconut and banana offerings round about the Buddha shrine—for the nats, not the Buddha. And scattered throughout Burma, often cheek-by-jowl with the Buddhist holy places, are full-scale nat shrines complete with images and attendants.

Nat worship has also its special festivals and celebrations. During the winter harvest season in the villages one may encounter many a nat-pwe, i.e. dancing-singing dramatizations to the accompaniment of the orchestra of drums, cymbals, clappers, and flutes. These are performed either by travelling companies of semi-professional actors and musicians, or on a more modest scale by local talent. The local populace bring their offerings to the nats in whose honour the pwe is held (bananas, coconuts, eggs, fruits) and sit about to behold the dancers who are usually painted, powdered, and dressed as women, whatever their sex.

There is a great deal of good festival fun involved for both performers and performees; considerable broad humour is bandied back and forth in the intervals between acts, and there appears to be some deliberate clowning by the actors. Nevertheless, the main purpose is quite serious. It is that the dancer should become possessed by the spirit of the nat whom he honours or seeks to placate. This possession is evidenced by a kind of hysterical excitement that grips the performers even when they are professionals, during which the magic-possessed words are spoken. Unless this occurs the pwe or performance has not been a success and the benefits of blessing on crops or deliverance from an evil spirit will not be received. Two contemporary newspaper accounts will indicate the important role of nat worship in Burma:

> *A Palaung villager, who ran amok, seized a dah [machete] and attacked a number of persons around him, was shot down and killed . . . during a nat festival held recently in Man-laing village, 26 miles from Hsenwi. Elders in the locality believe that the Palaung was possessed by the spirit of the Myosa's [district headman's] elder brother, who died some years ago. According to this belief, the Myosa and his people had incurred the displeasure of the "spirit" because the dead man had not been "invited" with the other nats to the festivities.*
>
> *. . . Whatever the reason, the festivities came to an abrupt end, and the contractors for the gambling waings suffered heavy losses.*[1]

[1] From *The Nation* (Rangoon), dispatch dated May 8, 1959.

Another and different type of incident, under Buddhist auspices this time, had been reported but a few days earlier:

For the past eight years, Henzada has been steadily eaten away by the Irrawaddy [river]. . . . In their desperation the townspeople have been reminded of an old Burmese couplet to the effect that "when the crocodile swims against the river, the banks are safe; when it floats downstream, the banks erode". Yesterday, the Pagoda Committee of the U Ba Yai Zedi, a well-known landmark in town, decided to try out the effectiveness of the old saw. They decorated a motor launch with the rainbow-coloured Sasana flag and chanted prayers in honour of Shin Upagok and U Shin Gyi, the patron nats of the waters. After the prayers, the motor launch steamed upstream, towing a wooden effigy of a crocodile, in the hope that the old saying might eventually come true. The wooden crocodile was later taken across to a sandbank opposite the town and buried there.[1]

A few words in passing may be said with regard to still another related phenomenon: the practice of astrology. Astrologers and fortune-tellers are often, though not exclusively, to be found about pagodas. (One of the newest and most splendid pagodas in Burma has lucky-sign decorations on outside pillars.) Many pious Buddhists, perhaps the majority, would not think of undertaking any important business without consulting their horoscopes or an astrologer to determine the "auspicious" occasion. Indeed Burma's Independence Day was set only after careful astrological calculations. The stars, as abodes of spirits or as powerful spirit-forces in themselves, exert a tremendous influence for material good or evil over human life, it is held.

All these "extra-curricular" accompaniments of Buddhism raise the vital question of their relation to the Buddhist teaching and practice itself. Is Burmese "Buddhism" a covering name for, or a thin veneer over, popular folk religion of pre-Buddhist origin? Or is genuine Buddhism of the essence, and nat worship only incidental to it? To this question, on which there have been different opinions, an answer may be better given after noting another important element in the situation, of which a person only slowly becomes aware after his initial bemusement with popular religion has worn off. This is what

---

[1] From *The Nation* (Rangoon), dispatch dated April 27, 1959. Sasana Flag is the "official" Buddhist flag, Sasana meaning "Buddhist religion".

may be called the traditional orthodoxy, which harbours within its somewhat harsh and rigid externals a core of live experiential religion.

Traditional Orthodoxy

If there is anything upon which Theravadins pride themselves more than another, it is their orthodoxy. Over and over it is affirmed that the Theravada doctrine and practice are the contemporary embodiments of the pristine purity of Buddhism —this with an emphatic and scornful glance in the direction of the "diluted" orthodoxy of the Mahayanist. Such is the firm conviction of both monks and laity.

The literary form of this conviction is the insistence that the Pali Canon or Tipitaka (three "baskets" containing the Vinaya rules for monks, Suttas or simpler discourses, and Abhidhamma or philosophical development of doctrine) represents the direct, perhaps even verbatim, teaching of the Buddha. It is staunchly maintained that the oral tradition, handed down for five hundred years through the Sangha or order of monks, preserved his words unaltered. The Mahayana tradition of a secret teaching made known only to a few and written down much later than the Pali scriptures, is deprecated as false and un-Buddhistic. Along with this is included, for practical purposes, the later *Questions of King Milinda* and a vast commentarial literature in which the works of Ceylon's Buddhaghosa (fifth century A.D.) are most highly esteemed as the orthodox interpretation of the orthodox scriptures.

The result is a Buddhistic scriptural Fundamentalism comparable to the conservative scriptural Christianity of some American groups.[1] Almost the same reasoning applies here as in Christian Fundamentalism, though there is, of course, no doctrine of a divinely dictated revelation. But the omniscient Buddha, who by his own efforts and insight arrived at absolute truth, spoke it to his monks; they repeated it faith-

[1] For non-American readers: Fundamentalism refers to those groups who, in the early part of this century, described themselves as standing by the fundamental doctrines of Christianity as opposed to the "modernists" who were undermining the faith. Today it is applied generally to conservatives who especially emphasize the literal inerrancy and truth of the Christian scriptures.

fully by memory century after century, mutually correcting each other in the public recitations of the successive councils. (The Sixth Synod held in Rangoon in 1954–6 re-edited the Pali Scriptures, with the slight variations in the several Theravada texts compared and corrected.) Thus the result is, for all practical purposes, an inerrant scripture and an infallible process of transmission which it is heresy to question. "Thus saith the Buddha", i.e. the Pali Canon, becomes equivalent to "thus saith the Lord", i.e the Bible, for the Fundamentalist Christian.

It is obvious that there has been almost no literary or historical criticism of any sort issuing from Theravada Buddhism. Now and then one meets a monk or scholar who will say that the *Jātaka Tales* (a large collection of folk tales, many of them obviously of pre-Buddhist origins, adapted to Buddhist use as portraying the former births of the Buddha-to-be) are in large part legendary, or the Abhidhamma, a development of Buddhist doctrine rather than the words of the Buddha himself. But by and large there is neither interest nor desire to analyze the Pali Canon in terms of constituent elements. The conclusions of those scholars who have done so, Indian and Western, are largely ignored. For the orthodox the Pali Canon simply did not develop; it comes direct from the mouth of Gotama Buddha.

Writes a devout layman:

> *Buddhist literature is the presentation of the Buddha's Teaching in the printed word. . . . What was expounded was in 84,000 titles which is estimated to be about eleven times the size of the Old and New Testaments. . . . It should be noted, however, that this [the Tipitaka] is not a gradual development. It has been brought down to this day in its original purity through the successive six Buddhist Councils.*[1]

This is matched by the general lack of speculative interest or new doctrinal developments. If one has the perfect truth perfectly transmitted and inerrantly written down, why should he seek to develop it in new directions? The danger of heresy lies in such attempts. Therefore the original deposit of truth is reworked over and over again; and since the Tipitika is of con-

---

[1] U Tun Hla Oung, *The Open Door*, Vol. II, No. 1, July 1959, p. 23.

siderable length this task can go on indefinitely, as the immense mass of commentaries and sub-commentaries testifies. Indeed this process of exposition still goes on at great length, with many a monk and latterly some laymen re-expounding the ancient truth. There are indeed some new practical emphases or restatements in modern contexts, but so far as he is able the Theravada expositor will keep well within the orthodox tradition, both in word and interpretation.

This attitude has had another side effect: complete immersion in the Pali-Buddhist tradition to the exclusion of interest in or knowledge of any other religious tradition, including Mahayana Buddhism. Such interest or effort is pointless to the average Theravada Buddhist since he has the perfect truth. Add to this geographical isolation, which in Burma's case has kept her apart from most of the tides of empire, emigration, and cultural change for the last thousand years or so, and the result is an almost completely parochial situation. Particularly is this true of Burma's religion since the scriptures are in Pali, a "dead" language largely untouched by living contact with other languages for nearly two thousand years, and even unknown to the average Buddhist layman. The Burmese monk, who is the religious mentor of his people, is thus doubly immured behind the walls of changeless tradition since with few exceptions he knows only Pali, and his own native language and isolated tradition. So it is that for many centuries Burmese Buddhism has stirred around only in its own circle of terms and concepts without genuine cross-fertilization of strange ideas of any sort. Such contacts as it has had with other religions through missionaries or minority groups have left it largely unaffected for reasons which we cannot explore here.

It is also true, rather curiously but understandably, that Theravada Buddhism has had little missionary impulse for many centuries. The Sangha has been neither disposed nor capable of speaking its gospel to other than its own countrymen. And though instruction which might well include missionary teaching, is part of the monkish discipline or duty, the monk's concern to achieve his own Nibbana tends to neutralize such effort. Besides, there is the consideration that only those whose kamma is ripened can hear the word with profit anyway; and if their kamma is sufficiently good they will be born into a Buddhist country, preferably Burma, where it is easy to hear the Buddha's true word.

We may consider also the orthodoxy of meditational practice. This is a tradition in its own right, or a tradition within a tradition as it were. For the universal Buddhist teaching, now especially emphasized in Theravada countries, is that only by the actual living of the Buddha-life can one "know" the truth. Even doctrinal correctness, necessary as it is, is not sufficient. "Book learning" can never substitute for direct, personal experience of truth.

To be sure there is a general and more external pattern of orthodox Buddhist practice. It consists of two parts, monk's and layman's. Theravada Buddhism, especially in Burma, sees in its monks the holy community of the faithful who preserve the truth both in its literary and experiential forms. Therefore in view of its staunch conservatism it holds its monks closely to what is conceived to be the aboriginal pattern of conduct. The 227 major rules of the Vinaya Pitaka, which prescribe the dress and the living habits of monks in great detail, are to be followed just as they are written in the scriptures without concession to modern conditions. Of course there have been some such concessions, so that even in Burmese Buddhism there are those brethren of the yellow robe who are looked upon by their more conservative brethren as being slightly worldly in their garb (brighter yellows) and living accommodations (wearing sandals, using rugs on the floor, smoking tobacco and so forth). But the true pattern, even with its slight variations is clear: a simple, abstemious, sober (though not sorrowful), studious, and devout life.

For the layman, too, the path is reasonably clear. He has Five Precepts which enjoin him to avoid killing, lying, stealing, sexual misconduct (though not polygamy), and intoxication. And on sabbath and festival days he may add thereto some further disciplines of fasting and abstaining from personal adornment. Thus at the minimum he will be a sober respectful citizen; and at the maximum he will add to his moral virtues, extra religious virtues of frequent pagoda attendance, gifts to the Sangha, and the attempt to raise the external observation of the Precepts into an inner spirit and rule. This sober, almost puritanical, morality of the good Buddhist layman combined with the primitive naturalness and childlike spontaneity which seems congenital to the Burman, results in a delightfully inconsistent and unpredictable type of behaviour which is one of the joys (and exasperations) of the Burmese Buddhist character.

But orthodoxy today goes beyond these outward forms; it includes the practice of private meditation. Since a full chapter is devoted to this subject, I shall only note it here. Formerly the almost exclusive privilege of the monk, whose whole life pattern is geared to make it possible, meditation is now being practised by many laymen according to a more simplified pattern. But in whatever form, and by whomever practiced, meditation is the heart of the Buddhist way of salvation. Apart from it morality and doctrinal correctness are dry husks; its practice alone, in addition to the externals, can produce the saint; without it the ultimate detachment which leads to Nibbana is impossible. Thus the truly devout Buddhist aspires to find both time and capacity within himself for its practice. Many a layman, especially when he comes to mature years, gives himself increasingly to this meditational discipline.

Such then are the lineaments of Buddhist orthodoxy. Intellectually it has championed the same scriptures and expounded the same doctrines for a thousand years or more. This rigid doctrinalism has been the structural steel of the Theravada edifice. Practically it has been the presence of a core of the inwardly orthodox and devoutly religious within the Sangha and among the laity that has kept Buddhism alive (sometimes more and sometimes less). They are the salt which has preserved the true Buddhist savour. Their inner gospel of the special Buddhist religious experience that has been handed down through the ages is Buddhism's vital heritage.

But what then are the relations of this rigidly traditional and pure Buddhist doctrine and practice to that popular Buddhism of pagoda cult and nat worship which we have previously described? To this question we now turn.

The Relation of Popular and Orthodox Buddhism

This relationship is no simple or easy matter to determine. It is full of seeming contradictions and dynamic complexities. But we may first try to unravel some of them by means of two sets of questions. One set has to do with the locus of orthodoxy in terms of *persons*. The other has to do with its locus in terms of *doctrine* and *practice*.

1. *Locus of Orthodoxy*

With regard to the first we may ask: Who is orthodox? Is orthodoxy to be found in certain specific groups, or given institutions, or is it to be thought of relativistically in terms of understanding, of "higher" and "lower" truths, that is? The answer is both yes and no in all three cases. There *are* those cultural levels, those institutional groups, and those levels of experience distinguished at great length by Buddhist learning, which are more truly Buddhist than others. But at the same time these same groups, institutions, and levels are permeated in a most confusing fashion with *"non"*-Buddhist attitudes, beliefs, and practices. One cannot say, for example, that all town dwellers or all persons with a college education disbelieve in nats, despite Christmas Humphrey's definition of nats as "the nature spirits of Burma still worshipped in village shrines."[1] This is too neat a solution as will be exampled at length below. While nats are more generally worshipped in the villages among peasants of small education, many an educated person still keeps some minor elements of nat worship about the house, or allows some member of the family to do so; and even though perhaps rather apologetic or secretive about the matter himself, he will invoke the aid of nats in emergencies. And in the reverse order we may find some much less educated villager who holds aloof from the more popular aspects of Buddhist devotion, and from nat worship in particular, practising rather the moralistic and meditative way of life.

If we turn to the institution of the Sangha the situation re-

---

[1] *A Buddhist Students' Manual*, Buddhist Society, 1956, p. 159.

mains ambiguous. To be sure one finds here, perhaps, the largest number of those who disdain nat worship, look upon pagoda worship as useful for others' progress but not their own, and seek to lead their followers toward a purer Buddhism. Yet even here Buddhist folklore and popular practice have their hold. Many monks still live in the marvellous world of fable and myth. There are those among them, as there always have been, who dabble in the arts of fortune telling and astrology, or amateur medical practice. And many of them seem to find the use of beads and the worship of images of the Buddha essential to their own spiritual lives. Indeed one sect among the monks (within the memory of many living persons) that sought to do away with the use of images and most of the external apparatus of pagoda worship, made no headway at all because of the hostility of laymen and monks alike to such iconoclasm. This sect has dwindled away almost to nothing.

With regard to the question of orthodoxy of doctrine and practice—which is only the other side of the coin from orthodoxy of persons—we may ask: What is orthodox Buddhism and what is folklore, when the latter has been incorporated so long in the Buddhist tradition that it cannot well be separated from the "original" or "essential" teaching? Perhaps at one level the *Jātaka Tales*, so popular in Burma, almost perfectly embody the actual working synthesis of orthodoxy and folk tale. There are three layers in the *Tales*. The first is an aphoristic couplet or short verse. To this has been added an explanatory or expository story, sometimes of considerable length. This story is sometimes comic, sometimes tragic, sometimes just interesting adventure, with an ever-present fabulous element. Through the five hundred and forty odd accounts move men, animals, and spirits, conversing familiarly with each other, playing tricks on each other, matching magic against magic. The best, wisest, or cleverest individuals (usually identical) come out best as the rule.

These *Tales* which are a kind of oriental Aesop's Fables, and may well have influenced the latter, are obviously of pre-Buddhist origin. And just as obviously they have been adapted to Buddhism in their present form. For the "winner" of the various contests in all the stories is held to be the Bodhisatta, or Buddha-to-be, who is perfecting his virtues through count-less existences. And to make the adaptation complete, there is a third layer of introductory story or incident and a conclu-sion, in which Gotama Buddha was reminded of the story by a contemporary happening, and went on to identify all the main characters as previous incarnations of himself and others there present.

Here then we have the pattern of reconciliation of folk-lore and orthodox Buddhism, at least on one level. The *Tales* have all the rich flavour of a primitive culture, and are full of the beliefs of simple people living near the soil: Spirits inhabit trees, caves, mountains; they now threaten, now help mankind —provided they are placated or forced by charms to do so. Marvellous events occur daily. Animals and men talk to each other. But through all the stories majestically moves the Bodhisatta, who will become the (Gotama) Buddha many exist-ences later. Here he is the most benevolent, the wisest, or sometimes merely the cleverest or strongest, beast, man, or spirit. But almost always he is the one who wins the battle of wits or proves right in the end. Usually the other characters, except for a few witless or unregenerate individuals, inevitably recognize his essential superiority.

This relationship of gentle dominance of the situation by the Bodhisatta—for he is never vicious or oppressive no matter how clever or strong—is one key to the relation of the Buddhist orthodoxy to accompanying folk-lores. The Buddha and his ways are held to be supreme over all other ways; even the most nat-ridden or animistic Buddhist villager feels this, though dimly. Nats and lesser spirits, as their images, always in worshipping position before the Buddha, attest, are sub-servient to the Enlightened One; for he alone can bring one to Nibbana.

But both the Enlightened One and the nat worshipper realize that there are many, many stages on the way to enlightenment, and that, alas, most individuals are far from ready for it. And in these many lives there are temporarily important matters such as health, happiness, physical and material welfare, and the companionship of other mortals. Thus it is that for these worldly interests the nats must be entreated—for the Buddha has no interest in them and his way leads directly to Nibbana. Yet he was tolerant of human weakness and knew that a man can progress toward Nibbana or receive the Higher Truth only when his good kamma is sufficient. Hence the lesser truths, lower ways, and inferior spirits are not outlawed; but the whole Buddhist structure is pervaded by the gentle and patient hope that in lives to come even the least of these who still worship nats and crave the gifts they can give, will in the end come to the Higher Truth that finally leads to Nibbana.

This interpretation accords with almost everything we know of Buddhism. It is consonant with its historical development, especially in the Theravada tradition. "Original" Buddhism was primarily, and perhaps only, for monastics; Buddha's message was: "Come ye out from among them (the householders) and be ye separate (and homeless)." So great was its success in some areas that family-conscious India was apprehensive that her communities would be ultimately depopulated. But slowly and somewhat reluctantly the role of the lay Buddhist was defined, and as the number of monks increased his role as supporter became more and more important. Yet strictly speaking he remained an outsider. The heart of the Buddhist gospel was the direct quest of Nibbana—and this was esteemed almost impossible for laymen, despite a few brilliant exceptions. For most of them the supreme and enlightening truth remained hidden; nor were they encouraged to seek it.

The result was in some sense a cultural and religious vacuum. Far above mundane concerns and capabilities stood the Buddha and Nibbana, within range only for the few. To them might be given the high, austere reverence men give absolutes; but what of some object for personal devotion, some emotional warmth, some guidance and help in practical living? For all this latter the Buddha way had little or nothing to offer. Even more: Religious symbolism, let alone wider cultural interests, was alien to this central loyalty. Interest in symbols or use of them in "worship", might even hinder the supreme quest for formless, detached Nibbana. Thus for several centuries the form of the Buddha was never represented in Buddhist sanctuaries; only indirect symbols of his invisible presence were utilized. While this partly rooted in the Indian reluctance of that period to picture or represent their deities, it also admirably accorded with the central Buddhist viewpoint.

But vacuums seldom remain unfilled. Nor did this one. Under the influence of Greek sculptural forms of the Gandhara style, Buddha imagery grew and flourished. The very avidity with which it was seized upon showed the layman's deep hunger for the tangibilities. And along with the growth of imagery came other elements to fill the vacuum: relics, sanctuaries, rituals, mythology. Much of this latter, since it was absent in the original Buddhist tradition itself, was supplied from whatever was at hand. In India this meant that the old gods became subordinate and helping spiritual forces, nearer at hand than Buddha in his Nibbana. Occultism, necromancy, astrology—all the esoteric wisdom of India—flowed into the vacuum and became the camp-followers of Buddhism wherever it went.

Thus it was that Buddhism came out of India. There in the centre, but remote and even inaccessible, was the Buddha and his high truth. But attached to him came a multitude of devas and a mass of traditional mundane wisdom. To this motley following each new country into which Buddhism entered added its own quota and made its own changes. In Burma the host of Indian deities was merged with the local nature spirits or nats. To Indian wisdom was added Burmese folk-lore. And the whole of it came to be known as Buddhism!

If we ask again whether this is indeed Buddhism, the answer is not much clearer than before. For though there may be a simple severe core of meditational moralism which we call "essential" Buddhism, the truth is that even here there is an affinity, a kind of softness, for the element which folk-lore supplies. Take the twin doctrines of kamma and rebirth, for example. According to these there is no ultimate distinction between animals, men, and gods. All are sentient beings who are passing on indefinitely from one existence to another according to the nature of their deeds. There are indeed some thirty-one planes of existence, with four below and twenty-six above the human state. The universe is literally teeming with sentient beings who were once human and may become so again. The only distinctive thing about the human status is its innate potentiality for the improvement of one's kammic inheritance. And Buddhism promises to those who as human beings mature their minds, unusual attainments, god-like in quality, by which minds of others may be read, knowledge gained of one's own past births, sounds and sights heard and seen at a distance. And even the ability to change bodily form, or project oneself through the universe instantaneously, may thus be achieved.

What then in such a melange shall be the "orthodox" Buddhist criterion for distinguishing between true and false, good and bad supernormal powers? How shall it draw a clear line between the Buddhist supernormal and the superstitious supernatural of the folk-lore? When does it become wrong to traffic with other spirits and seek the aid of the gods, or the wisdom of the astrologer? How can true Buddhist devotions be distinguished from superstitious prayers? Though answers to these questions may be clear to the expert, they are obviously not so to the rank-and-file Buddhist layman. The presumedly more orthodox Sangha has been able to do little but gently reprove or frown upon the excesses produced by folk religion, hoping to shame the faithful into control.

And to tell the truth, the Sangha itself has not always escaped such contamination. As already noted there has been through the years, a certain dabbling in the occult by Sangha members though often done with a bad conscience. Thus does Maurice Collis portray the royal chaplain under Queen Saw of Burma, in his novelistic adaptation of portions of the *Chronicles of the Glass Palace*:

> The Royal Chaplain was that rarity, an unworldly person who held an official position at Court. As a strict Hinayanist, he disapproved of the occult arts, though he did not disbelieve in their authenticity. He disapproved because they were irrelevant and distracting to his apprehension of truth in the Buddhist sense. . . . Nevertheless, he dabbled in them, unable to resist their fascination.[1]

And as significant as the dabbling is the statement that, though disapproving, the chaplain "did not disbelieve in their authenticity"—a statement which is roughly true with regard to Theravada Buddhists even today. How then draw the line against something whose reality one acknowledges and which is not positively evil—especially if practiced by others?

[1] *She Was a Queen*, Faber and Faber, 1937. Notes, pp. 243-4.

The attitude of the Sangha in these matters has been most important in Theravada countries. For in addition to a considerable degree of illiteracy among the general populace, not even the literate laity can read their own scriptures as the rule. True, the scriptures are written in the characters of their language, and numerous standard religious formulae are known by heart; but the significance of what they say is open only to the expert in Pali, that is, the monk or occasional layman. Hence the stabilizing orthodoxy of the scriptures, such as it is, has been largely denied to the laity save as the Sangha mediates it by word and attitude.

We may lastly observe that the easy tolerance for non-Buddhistic elements in the tradition is part and parcel of the general Buddhist attitude toward differing levels of spiritual attainment. This grows in great part directly from the kamma-rebirth scheme. For no man can appropriate more or higher truth than his present spiritual capacity allows him. And such capacity, of course, is the result of the deeds of all his past existences. Therefore it takes many ages of constant spiritual improvement to provide a saint who can appropriate the higher truths of the way to Nibbana. Meantime no man can be forced into such truths and must follow such light and truth as he has. In such a case even a faint and dim reverence for the Buddha, overlaid though it be by many a layer of folk-lore, is better than no reverence at all. Hence many a lesser and non-Buddhist truth receives tacit baptism into the "orthodox" tradition.

What can be said of the contemporary status of the folklore elements of the Buddhist tradition? The answer is that they are still flourishing in Theravada countries. One may example the matter of the high degree of regard for relics which continues unabated, even enhanced. The gift or enshrinement of a relic of presumed antiquity is an event of major importance in the Theravada world. In 1952 the then premier of Burma, the Honourable U Nu, was invited to Sanchi, India, to assist in the re-enshrinement of the relics of Sariputta and Mahāmoggalana, two of the Buddha's most prominent disciples. These relics, after residing in the Albert and Victoria Museum in London for nearly one hundred years, had been returned to India. A contemporary account of the procession in which the

Burmese premier bore the sacred relics on his head, reads in part as follows:

> *On November the 29th and 30th with great ceremony these sacred relics were taken again to Sanchi and re-enshrined by Premier Nehru amidst the chanting of hymns by yellow-robed Bhikkhus from many countries of South Asia and deafening cheers from nearly one hundred thousand people representing almost every country in the world. The relics were taken in a mile-long procession of devotees chanting sacred verses, offering flowers and burning sweet-smelling incense. The relics were placed on a gold-embroidered cloth for two hours for worship by delegates from many countries who bowed in homage.*[1]

If we consider the matter of nat worship, the same must be said: It is still a vigorous part of the "Buddhist" tradition. And if the Sangha does not worship nats, some of its members still believe in their presence and power. Thus we hear from the Mandalay area that a fireman at a fire station heard and saw the apparition of one of the firemen who had died a few days previously. A police search failed to find any actual stranger, physically speaking, on the premises. Therefore on "the next day phongyis [monks] were invited to the Fire Station to recite the 'Pareik' and exorcise the spirit.[2] Needless to say the idea of a dead man's "spirit" or "soul" hovering about his recent abode for a few days, is more folk-lore than Buddhism, but persists along with it.

Nor is it only in the villages that respect for the nats is found. Many are the houses in Rangoon which keep the coconut hanging in a wicker basket in the house or near the Buddha shrine to provide the local nats with food. One well-educated and devout Buddhist related to me that upon the family's moving to a new house, he found that his wife had placed the nat's coconut at a higher level than the Buddha shrine. He insisted that first things should come first; so the coconut was placed on a lower level—but typical of the harmony between Buddha and the nats, there was no thought of forbidding the nat reverence altogether.

But again we may not relegate nat worship to village peasants or the private foibles of a few housewives in the cities.

[1] *Light of the Dhamma*, Vol. I, No. 2, January 1953. p. 22.
[2] *The Nation*, dispatch dated July 15, 1958.

It is also a matter of significant public concern in Burma. Thus a newspaper dispatch dated February 22, 1959:

> *Led by the Daw Khin Kyi (Madame Aung San) President of the Union Women's League, and Daw Tin Aye, wife of Bohmu Aung, Vice-President of the League, members of the League visited the Shwedagon Pagoda.*
> *All took the Pansil (Five Precepts) and in one accord . . . prayed that for merits acquired from observance of the five precepts and the offering of flowers and libations in memory of the enlightened Buddha, the country and its people be spared from the fascist menace and that fair and free elections . . . be made possible. They also invoked the devas [i.e., heavenly beings including nats] to guard over the destiny of the country and its people and urged them to protect General Ne Win and U Nu from all evils engendered by ill-will and hatred of their enemies.*[1]

Some four months later the matter of nat worship was again called to public attention by two announcements, one from the Government (at that time the caretaker government of General Ne Win) and a responding one from the "Clean" AFPFL political party, that of U Nu. A newspaper reported thus:

> *The Clean AFPFL yesterday announced that it will hold Day-watha-bali ceremonies on July 18.*
> *The Government, it will be recalled, announced . . . that it would dispense with these invocations to nats in the future and, instead, observe the more orthodox* soon *offering to monks for the same purpose. The nats will only be called upon to "share in the meritorious deed" and no ceremonies will be held in their honour.*
> *In a statement issued to the Press, the Clean AFPFL claimed that the former Prime Minister U Nu had been able to "save" the country from disaster in 1948 when countrywide Daywatha-bali ceremonies were held while he, at the same time, obtained the co-operation of Army leaders and patriots in warding off defeat.*
> *Offering of food to the guardian spirits in no way conflicted with the teachings of the Buddha and U Nu still believes these ceremonies should figure with other religious observances such as* soon *offerings*

---

[1] *The Nation.* "Deva" is the classical Pali term referring to the "demoted" Hindu gods who came to learn of the Buddha. In Burmese Buddhism they have been generally merged with the nats, nature spirits and spirits of dead persons, but "deva" sometimes suggests the more blessed or heavenly spirits.

to monks and chanting of the scriptures, to call down blessings upon the country and its peoples.[1]

Two postscripts to the affair will give it the proper context in contemporary Burma. In a dispatch from the same newspaper, dated July 6, a speaker at the Solidarity Association of Army and Police officers said, obviously in a not-so-oblique reference to the above:

democracy and human rights were not obtained by people going up to the pagodas to pray. Democracy, he added, must be constantly strengthened if it is to endure.

But it is also true that U Nu and his party held their Day-watha-bali ceremonial as promised on July 18, and that in February of the next year the people of Burma gave U Nu and his party, who had promised to make Buddhism the state religion, an overwhelming endorsement at the polls.

On the level of defining Buddhism in terms of its orthodoxy, the situation seems relatively clear. There is a traditionally orthodox centre represented *literally* by the scriptures, *doctrinally* by the conservative tradition expounded by the Sangha and the orthodox core of lay-followers, and *practically* by the conventional Buddhist morality for laymen and meditational practice by the spiritually elite in both Sangha and lay ranks. Living cheek-by-jowl with orthodoxy, often frowned upon but never rigidly excluded, and hence become a nearly integral part of "Buddhism", is the religion of folk-lore and the popular devotional cultus of adorational worship of the Buddha image and prudential reverence to the nats.

2. *Dynamic and structural relations*

But this analysis does not do full justice to the Buddhist religious structure. It seems to find in "Buddhism" simply a collection of cultural diversities held loosely together by ancient historic association in one religio-ethnic tradition. Actually there is a deeper and more organic relationship— and a more Buddhistic one perhaps also—in whose terms we may view the structure of Buddhism.

[1] *The Nation*, June 16, 1959. There can be no doubt that this is the considered belief of U Nu. Also on the occasion of the building of the Great Cave and other buildings on the Peace Pagoda grounds, preparatory for the holding of the Sixth Buddhist Synod in 1954–6, when many trees had to be cut down, he led the ceremonies for placating their guardian spirits.

Dr. E. Michael Mendelson suggests that Burmese Buddhism represents a continuum between the extremes of nat worship and ideal (scriptural) Buddhism, rather than a set of disparate elements; one in which the high Buddhism of the Pali tradition is the ideal toward which Theravada strives rather than being a portrait of actual practice or a fully effective rule of behaviour.[1] I shall here adopt this general viewpoint with particular emphasis upon the drive toward the ideal, implicit at least in all the varied levels of "Buddhist" practice. That the practice often gets bogged down in nat worship at the far end of the continuum, or to use my figure, at the outer and lower levels of aspiration, goes with no more than saying. But it is also equally true, it seems, that it is the relation of the total mass of ideas and practices to the central ideal that holds the structure together in what is something of a truly organic unity, articulating its relationships, and making genuine intercommunication (or at least understanding) possible between the various levels.

We may put this striving toward an ideal Buddhism in a more specific form. We may call it a *nisus* toward Nibbana. We may conceive Theravada Buddhism in terms of a series of concentric circles, with the magnetic attraction toward the innermost circle holding the totality together. Thus:

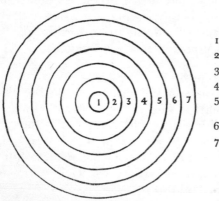

1. Nibbana
2. The Buddha
3. Meditational Discipline
4. The Sangha
5. Conservative Scriptural Orthodoxy
6. Pagoda religion
7. Popular cults and nat worship

---

[1] "Religion and Authority in Burma," *The World Today*, March, 1960. (Published for Royal Institute of International Affairs, by Oxford University Press.) Quotation, p. 117; "The fact remains that Buddhism, as understood in the texts, is not so much the religion of Burma as the religion to which she aspires."

A word may be in order about each of these items. Nibbana is the kingpin of the total structure; it is the dynamic centre toward which everything that can be called Buddhism tends. No Nibbana, no Buddhism! Buddhism itself is the historical projection and visible form of the hope of Nibbana. The Buddhist way is the actualized discipline leading to the attainment of Nibbana—essentially this and no more or less. Therefore insofar as we use the term Buddhist at all correctly, when applied to a set of beliefs or way of life it means that at the heart of this Buddhist entity, more or less affecting all its formulations, practices, and patterns, is the Nibbanic hope.

However, this hope is most difficult to appropriate directly. Only the saintly few can do so. Empirically considered, the hope, let alone the prospect, of Nibbana is often a very distant or even unwelcome prospect. There is neither emotional stomach for nor expectation of it—at least for many lives to come. In its quality as the ineffable Good, beyond time and space, it is unapproachable for most. Therefore it must be approached indirectly or in its incarnated forms. Hence each of the successively more distant circles represents the best, or most appropriable, form of the Nibbanic hope to be found at that point or level.

With regard to the Buddha it may be noted that Buddha-hood represents the primordial instance of "incarnated" Nibbana. The man Gotama became a Buddha or Enlightened One; he personally achieved that ultimate knowledge of things as they are, with its resulting detached calm, which is the essence of Nibbana-in-this-life and the absolute guarantee of Absolute Nibbana or cessation of individualized existence at the end of this present existence. As an actually existent historical individual, he became for Buddhism its supreme and highly concrete symbol of the Nibbanic quality under time and space conditions, which could be appropriated, in one way or another, by almost all Buddhists at any level of attainment. That many in the outer and lower levels have substituted and continue to substitute personalized adoration of the Buddha for the effort to achieve Nibbana directly, goes almost without saying. Gotama Buddha, as the human incarnation of the Nibbanic substance and experience, and as tangibly "present" in pagoda relics and images, is the most readily available way in which the mass of Buddhists can express their own hope of ultimate Nibbana.

But there is another and more difficult way of approaching Nibbana quite directly. It is not absolutely exclusive of reverence for the Buddha, though practically it becomes an alternative for his personalized adoration or sharply modifies the quality of such reverence. This is the practice of the Buddha's own meditational discipline. For theoretically Buddhahood is not absolutely unique, though very rare; and in terms of its quality as the achievement of Nibbana itself, it is universally appropriable. That is, there may be arahats, saintly experiencers of Nibbana-in-this-life, apart from Buddhahood. For all who desire thus to attain, the Buddha's own experience and teachings about it are both guarantee of and sufficient guide to success. Meditation is thus the essential technique of salvation; and it is also an embodiment of Nibbana, this time in an available spiritual technique of which Gotama Buddha is only the latest supreme example.

But to whom is meditation available? Not to all men, either because of personal historical circumstances or internal incapacity. But to those who have the disposition and power to leave ordinary life and join the holy brotherhood of monks, or *Sangha*, the way is open. For the monk upon entry in to the Sangha dedicates himself to the direct pursuit of Nibbana. His life-pattern is geared to its achievement—free from mundane worries or responsibilities, providing him with solitude for study and meditation. While today many laymen are attempting meditation—and this may indicate a basic shift in the quality of the Buddhist pattern—traditionally the Sangha represents a select body of direct Nibbana-seekers who are honoured as such by the layman who has no ability or desire or opportunity to aim that high at present. Here again then is Nibbana-incarnate, incarnate in a devoted brotherhood who show by dress, mode of life, and character that they believe in the reality of Nibbana and the possibility of its attainment; and through whom—by honouring and supporting them—the layman may also strive toward their same goal, though indirectly and vicariously as it were.

Enclosing the Sangha, as the fifth level of incarnate Nibbana, is what has been termed traditional scriptural orthodoxy. This can scarcely be called a grouping like the Sangha. It is rather a context of belief, emotion, and practice which includes both layman and monk, and reaches practice-wise well into the area of pagoda religion. That is to say, Theravada orthodoxy has reached out to include pagoda worship within its circle of orthodoxy and goes to considerable length to provide a scriptural basis for it. Yet this context of orthodoxy does not include all of the pagoda elements; it often de-emphasizes or even frowns upon the folk-loristic and super-stitious accompaniments characteristic of pagoda religion; and it points toward the higher way of meditation as the truly Buddhist way, to be followed by all those are are able to do so. But practically speaking this range of orthodoxy also recog-nizes the need for external forms and standards in religion. Hence it is an orthodoxy composed of scripture and tradition, as safeguards and vehicles of the persistence of the pure Nibbanic hope. Thus in turn do scripture and tradition represent a type of Nibbana-incarnation; for scripture and tradition, as the visible containers of the holy hope of Nibbana, offer to the believer, by his reverence for them and hopefully in his observance of their precepts, a way to strive toward Nibbana itself.

Pagoda religion represents the most concrete physical means of honouring the ultimate but ineffable hope of Buddhism. For the pagoda, enshrining the relics of that One who first showed men the way to Nibbana in this world age and containing His image, offers a tangible means of expressing that hope, however imperfectly. Emotionally speaking the pagoda and image represent the contemporary embodiment of the hope of Nibbana, made visible in the Buddha. The worshipper can see his hope with his eyes, feel it with his hands, offer audible prayers and visible symbols to this hope. In an emotional sense he overleaps all the intermediate stages of hard discipline and uncounted future lives of effort to the heart of the hope itself; he feels in the presence of the Buddha image something of the presence and glory of ultimate Nibbana.

But, of course, to this tangible Buddha-worship of the pagoda it is easy to add a multitude of other tangibilities, not actually Buddhist, but consoling and helpful along the way.

For most men need to live numerous lives yet before they are within striking distance of Nibbana itself, or membership even in the body of those who seek it. And the forces and spirits of the universe must be lived with in the meantime; indeed they may on occasion even help along the high way to Final Nibbana. Hence, side by side with the Buddha's shrine stand the nat or spirit shrine, the good-luck symbol, the astrologer's stall and the sacred trees. Most Buddhists feel no antagonism between the two but appropriate to themselves that kind of loyalty to "Nibbana" which seems most suitable under their present circumstances.

We may, in conclusion of this section, make a slight alteration in the previous diagram to suggest the quality of fluidity and progression from one "level" or "stage" to another which is present in the living Buddhist structure. Here we will use a spiral of upward and inward steps toward the supreme hope rather than concentric and closed circles. Particularly is this more appropriate when we think in terms of that succession of lives in which Theravada Buddhists so devoutly believe, by which one progresses slowly step by step from the outer and lower level to those higher levels or superior forms in which he is able to strive for Nibbana at ever closer range. It still distinguishes levels of attainment but sees them as stages on the same way to deliverance, a living hope that binds the total structure together.

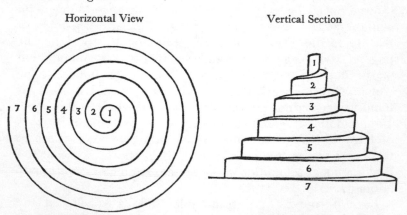

Horizontal View   Vertical Section

1. Nibbana 2. Buddhahood 3. Meditation 4. Sangha 5. Scriptural Orthodoxy 6. Pagoda Religion 7. Folk Religion

Critics and Doubters

While the mass of people are still loyal to the old Burmese Buddhist tradition as sketched above, there are those who sit loosely to some of its aspects at least and form a fluid group "outside" Buddhism or not to be located easily within any of its specific circles or levels. Some of the more scholarly and the more orthodox Buddhists, both among laity and Sangha, decry the excesses of nat worship, and even its practice as such. They have been very critical of U Nu's position and the injection of such matters into politics. Yet their voices will remain muted in the immediate future because the new wave of patriotic and religious fervour arising in the wake of Communist attacks upon Buddhism, both within Burma and in neighbouring countries, will not brook any criticism of any part of the Burmese Buddhist heritage, nat worship included. Therefore scholarly historical analysis and self-criticism—save in the flavour of "Let us be more faithful Buddhists"—will be deferred for a while longer.

But this does not help the situation of another group who belong, predominantly, to the "younger generation" and find themselves between two worlds; or to change the figure, they are in a cultural and religious vacuum. There are the rudiments of traditional Buddhism in their home background. But even this influence is weakened with the passing of many of the monastery schools, where in the past every Burmese child, particularly the boy, was indoctrinated in Buddhism along with his elementary education. Today many Burmese children are educated in the secular government schools or in Christian missionary schools, where devout Buddhists, especially of the upper classes, send their children to secure a modern education and to learn English.

What happens then to the child? His belief in the nat-worshipping, relic-honouring Buddhism of his parents is often undermined. (Indeed it will be the force of technical and scientific education which will undermine nat worship more rapidly in Burma than the orthodox "disapproval".) And when he reaches university level he finds himself faced with four alternatives: (1) He may adopt another faith—but this is made almost impossible by the strong family pressures in Burmese society; (2) he may compartmentalize his religious observances and intellectual life, as many undoubtedly do; but the result will be a devotional Buddhism which is largely irrelevant to his important practical decisions; (3) he may remain a cultural Buddhist (equivalent to the Christmas and Easter Christian) who nominally accedes to the traditional usages, but knows little of its doctrine or inner experiences; and there are many of these; (4) he may become religiously neutral and concern himself only with the secularities.

It is with respect to such that many earnest Buddhists today are concerned. They believe that not only is the vitality of the faith threatened, but that the moral character of the younger generation will deteriorate. This has always been the concern of the older generation from the beginning of the world, of course; but of the fact that today the specific Buddhist moral values are being rapidly eroded from among the younger generation there can be no doubt. And the Sangha sees in this situation the foreshadowing of the extinction of the Order itself, through lack of suitable candidates.

To right this situation many remedies have been suggested. A commission was appointed in 1959 to study the entire educational situation, with a view to strengthening its Buddhist character. The reinstitution of the monastery schools, providing education through the first five years or so, and the compulsory study of Buddhism (by Buddhist pupils) in the government schools, have been most insistently urged on this commission by interested monks and laymen. Though the new government (elected in 1960) achieved the recognition of Buddhism as the state religion, neither of these measures was ever effected. And the Ne Win regime is religiously impartial.

Buddhist resurgence

One more feature of contemporary Theravada Buddhism remains to be noted: the so-called Buddhist resurgence. This has been extensively discussed within recent years and it is not the intention here to do more than briefly to sketch the nature of the resurgence, most particularly as it can be observed in contemporary Burmese Buddhism.

That it is in considerable part nationalistic in impetus and in orientation cannot be doubted. The average Burman cannot tell where Burmanism ends and Buddhism begins, because the two are so intimately linked in his culture and history. What helps one helps the other. And with the enthusiasm of recent independence still fresh upon her, Burma hopes to achieve both a significant political and religious expression heretofore denied her as a colonial possession.

But it is more than this. There is a new missionary stirring in Buddhism which has not been known in Theravada Buddhism for perhaps a thousand years, if ever. Its components are varied. Partly it is the East rising in cultural self-assertion against the long-dominant West. In part it is the increasing contact with foreign cultures brought about by contemporary political currents and technical requirements. There is also the interest which Western scholars have been showing in the scriptures and doctrines of Buddhism; and that small but perhaps significant number of Westerners who have become Buddhist converts. All these together have roused Buddhism from its age-long slumbers to re-examine its message, and ask itself whether it may not have the gospel that the modern world, materially rich but spiritually uncertain, so desperately needs.

In this connection one of the above-mentioned groups needs particular noting—Western converts to Buddhism. The number of these is small, particularly those who choose to become residents of Theravada countries and attempt to become integral members of the Buddhist community there. Ceylon has attracted the largest number, mainly from Germany, a half-dozen of whom have become monks and have contributed substantially to English-language expositions of Theravada doctrine and practice and translations of Buddhist classics into English. There was at least one Italian (ex-Roman Catholic) Buddhist monk in Burma to the author's knowledge; one American who had taken the yellow robe for a period of some years; and two Englishmen who have been writers, editors, and founders of Buddhist World Missions to the West.

Their position seems to be ambiguous. The Buddhist community welcomes the convert, but at the same time looks upon him and his efforts with some apprehension. Perhaps the most significant of this group are the Sinhalese group who appear to have become integral members of the community there, and trusted interpreters of Buddhism to the West. Others, speaking and acting out of a convert's completely uncritical enthusiasm for his new faith and his absolute rejection of the old faith (Christianity in these cases), sometimes become embarrassing to the birthright Buddhists in the extremity of their statements and actions. Their aggressive propagandist attitude toward the West is welcomed by a Buddhism which finds itself rather inexperienced in this respect and unable to meet the West on its own philosophical and scientific grounds; yet the very missionary urgency and absolutist quality of statement is uncongenial to the Buddhist temperament.[1] Notwithstanding, their anamolous position in the Buddhist community these converts remain the most cogent and able expositors of the Theravada tradition to the West.

But though the convert may have a temporarily useful function in the current Buddhist resurgence, he does not represent the whole of it nor the most important part of it. Important missionary stirrings are to be found within the Sangha itself. Some of them have been sent on missions of interpretation to the West, as lecturers at Western Buddhist centres, universities, and to religious conferences; and there are those in Burma who hope to organize Sangha universities, i.e. universities for monks, which will give them the equivalent of a B.A. degree, now denied to them in the public universities. The express purpose of such universities, modelled somewhat on

[1] Thus one member of this group flatly asserts that the Buddha clearly taught that if a man kills even a single insect, he will inexorably go to hell—a statement which a birthright Burmese Buddhist finds rather overdrawn and which embarrasses him as an exposition of his Buddhism. The Catholic convert sought to make a Buddhist of the author on the spot, encouraging him by the counsel that if *he* had given up his Catholicism for Buddhism, how much less had a mere Protestant to give up! He likewise makes the non-killing of animals his central message, asking native Buddhists to hold up their hands if they think they can express their love for animals by eating them. A third found himself without a following, though he is used as an expositor of Buddhism to the West in official publications, because he was suspected of wishing to use Buddhism as an anti-Communist tool. While many birthright Buddhists see Communism as the enemy of Buddhism, such aspirations by an outsider are looked upon askance.

the Thai and Sinhalese Buddhist universities, is to broaden the scope of the monk's education to fit him better to teach his own people and to spread the Buddha's teaching to the English-speaking world.[1]

But the real core of the missionary emphasis, and perhaps the central force in the most significant developments in Theravada Buddhism today, is to be found in the new lay-man.[2] This new layman, to be sure, is hard to define or point out, because he is both few in number and varied in background. And he is not formed into a self-conscious association as the rule. But he is there. Sometimes he is a member of the conservative orthodoxy, who by virtue of his position in the economic or political life of his country has been in greater than average contact with the outside world and is more aware of the contemporary currents of international life and thought. Sometimes he was educated abroad or in local mission schools, and now in his middle-age period is returning to a more fervent study and practice of his childhood faith.

This group, if it can be called a group in any genuine sense, is in general concerned with two aspects of the contemporary Buddhist situation: (1) the need to spread the teaching of the Buddha abroad as well as making it more effective at home; (2) the inability of the Sangha to undertake major responsibility in this task. (They find the Sangha members hampered by the Order's cramping regulations, the doctrinnaire traditionalism of their views, and their narrow and mono-lingual training.) To remedy the situation they seek, as earnest laymen, to spread the message of the Buddha themselves. Some write and publish extensively in English: pamphlets, articles, and small magazines. Sometimes they meet in discussion groups for the purpose of purifying and propagating the Buddha Dhamma or teaching. In another case a well-known government servant conducts a meditation centre for other laymen, including non-Buddhists, and is much concerned to direct the inner Buddhist experience into practical channels.[3] On the whole these laymen are much more aware of the prac-

[1] Notably: the Venerable U Thittila, who has made lecture trips to England, the United States, and Australia; the Venerable U Pyinnya Dipa who founded a Sangha University in Rangoon nearly 4 years ago.

[2] See also author's expanded discussion in volume: *In the Hope of Nibbana*.

[3] See the later chapter on Meditation.

tical and the outside world than the ostensible leaders of Buddhism, the monks. It is they who seek to emphasize the practical this-worldly value of Buddhism, to enable Buddhism to meet the modern challenges of Western technology and the Communist socio-economic gospel. But will they be able to secure a following among the younger men—for their following among younger men seems slight? Do they truly represent the "wave of the future", or are they only a thin intellectualized and Anglicized group who are separated from their own co-religionists by this very fact? And what will be the response of the still dominant Sangha to the layman who seeks to assert leadership in Buddhism; hostility or a new effort of its own?

It is interesting to speculate, even momentarily, upon what a layman's version of Buddhism would be. Most of these groups seek to be absolutely orthodox in their activities and profess only to be studying the already received gospel of the Buddha. Yet the very fact that it is a lay leadership means that its doctrinal grounding will not be as deeply traditional as the Sangha's. Will this mean a new "practical" Buddhism for the man in the street or the non-Buddhist, which will emphasize meditation and sincerity of life and conduct, rather than the technical training in Abhidhamma which is the pride and joy of the monks?

Finally, we may note an organization that tends to draw Burmese Buddhism into the international orbit. This is the World Buddhist Fellowship which is about 14 years old, holding its fifth biennial meeting in Bangkok in 1958. It involved some of the leading Buddhist laymen and monks of Burma; a Burmese judge was elected president for the 1958–60 term. The avowed purpose of this organization is two-fold; first, to overcome the divisions in the Buddhist world and remind Buddhists, Theravada or Mahayana, that they are Buddhists; second, to spread the teaching of the Buddha to the entire world. Their words are brave: the world is breaking down morally; all other religions except Buddhism are proving insufficient to counteract the mood of materialism and religious scepticism which is sweeping it toward global war. Now is the golden opportunity for missionary Buddhism!

And what is the future of this organization? Its most active

members appear to be laymen—which suggests the conclusion
that if Buddhism is spread to the world it will be the laymen,
not the monks, who do it. And its meetings are attended by
Buddhists from all over the world, literally. But do the dele-
gates represent vital movements in their own respective
countries? So far as Burmese Buddhism is concerned it might
be said that rank and file Buddhists were not much stirred.
Some of the internationalists among both laity and Sangha
attended, but the majority were almost completely oblivious
to it. And there was even some local Burmese criticism of this
fellowshipping with the Mahayanist heretics! . . . Perhaps in
time it will stir a greater response even at Theravada grass-
roots; perhaps even the more sectarian-minded will in the end
take up the missionary task in a spirit of unity with the somewhat divergent Buddhism of other lands, but this day is not
yet.

It may be observed in passing that such missionary plans for
the most part are both optimistic and naive. Believing that the
world is now in need of Buddhist teaching, and being encouraged by present Western interest in the East, Theravada
Buddhist leaders tend to think that the West is waiting only to
hear some of the simple words of the Buddha to convert it to
the Dhamma. There is almost no real appreciation of the depth
of cultural and intellectual difference between Theravada
East and Christian-secular West, nor of the fact that the
Theravada tradition will need to re-think and re-present its
message in radically different fashion from that of the traditional past if it is to receive more than a polite and scholarly
hearing on the part of those it hopes to convert. Burmese
Buddhists, for the most part, fail to understand that on the
lower level, popular pagoda-centred and nat-infected Buddhism may seem like superstition to the West; and on the
higher level, Abhidhammic studies, their pride and joy, leave
the Westerner cold because they make no real contact with
his philosophical or religious categories and seem to him to be
an infinitely exhaustive and infinitely dry enumeration of
unfamiliar and unimportant distinctions.

Conclusion

Such is Theravada Buddhism: an organic doctrinal structure and way of life finding its dynamic centre on many different levels in the hope of ultimate Nibbana; and yet also an amalgam of many different groups and forces whose relationships are full of tension. To this we must add the factors of Theravada Buddhism's new membership in the wider world—particularly in the case of Burmese Buddhism—and note the powerful disruptive influences of the world context upon Buddhist cultures and peoples. That changes will occur, both inwardly and outwardly in the Buddhist structure can scarcely be doubted. What they will be it is impossible to forecast in detail. Nor do the following chapters attempt such a forecast. They rather discuss some further features of the Buddhist structure and efforts to adjust that structure to the contemporary world scene.

Appendix

One further aspect of the organic structure of Buddhism may be noted. It is the inter-relation of the physical and spiritual power structures within the Buddhist teaching which has been mirrored to a degree in the actualities of the social and political world of Buddhist cultures. There are two elements here. One is the doctrine of kamma, which tends to bind virtue and power together. That is, power, along with wealth, health, social position and other mundane goods, is presumed to come to a man because of his virtue. The problem of the relation of physical power to spiritual worth is somewhat complicated by the fact that present virtue does not always go hand-in-hand with present power, or vice versa; hence it is often held that present power and prosperity are the result of past virtue, i.e. good done in past lives. And, conversely, that present virtue may not receive its reward till a future life. Nevertheless the equation which brings virtue and worldly station together in some sort of congruence is implicit in the Buddhist structure.

The other element is the relationship of this virtue-power connection of the kammic order—that of successive rebirths— to that absolute scale of worth which leads out of the worlds governed by kamma to Nibbana. That there is some disparity here cannot be doubted. The way to Nibbana is the way of the renunciation of the world of kamma as essentially worthless; Nibbana is a complete detachment from kamma's most cherished rewards. Hence there is, generally speaking, no Buddhist basis for an ecclesiastical power structure. The monk as a Nibbana-Farer is the most unworldly of persons in the sense of desire for political power, social position, and ecclesiastical authority; the more spiritually mature, the less concern he has for such elements.

But, on the other hand, there is a correlation even here. Presumedly the developing saint, i.e. that individual who is progressing toward arahatship or the achievement of Nibbanic liberation, is also one who has developed a considerable degree of psychic power. Though the Buddha warned against a vain demonstrative use of such powers, the saint is presumed to be capable of such miracles as assuming one or many forms, projecting his presence to a distance, and so forth. (See Chapter V.) Such supernormal feats are constantly being reported of revered monks, even today. Thus we might say that progress toward Nibbana is also somewhat proportionate to increase in magical or psychic powers, whose exercise might have tangible effects in the social and political worlds.

Psychic gifts do not directly transform themselves into political and social power and position, of course. There are few cases if any on record where a Buddhist saint through his psychic attainments has obtained political eminence. On the contrary, saints are more likely to be forest hermits than rulers or ecclesiastics—perhaps necessarily so. Yet there is an almost complete correlation at the very highest level between the physical and spiritual (and also the kammic and nibbanic) orders; at this level the separate orders converge or even blend into one order in a given individual. This is illustrated in the birth stories about the Buddha. A sage is called in to look at the baby Gotama. He notes that the child is possessed of the thirty-two marks of the supernormal individual and proclaims that he will be either a great sage—which in the Buddhist

F

tradition meant a Buddha or Enlightened One—or a universal monarch.

Now a universal monarch had long been in Indian tradition and represented an idealized world-monarch who, in some semblance to the Hebraic Messiah-King and his golden age, would rule over the whole earth, or a goodly portion thereof, in splendour, justice, and mercy. Should we understand that Gotama presumedly had the opportunity to make a conscious choice between the two careers, one of universal political-social power and the other of spiritual achievement? This is hard to determine and probably should not be put in that exact way. It is rather to say that the kammic merits and spiritual attainments necessary to be either one or the other are of the same order and magnitude, and that Gotama possessed them, even though he was destined to be a world-saviour rather than a world-ruler.

Usually this coalescence has remained only in the realm of sacred scriptural "history". But now and then the coalescence of these two orders is recognized on the actual historical plane. Thus in Thailand it is generally assumed that the reigning monarch will become a Buddha in his next, or a very proximate, rebirth. And in Tibet the Dalai Lama was considered a living Buddha-King. The relation of the two orders may be diagrammed thus:

THE POWER PYRAMIDS IN BUDDHISM

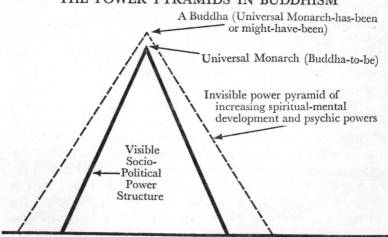

A Buddha (Universal Monarch-has-been or might-have-been)

Universal Monarch (Buddha-to-be)

Invisible power pyramid of increasing spiritual-mental development and psychic powers

Visible Socio-Political Power Structure

In Burma this coalescence of the two orders has never taken either the modified Thai form of the King who is a Buddha-to-be or the living-Buddha incarnation of the Tibetan schema. This may be because a hierarchical church pattern similar to the Tibetan never developed in Burma for a variety of reasons; and because the political history of Burma was more turbulent than that of Thailand. The actual area of Burmese dominion varied widely, and Burma never had a long-enduring succession of monarchs from one well-established dynasty. Many adventurers and strong-men rose to power as king during the centuries of pre-British rule, by the simple expedient of grasping it by force. Hence the royal house could not be invested with the mantle of Buddha-to-be sanctity quite so easily as elsewhere. There were at least one or two kings who audibly cherished hopes of becoming universal monarchs, and it may well have been the secret hope of many others. And one there was who wished to be thought of as some sort of living Buddha. But circumstances and the hostility of the Sangha effectively discouraged Burmese kings from habitual indulgence in such pretensions.

There is a residue of this, however, in contemporary Buddhism. There exist in the Burmese Buddhist community various circles of disciples or *gaings*, evanescent and seldom reported publicly, that follow past and present religious leaders who presumedly (in the eyes of the faithful at least) possess a privileged position in some forthcoming new spiritual-social order of the world and will favour their faithful disciples when that time comes. These groups hover somewhat ambiguously in the intermediate regions between traditional orthodox Buddhism, and the folklorist elements of popular superstition. Yet such diluted apocalyptics are given some air of Buddhist legitimacy by the following elements in the central Buddhist tradition itself (see also Chapter III): The hope of Maitreya the coming Buddha (next after Gotama) who is perhaps, even necessarily, now somewhere in existence as a Bodhisatta or Buddha-to-be; the popular expectation of the end of the age of Buddha-influence in another 2,500 years, that is at the end of the reputed 5,000 years of influence of his teaching supposedly predicted by the Buddha himself. When this epoch ends, destruction or radical alteration of this present order may take place. Many there are who hope by some sort of inside-track effort, either of intensified meditation or by occult devices and adherence to special "messianic" leaders, to find themselves in a favoured position when the new era, whatever its nature is, shall come.

III

WORLDS WITHOUT END

THE ATTITUDE OF THERAVADA BUDDHISM TOWARD ITS cosmology is ambivalent. Traditionally and theoretically it scorns the rather avid Mahayanist enthusiasm for celestial geography and matters metaphysical. Staunchly adhering to the Pali Canon as authoritative, Theravadins tend to take those Sutta passages that portray the Buddha as disinclined to discuss metaphysical questions of any sort with his disciples (in particular the indeterminables)[1] as definitive of the proper orthodox attitude toward all matters of cosmic concern. They would hold that in keeping with the parable of the arrow, the Buddha's only concern was with man's moralistic and psychic training, not with metaphysical or cosmological theorizing.

Yet this disdain for metaphysical questions, at least on the secondary level of cosmology, has not been maintained in Theravada Buddhism in anything like such pristine purity as the above would suggest. The Indian metaphysical heritage of Buddhism was too strong for a complete abstinence from theorizing; nor was the Hinayana–Theravada tradition untouched by those speculations that were carried to greater lengths in the Mahayana tradition. To be sure there is a verbal adherence to the ban on metaphysics. Absolute beginnings of the world of existence and the final end or destiny of all Being, are seldom if ever discussed; and by and large philosophical speculation in its wider ranges, as found in Hinduism and the West, is mostly absent in the Theravada tradition. But if we extend the term "metaphysical" to include theories about the nature of man, his consciousness, his destiny, and of the rise and fall of universes, then there is much of this even

[1] See above, p. 16.

in the midst of a tradition that professes to be completely non-metaphysical. We might say that Theravada has a working or virtual metaphysic which is taken for granted, assumed to be true, and very important to its religious life, even though some ultimate questions may be avoided.

There are indeed some contemporary Theravadins who believe that the cautious, non-metaphysical emphasis of their tradition has been overdone. Thus writes a Sinhalese Buddhist:

> *There is a section of Buddhists in the world who, probably, have never had the opportunity to study the Higher Truths contained in the Abhidhamma the third, latest, most philosophical section of the Pali Canon. All that they see is the Sutta philosophy, and in it they would find only a good and rational moral science. Many Buddhists who study Buddhism in this manner seem to think that the Buddha had put all the problems of the universe amongst "the truths he knew but did not explain". But the universe is not amongst the things he did not explain. In fact, the universe is all that the Buddha has explained. . . .*
> *It is wrong to say that the Buddha did not explain the physical universe and quote in support of this view the instance in the Sutta Pitaka when the Buddha kept silent. No student of Abhidhamma tolerates this view, because the Abhidhamma is full of explanations of the universe.*[1]

This is a most interesting comment coming from a Theravadin, since it is quite parallel to a favourite Mahayanist teaching that is usually rejected by Theravadins: The Buddha had a higher truth which he did not reveal to all. The difference, of course, is that the Mahayanist identifies his secret truth either with special Mahayanist scriptures or the oral-mystical tradition handed down through the ages apart from written scriptures; and the Theravadin identifies his higher truth with the Abhidhamma Pitaka which is indeed completely written down but is hard to understand.

In any case, acknowledged or unacknowledged, semi-metaphysical elements are solidly and centrally in the Theravada tradition. And indeed they have been there almost from the beginning. Whether the Buddha himself spoke these words

[1] *The Buddha's Explanation of the Universe*, C. P. Ranasinghi, Lanka Buddha-Mandalaya Fund, Colombo, 1957, p. 350.

—Theravadins would say that he did—one finds in the Digha-Nikaya itself extensive passages that portray the manner in which virgin-new worlds are populated and then deteriorate to their present sorry state, with worse yet to come.[1] And while the Abhidhamma is highly psychological in most of its categories, it is also metaphysical in essence. For here mental states are considered to be originative of physical conditions, perhaps even of "being" itself, so that an investigation of mental states is in reality an analysis of the nature of being in general. And even more specifically there are some discussions of the structural features of the cosmos, the planes of existence, and the universal operation of the law of kamma.

Thus it is that one cannot think of Theravada Buddhism apart from its theories of the structure and nature of the universe. There is the law of kamma or action which em-bodies the moral governance of the world-process of endless rebirth. It is inexorable, and intrinsic to the universe. By virtue of its operation every sentient being upon death finds his proper, i.e. morally deserved, place in one of the thirty-one planes of existence into which all beings in all universes in all ages are fitted. And, of course, it is taken for granted that innumerable universes have already come into existence, deteriorated, and eventually disintegrated in past ages, and will continue to do so. To a description of this rich cosmology, so essential a part of the Theravada tradition, whatever its non-metaphysical profession, we now turn.

The Established and Vertical Universe

It is perhaps easiest to begin with that somewhat stable order of which we are now working members. For though the elements of existence are in essence only fluxing processes, and universes come and go like grains of sand in an hour-glass—if only we think in sufficiently long enough time spans—there is an established framework or structural order into which even these changes fit. The two orders, the static and the dynamic,

---

[1] *Dialogues of the Buddha*, P.T.S. edition, Suttas 26 and 27. See also similar statements in the *Anguttara-Nikāya*, or *Gradual Sayings*, P.T.S. edition, Book of the Fours, Chapter XIV, Section 156 (Text ii, 142); and Book of the Sevens, Chapter VII, Sections 62, 70 (Text iv, 10, 99, 137).

do not in truth fit neatly together and in some ways even cancel each other out. And the reason for this, of course, is a double heritage. From pre-Buddhist Indian mythology comes the structure of the framework; and into it was fitted the Buddhist universe of flux and momentariness. The first is a series of levels of existence that includes all sentient creatures in all of the whirling universes of all time. It bears many marks of its primitive mythological origin. The second is the dynamic realm of world evolution and devolution in which sentient beings work out their destinies and proceed to a higher or lower level of being in their next existence. Thus the two realms intermingle and affect each other, and beings are involved in both of them; yet they are also to a considerable extent independent of each other in their operation. For practical religious purposes, however, it is the static universe of many-levelled existence that is the more important.

The static universe of many levels, i.e. thirty-one planes, clearly rises out of the Indian mythology of the Himalayas. For its centre is Mount Meru, a great cosmic mountain beneath which, on whose slopes, and above which, are found the various planes of existence. And "south" of it is the island-continent of Jambudvipa that is the home of the Buddhas— an obvious reference to the sub-continent of India. This mountain is reputed to be 80,000 leagues above the level of the seven seas that surround it, and 80,000 leagues broad.[1] Around it in concentric circles or rings are seven broad seas, each separated from the other by high mountain ranges of gold, also concentric to Mount Meru. The outermost sea, which contains the earth-islands, is the largest of all, some 322 leagues in width and bounded in turn by the Chakravala iron-mountain ranges at the very fringe of the universe.[2] The earth islands are 600,000 leagues distant from Mount Meru. And of all the earth-islands the aforementioned Jambudvipa is the most important, Buddhistically speaking.

Thus is the horizontal universe. Vertically, and more fundamentally, we may think of successive layers or levels, each

[1] Such figures were perhaps originally only indications of tremendous size; but in Theravada Buddhism they have often been taken in all literalness.

[2] The general materials here are drawn from the relevant articles on Buddhist Cosmology and Cosmogony in Hastings, *Encyclopedia of Religion and Ethics*. The organization and some of the particular items are the author's.

representing a realm or sphere of being, the whole of it resting upon a vast cloud or mass of water that floats in space. Thus does the scripture describe it:

This great earth, Ananda, is established on water, the water on wind, and the wind rests on space.[1]

The whole universe is then a kind of water-earth mass upheld by cosmic space-winds. And commentators have calculated that this "wind-circle" is 1,600,000 leagues in diameter (each league 7 miles), and that it supports a golden sea, 1,203,450 leagues in diameter, and 1,120,000 leagues in thickness. Wind and sea in creative action churn up the water circle to a depth of 800,000 leagues and out of this and floating upon it comes to be the earth, some 320,000 leagues in thickness, with Mount Meru on its top surface.

Now the thirty-one planes of existence (see diagram) proceed vertically upward from the depth of the earth, into the vasty space beyond. Generally speaking a physically upward direction implies also an improvement in status or condition. The hells or purgatories are 20,000 leagues under Jambudvipa. Their suffering is not eternal but it is most painful and it is age-long. A general name for these lowest of the nether planes is Niraya, which means in essence, death or destruction, and connotes pure suffering without any admixture of pleasure or relief. Later it came to mean a specific hell. And while there were subsequent elaborations (see below) the purgatorial theme is quite in evidence even in the early Pali Canon. This in the *Majjhima-Nikāya*:

Then, Evil One, Dusin the Mara, having visited a certain young man, having taken up a stone gave a blow to the venerable Vidhura's head; his head split . . . Dusin, the Mara, deceased from that place and arose in the great Niraya Hell . . . Then, Evil One, the guardian of Niraya Hell . . . spoke thus: "When, good Sir, spike shall meet spike within your heart, then you shall understand this: There will be a thousand years of boiling in Niraya Hell for me. . . . After ten thousand years of that Great Niraya Hell . . . I was boiled in Ussada (Hell)."[2]

[1] *Dīgha-Nikāya (Dialogues of the Buddha) Mahāparinibbāna*, Sacred Books of the East, Vol. III, Chapter III, Section 13 (Text ii, 107), 1951 edition.

[2] *Middle Length Sayings*, PTS edition, Vol. I, Sutta 50 *(Maratajjaniva Sutta)*, Text i, 337. Ussada was a sort of cooling off room *on the way out* from the deeper, hotter hell.

Such is the punishment for striking a holy monk and drawing his blood. But for that matter the punishment for defaming a saint in extreme terms is also very severe. It is related in the *Samyutta-Nikāya* that a Kokalikan monk defamed the great saints Sariputta and Mogallana. Because of this he took sick, died, and was reborn in the White Lotus Purgatory. When a deva inquired what his time therein would be, the Buddha is portrayed as replying:

> *Suppose there were a load [i.e. a cartload] of twenty kharis... of sesamum seed. And suppose at the end of every century a man were to take out one seed at a time. Sooner, bhikkhu, would that same load be used up and finished than [a term in] the Abbuda Purgatory.*[1]

The passage goes on to specify that the Abbuda Purgatory is the first and shortest-term purgatory. A term in each of the lower purgatories is twenty times that of the preceding one, so that a term in the White Lotus Purgatory to which the defamer was condemned would be the sum of an eight-fold successive multiplication by twenty of the length of the Abbuda-Hell term. For the White Lotus Purgatory is the ninth in order.

Whether this passage is to be attributed directly to the Buddha himself, will not be decided here; such is the Theravada belief. In any case it presented a broad basis for later elaboration which was not lacking even in the literalistic Theravada tradition. The number and horrors of hells were increasingly specified in gruesome detail. Avici was the worst of all; but in various of them the victims might be cut to pieces and revived countless times, crushed by mountains, pierced by burning weapons, cast on burning stakes, and burned by unceasing flames for thousands of years. Northern or Mahayana Buddhism added to the hot hells some eight cold hells; and in Tibet the purgatories were multiplied by 84,000.[2] Often elaborate masses were said for the departed-into-hell. But even so, there is here only a difference in the degree of elaboration of Mahayana and Theravada purgatorial beliefs—though in practice the latter has never encouraged any prayers for the

[1] *Kindred Sayings*, PTS edition, Vol. I, Sutta 1 *(Brahma Sutta)*, Section VI, Parts 1, 10 (Text i, 150).
[2] *The Buddhism of Tibet or Lamaism*, by L. A. Waddell, W. Heffer & Sons, 2nd edition, 1958, p. 96.

victims of hell, who must suffer there till their evil kamma is exhausted.

The next plane up from the hells is that of the animals who theoretically were supposed to have a particular part of the earth-universe for their home but obviously mingle with human beings. (Cf. Sutta 129 of the *Majjhima-Nikāya* or *Middle Length Sayings*.) Why the animal plane is considered next to the lowest is not clear, for in terms of suffering the animals are far better off than the inhabitants of the hells, and even more fortunate than the *Petas* (Sanskrit *Pretas*) or disembodied ghosts of the plane next above them. In any case it is held that many human beings are reborn as animals in a form roughly equivalent to their ruling disposition as a human being. Thus a gluttonous person may well become a hog, a rapacious one a tiger, etc. Buddhist literature, particularly the *Jātaka Tales* and many of the Commentaries, is full of stories of such appropriate animal rebirths.[1]

Next above the animals, as before noted, are the petas. Petas are disembodied ghosts whose appetites and desires outrun their capacity to fulfil them to an extreme degree. A favourite portrayal of a peta is that of a ghost whose belly is as big as a mountain (with a correspondingly tremendous appetite) and whose mouth is only the size of a needle. Why a disembodied spirit needs to eat at all, is never explained. Perhaps it is because all things this side of Nirvana are sometimes thought of as utilizing a type of nourishment appropriate to the plane on which they exist; or, perhaps more importantly, we have here expressed in terms of poetic justice the ruling concept of the Peta-state as a state of punishment appropriate to one's peculiar "sins" in past lives. Such ghosts are "at home"

---

[1] On the basis of sheer mathematical probability it would seem that all animals might be considered as once-upon-a-time human beings—given as we are infinite time, infinite numbers of worlds, and the see-saw character of the rebirth process. Yet human beings are few (proportionately) in number, and the Buddhist tradition implies that some animals have always been animal, never debased men. In any case the potential memory of *all* previous existences, which may be revived or made explicit to consciousness at some future time, persists even through animal existences. So also it is implied that even animals can perform "good" or "bad" deeds. Thus a tiger sins by killing, and a cow cropping daisies is relatively virtuous. It is a part of the doom of the rapacious animal that it is thus condemned to make its load of crime even heavier, and its term as animal, or later in hell, even longer.

in the Yama Realm some 500 leagues below Jambudvipa, but often wander at cross-roads, outside fences and city walls, and in the desolate places on the human earth, hoping against hope that some compassionate soul will share with them his merit and thus lift them from their miserable existence to a higher plane. Alone of all the beings in the nether planes they can be helped by human deed, according to the Theravada tradition (*Vide, Peta Vatthu*, PTS, *Minor Anthology*), though in the Mahayana tradition in China, even those beings doomed in the hells may be redeemed by human kindness. The last and highest of the nether planes, that is of the planes below human status, is that of the Asuras, or in terms of Greek mythology, Titans. These powerful spirits, often at war with the gods in the planes above them, dwell in the caves beneath Mount Meru in four realms, all of them below sea-level. To this general plane likewise belong a host of earth, air, and water spirits who may be of help or hindrance to human beings in many practical and physical ways. Somewhere in this area we may place the lesser Burmese nats, though the more important nats seem to rank with, and perhaps are synonymous with, the devas or ex-Indian gods in the higher realms.[1]

Next of course comes the human realm which is one of mixed woe and bliss, with less of woe than the nether planes, and less of bliss than the heavenly plane above the human one. Human beings live on the four earth islands in the seventh sea out from Mount Meru, and those who are most blessed because of their past good deeds are born in the South Island, Jambudvipa, which is also the land where Buddhas are born. While human life is thus mixed woe and bliss, it must be remembered that the human realm has one unique feature: Only here can a man strive for Nibbana. In the hells there is little or no hope for positive striving because of the pain; there is only the hope of finally wearing out the force of bad kamma, and rescue therefrom by the fruition of some long-past good

---

[1] In his book *The Thirty-Seven Nats* (W. Griggs, 1936), R. C. Temple suggests that *Thagya Nat* of Burmese tradition is the Sakka of the Pali scriptures, who in turn was one of the former Brahmanical pantheon, perhaps Brahmā himself. And *Man Nat* appears to be the traditional Buddhist Mara, or evil tempter of the Buddha, who lives in the sixth heaven above the human plane, supported there by the multitude of past good deeds.

deed. And in the heavens (see below) there is too much pleasure for their inhabitants to feel the need of liberation. Indeed it is because of the mixed quality of life in the human sphere that a being therein can fully realize the emptiness of all existence and yearn for deliverance.

It is not necessary to discuss all the remaining planes of existence in detail; there are some twenty-six of them above the human level, and their names roughly indicate their quality. (See diagram.) We may note, however, that there are three main divisions of these higher realms and briefly characterize each division.

There is first the *Realm of Sensual Bliss*, or perhaps better, of Sense Enjoyment. This includes the human plane and the six deva-worlds or planes above it. Human Life is, of course, lived upon the earth, or perhaps we should say upon some earth or other; the four great kings' plane is well up the sides of Mount Meru; the Thirty-Three gods live on top of the Mount; and the remainder live in successively and infinitely higher planes in the space above the Mount beginning at 84,000 leagues' distance and extending to 1,200,000 at the highest.

Now the quality of life in the Deva planes has a two-fold difference from human life. It is much longer than human life and it is filled with the unalloyed bliss of supreme sense enjoyment. As to length of years it is said that one day of life in the realm of the Thirty-Three Gods equals one hundred years of human life; and that a thousand god-years equals the life-span of the gods here. How this adds up can be seen on the diagram, though when we come to deal with *kappas* (Sanskrit *kalpas*) by which the highest levels of all are measured, we are in the realm of the incommensurable. A kappa may only be described by analogy:

> *Suppose, O Monks, there was a huge rock of one solid mass, one mile long, one mile wide, one mile high, without split or flaw. And at the end of every hundred years a man should come and rub against it once with a silken cloth. Then that huge rock would wear off and disappear quicker than a world-period, i.e. kappa.*[1]

[1] Quoted from *Samyutta-Nikāya* (Samyutta XV, Sutta V), in *Buddhist Dictionary*, Nyanatiloka, Frewin and Co., Colombo, 1956, p. 70. However, L. de la Vallee Poussin in ERE suggests that a kappa is anywhere from a 1 followed by 17 ciphers up to "352 septilions of kilometres of ciphers, allowing one cipher occupies a length of .001 metres"—in various Buddhist traditions.

And in another passage when a sceptic inquires why the gods (devas), who have become such because of good deeds as human beings, never come back to tell human beings of their pleasures, he is reminded that a god's day is much longer than man's. Thus a man who has become a god has perhaps lived only a "day" or two in his new world and not yet got around to go back to his human friends, forgetting that for them centuries have passed.

Besides, the new godling may have been so busy enjoying himself that he has not had time to think of anything else. For the deva planes are planes of pure bliss. In the *Vimana Vatthu* portion of the *Minor Anthology* there are many glowing descriptions of the glories of the deva-worlds. There is abundant food in endless variety; changes of sumptuous clothing beyond imagination, a thousand new garments for every day; servants to minister to one's every whim; magnificent and spacious mobile mansions and gardens that float at the owner's will through infinite space. Indeed, so busy are those who have been thus rewarded for good deeds on earth now enjoying those rewards, so little the suffering they see, that they know not how to perform a morally good work any longer but must look earthward for an example and inspiration:

> *The Devas who are not too addicted to indulging themselves in sensual pleasure, devote part of their time to extend their vision on our Earth and watch human beings at work. If these searching Devas manage to catch the human beings doing good deeds, they form in themselves thoughts of delight and thereby accumulate impressions of good thoughts in their own minds.*
> *The reason why these Devas look down towards Earth for people doing good actions is that they have no opportunity in their world to perform an act of goodwill. This is because everyone amongst their fellow-beings is so well provided with all the comforts, that there does not exist a beggar to give alms to, nor a life to save. . . .*
> *When Devas grow old and near the end of the force of the merit they were born with, they cast eager eyes on Earth in the hope that by gazing at the people doing good work, they might be able to gather a little more merit to live in the world of the Devas a short while longer.*[1]

[1] *The Buddha's Explanation of the Universe*, C. P. Ranasinghi, Lanka Buddha Mandalaya Fund, Colombo, 1957, p. 309.

One further note may be added here. The fourth plane above the human plane, that of the "Satisfied Gods", or Tusita Heaven, is the one in which Bodhisattas (future Buddhas) live prior to their incarnation in human form. It was in this heaven that the Bodhisatta who became Gotama Buddha was living just before his descent into the womb of his mother; and it was the other gods living in this realm who entreated him thus to descend in order to liberate mankind.

The second great division of the thirty-one planes is called the *Fine Material Realm* and consists of sixteen divisions or levels. Sometimes it is also called the *Realm of Form*, and the highest five planes in it are called the *Pure Abodes*. The significance of the term "fine material" is that as one progresses up through these planes the materiality of his form or embodiment is progressively finer, i.e. more nearly immaterial. Physical forms and functions are more and more attenuated, so that some of these radiant beings are practically self-sustaining, i.e. needing no physical food. The sense organs practically disappear, and in place of sexual relations a mere touch or even a glance suffices.

At this level another distinction may be made. The sixteen levels here may be divided again into successive sub-groups of 3, 3, 3 and 7. When thus grouped these heavens are also called *Jhanic Heavens* because they are directly related to the Jhanic meditational trances. Those human beings who achieve mastery of Jhanic meditations, or the various Absorptions as they are sometimes called, will be reborn into corresponding Jhanic Heavens, upon death. The first three Jhanas lead respectively to the first three sets of three, and the Fourth Jhana mastery admits to the highest seven planes. And within the groups of three, the three-fold division represents bare, medium, or complete mastery of the respective Jhana.[1] Mere good works, that admit their doer to the deva worlds, do not admit here, but only that psychic development obtained through meditation.

We may note in passing that the Pure Abodes have one peculiarity: it is to these highest five that the *Anāgāmin* or Non-returner is born upon his human death. He has reached a degree of sanctity just short of that of arahathood, which

[1] See chapter on Meditation, also.

would have admitted him directly to Nibbana. Therefore he must be "embodied" in some form or other for a time yet, but will not return to human form again. After indefinite periods of time in each of these planes he will rise through them and those of the highest level as well (Realm of Formlessness) into Nibbana itself.

Finally, there is the *Realm of Formlessness*. Existence here is without form, i.e. physical components; it is a purely mentalistic existence—yet not of the absolute and unconditioned quality of Nibbana itself, though tending toward Nibbana as an absolute limit. Thought here—or should we say existence, since the only existence here is thought-existence—reaches an almost imperceptible purity and immateriality at the highest level. And entrance to this realm of four planes is gained only by the mastery of the four so-called formless meditations (Infinity of Space, Infinity of Consciousness, Nothingness, Neither Perception nor Non-Perception) when in human form.

Thus we have reached the highest level, highest both in physical elevation and in mental attainment, to be found this side of Nibbana. But except for the Anagamin there is no entry from even the highest plane into Nibbana, unless one has at the same time engaged in another (Nibbanic) type of meditational discipline. (See chapter on Meditation.) For even the Formless Realm, ethereal as it may be, is still within the realm of Samsara (birth-death) and under the control of kamma. Therefore no matter how many kappas life there may endure—84,000 in the very highest plane—finally it must end; for even the almost infinite amount of good kamma needed to secure rebirth there is exhausted at last and the "Formless" being descends again to embodiment on the human level, or even to the nether planes.[1]

The Dynamic Universe

The universe that has just been described, inherited from Indian mythology, might be called the spatial universe. It can

[1] Some references to these realms are to be found as follows: *Dīgha-Nikāya* (*Dialogues of the Buddha*) PTS edition, Sutta 20 *(Mahā-Samaya Suttanta)*, vs. 16, Text ii, 250; also Text 1, 218; *Itivutakka* 14; *Path of Purification*, p. 225, Nyanamoli edition, Semage (Colombo), 1956.

scarcely be said to be affected by time and its passage; for even the envolving universes somehow fit into its pattern or conform to its shape during their evolution and devolution. Though universes come and go, the planes of existence remain and characterize existence in any and all of them. To this extent it seems scarcely Buddhist in its everlasting permanence, unless one thinks of it only as form and not substance.

But there is another and more Buddhist conception of the universe that does not always accord with the static universe but has been fitted into its framework nonetheless. We may call it the dynamic or temporal universe, for it is a universe of continuous activity, of the rising and falling of worlds in cyclic rhythm. This, too, is Indian in origin but peculiarly adapted to the Buddhist viewpoint that all things and beings in existence are characterized by anicca (impermanence) and anatta (no genuine substance or reality). And this character may be extended to world ages and universes as well as to the moments of an individual life or successive human lives.

Here we need to raise a question or two with regard to the relation of the static and the dynamic universes. We may observe first of all that Buddhism modifies the ancient terms for the constituents of the physical universe in accordance with its theories of insubstantiality and change. Thus "earth" means extension in space, "fire", combustion or heat, "air", movement, and "water", cohesiveness. These are viewed as qualities rather than substances, essences rather than being. Hence the existing universe at any moment is only, so far as we know, a collection of such qualities. While one may say that the question of substance, or at least substantial form, is thus bypassed rather than being dealt with, it opens the door for a less primitive interpretation of the earth-air-fire-water categories. Mount Meru, the planes of existence, the beings in them, and the whole static universe may thus be regarded as subject to change and dissolution, or even (see below) be regarded as less than physically real by modern Theravadins. They are but series of mental-physical vibrations.

It must also be noted that the shadow of a suspicion of absolute idealism always hangs about the Buddhist philosophy of the physical universe. There is for instance a passage in the Buddhist scriptures which suggests that in this fathom-long

G

body is all the world that there is.[1] Whether it quite means that the actual physical universe is thought to be dependent upon my personal perceptions, or the totality of the perceptions of all sentient beings—and would disappear if they were lacking—is not clear. Perhaps it means only that the world ceases to be for me, when I escape bodily existence. This whole matter was in fact discussed by several generations of Buddhist philosophers and various answers arrived at, ranging from an absolute idealism to a realism of individual elements. Some scholars believe that the Hinayana ancestors of Theravada Buddhism espoused this latter position: the "atomic" elements which composed the universe were real, but their patterns and combinations were ever fluxing.

Whatever the case historically, we may say that contemporary Theravadins strongly emphasize the role of mind in the physical universe. There is of course no supreme Deity who created the world; and, as before noted, questions of absolutely first beginnings are out of order in Buddhism. But with regard to any particular universe—and there have been myriads of them and will be myriads more—it may be said that "mind" is its creator and sustainer. Whose mind, or what mind? No one's in particular, or else everyone's lumped together in a totality of mind-force. For worlds rise and pass away, Buddhists hold, not merely because of physical actions and reactions—the solidifying of clouds of atomic-vapour and their physical deterioration—but in direct relation to their component mental-moral forces. It is the cumulative and total mind force present in a given universe at any moment that actually holds it together as a universe. And when this decays, that universe deteriorates and finally dissolves until such time as the mind-force resident in the higher planes of being is able to produce a new universe.

Sometimes it is suggested that such a new universe can come into being following a period of disintegrative chaos, only if a Buddha-to-be is ready for rebirth in this new epoch. The new universe, so to speak, coagulates around the mental-moral power of the Buddha-to-be as a centre. A contemporary statement of the role of "mind" in world "creation" follows:

[1] Cf. J. Evola, *The Doctrine of the Awakening*, Luzac, 1951, p. 91 on this passage.

"MIND BUILDS AND MAINTAINS THE UNIVERSE"

Each unit of mind, according to the strength of its evolution-current, develops a gravitational force so as to keep in concentration a measure of units of abstract elements. Each being in the material universe which exists above levels of elementary life, contributes a measure of gravitational force to the universe. The higher beings, such as the human beings and the animals, contribute a larger measure, and the lesser beings contribute a proportionately smaller measure. . . . And if all the beings existing on this Earth disappear from it, there would be no gravitational force on this Earth. . . . Heat would concentrate and, ultimately, the Earth would blow up and dissolve in space.[1]

The life-cycle of a world or universe, or a kappa, is, as we have seen, of almost infinite length in time. And it is divided into four successive periods: (1) that of deterioration to the point of chaos or destruction; (2) that of the duration of this chaos; (3) that of re-development or renovation; (4) that of the maintenance in the renovated or coherent state. Sometimes this group of four sub-cycles is called a Great Cycle, or a kind of super-kappa.

Since presently a universe seems to be in existence, we may begin as above with the period of deterioration or destruction. The cause of this dissolution into chaos is as follows:

Why does the world perish in these particular ways? It is on account of the special wickedness that may be at bottom. For it is in accordance with the wickedness preponderating that the world perishes. When passion predominates, it perishes by fire; when hatred, it perishes by water. . . . When infatuation preponderates, it perishes by wind.[2]

There is a periodic rhythm in these destructive epochs. Buddhaghosa goes on to say that a world order perishes seven successive times by fire, and the eighth by water. This continues for seven such successions, fifty-six perishings in all; then after seven further fire-perishings, the sixty-fourth and mightiest perishing of all occurs by the agency of the wind.

These destructions are tremendous in spatial scope, reaching out horizontally through thousands of worlds (sun, moon, star

[1] *The Buddha's Explanation of the Universe*, p. 254.
[2] From Chapter XIII of Buddhaghosa's *Path of Purification*, quoted in *Buddhism in Translations*, H. C. Warren, Harvard University Press, 1953, p. 329

systems). And they are also cataclysmic in nature; all the physical universe as we know it is convulsed thereby. In further passages in the same chapter of his *Path of Purification* Buddhaghosa (fifth-century A.D. commentator of Ceylon, much revered in all Theravada countries) describes the various types of destruction at length. In the fire cycle several hundreds of thousands of years pass without rain and seven successive suns appear that dry up the clouds, the streams, the great rivers, and finally the ocean "so that not enough water remains to moisten the tip of one's finger". The earth is filled with smoke and then bursts into flames and consumes even up through the heavens of the Great Brahmas, or the ninth plane above the human.

In a period of water-destruction, there arises in place of the second sun a great cloud of salt water that gradually fills "one hundred thousand times ten million worlds, and the mountain-peaks of the earth become flooded with saltish water, and hidden from view".[1] The winds carry the destroying water up to, but exclusive of, the heavens of the Completely Lustrous Gods, or fifteenth plane above the human.

The great climatic period of destruction by wind, at every 64th Great Cycle, is thus described:

First the wind raises a fine dust, and then coarse dust, and then fine sand, and then coarse sand, and then grit, stones, etc., up to boulders as large as the peak of a pagoda, and mighty trees on hilltops.

This mighty tempest continues, increasing in force, until it tears apart the whole earth, i.e. Mount Meru and all its surrounding mountain and sea rings, grinding them all to powder. "Worlds clash with worlds, Himalaya Mountains with Himalaya Mountains, and Mount Sinerus [Merus] with Mount Sinerus, until they have ground each other to powder and perished".[2] A hundred thousand times ten million worlds and all the heavenly planes, including that of the Completely Lustrous Gods, perish together.

Even though there is a predictable rhythm in these periods of world destruction, their respective lengths, as well as the length of the other three phases of the world cycle, appear to be somewhat indeterminate. Thus:

[1] Warren, op. cit., p. 327   [2] Ibid., p. 328.

How long a world-dissolution will continue, how long the chaos, how long the formation, how long the continuation of the formed world, of these things, O Monks, one can hardly say that it will be so many years, or so many centuries, or so many millenniums, or so many hundreds of thousands of years.[1]

This passage, much less explicit than later writings, perhaps indicates the essential disinterest of the Buddha in such matters, or the early Buddhist caution with regard to cosmic calculations, or perhaps merely the impossibility of speaking of such periods of time in human terms, except as "incalculable", which is another term for kappa.

A practical question immediately arises: What happens to those beings existing in the various worlds and planes of existence when they are destroyed? There is at least some emptying of these worlds destined for destruction. Thus when the end of a world cycle approaches close at hand, say an odd 100,000 years or so away, some of the lesser gods from one of the heavens of sensual pleasure.

wander about through the world, with their hair let down and flying in the wind, weeping and wiping away their tears with their hands, and with their clothes red and in great disorder. And thus they make the announcement?
Sirs, after the lapse of a hundred thousand years . . . this world will be destroyed; . . . Therefore, sirs, cultivate friendliness; cultivate compassion, joy, and indifference, i.e. equanimity; wait on your mothers; wait on your fathers; and honour your elders among your kinsfolk.'[2]

This revival preaching has its effect, and earth-spirits and people cultivate the moral virtues. Thus when the end comes, some have already been reborn in the worlds above the reach of fire, water, or wind, including fishes, turtles, and even some of the inhabitants of the hells. However, according to Buddha-ghosa, there is some doubt about these latter for "some say the inhabitants of the hells perish with the appearing of the seventh sun".[3] What he meant by "perishing" is not clear, for there is no annihilation in the birth-death cycle according to

[1] From *Buddhist Dictionary*, Nyanatiloka, p. 70, quoting from *Anguttura-Nikāya (Gradual Sayings)*, Sutta IV, section 156.
[2] *Buddhism in Translations*, p. 322.
[3] *The Buddha's Explanation of the Universe*, p. 255.

Buddhism. A contemporary writer interprets Buddaghosa's perishing as signifying re-birth in other hells, or perhaps re-birth as "elementary" life—it may be at amoebic level. Thus:

> *Those beings who understand the impending disaster at that time would make haste to increase the force of evolution in their minds and thus escape into a spiritual sphere of existence, but the majority would sink lower and lower in strength of evolution and, ultimately, establish themselves in elementary life.*[1]

Why is it that this latter-age repentance does not produce an earth-renovating change, and lengthen the life of the deteriorating universe? I have never received a clear answer to this question. Presumably the total force of deterioration is so great, or perhaps the Buddha-influence has so waned or even disappeared in that world cycle, that nothing can arrest the slide to chaos.[2] It may be theoretically conceivable that a widely prevalent revival of right living could delay the progressive dissolution of a world in its period of decline. (Will the Maitreya "revival" do this?) But the seemingly inevitable tendency of universes is to deteriorate always and everywhere, sooner or later, from their fresh new radiance in which

---

[1] *The Buddha's Explanation of the Universe*, p. 255.

[2] There are five stages of the disappearance of Buddhist influence in certain epochs, taking place roughly every thousand years in succession. *First*, there is the disappearance of spiritual attainment above the grade of Sotapanna or Stream-Enterer. (The once-Returner to human life, the Non-Returner, and the Arahat who goes directly to Nibbana upon death, no more appear.) *Then*, good Buddhist conduct disappears from the earth; *then* Buddhist learning itself beginning with the Abhidhamma, proceeding "downward" through the *Anguttara, Samyutta, Majjhima, Dīgha, Kuddaka-Nikāyas,* and lastly through the *Jātaka Tales* and the *Vinaya Pitaka* (or monk's-rules portion of the scriptures). And in the *fourth* period there are not even any monks left. *Finally*, the last and greatest Buddhist treasure, the relics of the Buddha and his saints, all come together to form one Buddha image, but this can be seen only by the devas, and finally disappears altogether. Thus is the universe in five thousand years bereft of all Buddha influence, and thus it becomes impossible for any living being to make any progress toward Nibbana, even though the universe itself may not immediately disintegrate. Currently it is held that the teaching of the Gotama Buddha is half-way (2500 years) towards its ultimate disappearance. Hence Buddhists must now exert themselves individually to escape the catastrophe of its total disappearance on this planet, to be born in a more fortunate one. So also some suggest that such an end-of-the-age situation calls for social efforts. Thus, in a dictated note, the Honourable U Nu: "The Buddhists believe that the present age is Kaliyuga, that is, the age of vice, misery and misfortune. And, therefore, it is all the more necessary to make efforts for the minimization of social ills."

sentient life is long and conditions relatively ideal, to the radically opposite condition.

But, given a period of dissolution lasting for an indefinite length of time, how does a new universe get started again? According to our contemporary expositor, though it is never quite so stated in the scriptures, no units either of mind or "abstract units of matter", i.e. the basic four elements, are actually destroyed. Only the "material formations" of being perish. This process takes "matter" down through atomic dissolution, however, until there is only "free abstract heat" (pure caloric energy?) without mass. The mind units—apparently not exactly sentient beings or minds as we know them, yet capable of feeling—suffer intensely in this heat and are thereby purified. After their defilements, apparently moral in nature, are thus purged,

> *many units of mind acquire a sufficiency of evolutionary strength to cover their suffering physical systems of free abstract heat with a few units of the other abstract elements.*[1]

Thus has a kind of material condensation of material units about a centre of mind-feeling units begun. As this process continues it gains cumulative power, gravitational force comes into being, and a new universe is on the way to existence. This is the second period of earth renovation that is

> *The result of co-operative effort of all the units of mind existing in the bringing into being of this universe. . . . Every being in the universe according to its strength, wields an oar to move this universe, and . . . we are also riding on the efforts of all the other beings of the universe.*[2]

It may be noted in passing that our interpreter does not consider that this new universe is a real triumph of creative power at whose fresh and full appearance creative Mind sees "that it is good". It is only a reshuffling of the old elements and the beginning of the weary cycle again:

> *for the very thing they made and nurtured bites and kills them, i.e. mind-units or sentient beings. . . . Therefore let them escape from matter, the ever-clinging devil that pulls all beings toward suffering all the time, and enter into that peaceful and pleasant plane of*

[1] *The Buddha's Explanation of the Universe*, p. 258.
[2] Ibid., pp. 259–60.

existence where the inferior and low matter does not gather and existence is perfect.[1]

Is this perfect, non-material state "charged with the maximum forces of purity" to be identified with Nirvana? Since it is viewed as a final escape from materialized existence, it would seem to be so; though the use of the terms "peaceful", "pleasant", and "existence" with regard to Nirvana seems strange.

The process of world-renovation begins from the top down. From the lowest heavenly plane that remains after the destruction of the still lower ones by fire, water, or wind, the destroyed heavenly planes in space above Mount Meru are re-created. Then the wind and water circles are formed, which by their interaction again churn up "matter" and form a new physical universe, including Mount Meru and its surrounding seas, mountains, and continents. This third period of renovation and re-formation is sometimes divided into nineteen successive parts in which the universe is gradually repopulated by beings from the higher planes whose good kamma has run out, as it must for all, even though in that highest plane of Neither Perception nor Non-Perception where the life-span is 84,000 kappas long. Presumably the hells are re-created also, large and capacious because their inhabitants in the end, at least, will be far more numerous than those of the higher realms. And it may also be that unfortunates from other perishing universes are transferred here too.

Thus, having come through a period of deterioration, one of chaos, and one of world-rebuilding, we come to the fourth period in which we have the world at its highest and best, with the earth and lower heavens populated by radiant beings newly descended from the higher realms.[2]

And although life on earth may be evil compared to immaterial "existence" in Nibbana, yet judged by human standards it seems almost ideal. Those descended beings who populate it, are "made of mind, feeding on rapture, self-

[1] Ibid., pp. 259–60

[2] This descent leads to delusions of grandeur. That being who first descends to a newly created heaven thinks that he is the "creator" of all those who descend after him, and calls himself "Almighty God" according to Buddhism. Thus is Sakka, the mightiest of the Thirty-Three gods, sometimes deluded.

luminous, traversing the air". The earth-substance itself at this period is sweet-tasting and nutritious, though not needed for food. How long this continues we do not know. But some curious ones among the radiant beings, not satisfied with feeding on ethereal rapture, or unable to do so longer because of exhausted good kamma, put their fingers upon the earth and taste it. Thus is greed born again—because the new-earth taste creates desire. The corruption of desire spreads; the beings gradually lose their radiance and become more grossly physical or material. Having lost their radiance, sun, moon, and stars are needed for light and thus the day and night cycle begins.

Gradually over a long period of time the progressive deterioration is intensified. As beings continue to feed on the good earth, that good earth loses its sweet taste and nutritious quality; hence plants spring up for food. Some beings become less and less good-looking, even ugly sex differentiations appear and lust is generated. Due to increasing greed, these now completely "human" beings, begin to covet each others' mates, and possessions, set up organized societies, institute necessary laws to prevent robbery and murder—and life on earth approximates its present condition. Presumably in the end utter destruction will again ensue.

In the twenty-sixth Sutta of the *Digha-Nikāya* (*Dialogues of the Buddha*) this process of deterioration is described somewhat differently. Here there is not a total destruction of the earth consequent upon its corruption, but only deterioration to an unbelievably low point before the ensuing improvement sets in. At this lowest point human life is only ten years long and a woman is married at five years. Food is coarse and scarce. The good old customs are neglected. Sexual promiscuity abounds, including the sexual use of animals. But seeing the evil of their ways, human beings repent and amend their conduct. As they begin to practice the virtues again, life, health, and wealth increase. The life-span doubles to twenty years, twenty years to forty until at the apex.

Among humans living 80,000 years, brethren, maidens are marriageable at 500 years of age. Among such humans there will be only three kinds of disease—appetite, non-assimilation and old age. Among such humans (Jambudvipa) will be mighty and prosperous, the villages, towns and royal cities will be so close that a cock could fly from each one to the next.[1]

And there arise then the Maitreya Buddha and his fitting companion, a wise, "wheel-turning", i.e. Buddhist, universal monarch who rules in peace and plenty. But even this glorious state of things cannot last for ever. The universal monarch, realizing that human virtue and prosperity alike are passing, takes upon himself the robe of a monk and leaves the world.

It is obvious that these various accounts must have come from different sources and cannot be fully reconciled with each other. For some versions speak in one-world and others in many-world contexts. Perhaps we have small cycles of deterioration and self-regeneration within the greater or master cycles of total destruction and renewal from the heavenly spheres above. But in any case there is evident here that general cyclical pattern, so characteristic of Eastern cosmologies: First an Eden-like paradise of long life, health, and wealth; then the gradual deterioration of conditions through the entrance of "sin"; and finally a nadir-point of debasement, and perhaps destruction, before the new cycle starts again.[2]

The Function and Importance of the Cosmology

In his article on the Buddhist "Ages of the World" in the *Hastings Encyclopedia of Religion and Ethics*, the late Louis de la Vallee Poussin is of the opinion that its theory of world ages is not "essential" to Buddhism. The cosmology, he believes, is a kind of non-Buddhist impedimentum that became attached to the faith historically, and into which a few bits of Buddhist philosophical and religious beliefs were stirred.

That much of the cosmology is non-Buddhist and accords very unevenly and imperfectly with classical Buddhist teach-

---

[1] Sections 22, 23, of Sutta XXVI, Text iii, 75. Volume IV, SBB.

[2] The contrast here with Christian apocalyptic is obvious and interesting. Historical movement there is more or less straight-line and irreversible, a once-for-all proposition; and the final state will be a permanent solution of all social and personal destinies. Here the movement is cyclical and repetitious. The "same" individuals may live repeatedly in the same minor or major cycle, and in subsequent cycles. The predicament of the universe as a whole will never be solved; it is essentially unimprovable. And individuals can achieve their salvation only by escaping from all the cycles into super-cyclic Nibbana.

ings, is quite evident. But with Theravada Buddhism, particularly as it is found in Burma, this cosmology is so congenial to the tradition, indeed so long a part of it, so eminently useful, and even of so much contemporary influence, that to speak of it as "non-essential" seems wrong. Its elimination would mean nothing less than a major reconstruction of the total religious structure. That there are today some new qualifications and interpretations in process may also be true; but take away his thirty-one planes of existence from the Burmese Buddhist, and he could scarcely call himself Buddhist in any recognizable sense. Besides this, the cyclic theory or the dynamic interpretation of the universe is now being hailed as in full accord with the latest teachings of physical science—a remarkable anticipation that proves the omniscience of the Lord Buddha.

It is quite evident, for example, that the static universe and its planes of existence fit in admirably and perhaps essentially with the doctrine of rebirth. Indeed how can one think of rebirth without some such structure to provide a proper and fitting destiny for each reborn being? The varied conditions of human life give only inadequate scope for the play of kammic destiny. But provide thirty-one planes that vary from the deepest hells to the highest immaterial spheres, and provide an infinite succession of universes, and the scale becomes of heroically satisfying proportions.

To deal with the same elements in a slightly different context: In such a cosmology we have the complete enthronement of kammic justice. Kamma, the moral governance of the universe, is placed at the very heart of the whole psychophysical scheme of reality. For is it not true that individual beings rise and fall though the massive reaches of the planes of existence solely according to their merits? And is it not equally true that the universes, even up to ten thousand millions of them, are destroyed and re-created by reason of the moral wickedness or virtue of the inhabitants hereof? It must be remembered that the governance of the universe by kammic justice is as essential to the Theravada Buddhist as belief in the process of dialectical materialism to the Communist or Divine Providence to the Christian.

One further important function of the cosmology in Theravada Buddhism is to be noted. This is the correlation of the higher planes of existence with meditational attainment. As noted before, the mastery of the several jhanic states of consciousness and the formless meditations admits the meditator to the corresponding plane upon his rebirth. No doubt this is of more theoretical than practical importance, since only the very few will ever be able to attain those high planes; and, further, even their attainment is in some sense a detour from the straight road to Nibbana. Nonetheless this correlation of the planes with meditational competence is an integral part of the whole Theravada viewpoint and of some contemporary interest in view of the new emphasis upon meditation now found in Burma.

Not only so, but the dynamic conception of the universe is in complete agreement with those most basic Buddhist doctrines of the impermanence, suffering, and insubstantiality of all things. They are here exemplified not only within the life of the individual but on a grand cosmic scale. One's life on this earth is not his only life; it has been preceded by a multitude of lives upon this earth, or upon other planets. Those other heavenly bodies provide the stage upon which all the infinite number of his past lives have been lived, each one representing only a link in the endless line of causes and effects. Nor, of course, is this earth-universe the only universe. The number of universes in the past is infinite; and so will be the number in the future, again the result of the inexorable casual sequence governed by kammic justice. How fully all this exemplifies the fleeting impermanence of all states and conditions, and exposes the vanity of ordinary human hopes for some attainment beyond the reach of change and decay! It gives point to the exhortation of the Buddha:

Thus, impermanent, thus unstable, thus insecure are all compounded things. Be ye dissatisfied with them, be ye repelled by them, be ye utterly free from them.[1]

To repeat the first assertion: Theravada Buddhism is almost unthinkable without its cosmology, whatever the relation of cosmology and Buddhist practice in original Buddhism. Should one attempt to remove it by some sort of theological surgery, the remaining corpus might well become a corpse instead!

[1] *Anguttara-Nikāya*; or *Gradual Sayings*, P.T.S. edition, Volume IV. Book of Sevens, Chapter VII, Text iv, 99, 100.

And so strong is the rootage of this cosmology in the tradition that the majority of orthodox monks and laity even today would resist any attacks upon or alterations in the Mount Meru cosmology. For them this cosmology represents the clear teaching of the Buddha as interpreted by the orthodox commentators, and this is the end of the matter. Has not the Buddha spoken and does not Theravada tradition, pristine in its purity, so affirm?

Thus it is that even those who do not believe in the literality of the static cosmology must keep silent. To proclaim publicly that one did not believe in the existence of Mount Meru, the hells beneath it and the heavens above it, and their literal destruction by fire, water, or wind, would be considered by many as tantamount to a declaration of heresy. When a young scholar just a few years ago wrote a paper suggesting that the thirty-one planes might be symbolically interpreted as the differences in the condition and degree of attainment among human beings in this present life, he was sternly reprimanded by those of high ecclesiastical and civil standing and warned to desist from such dangerous speculations.

Yet there is some adaptation of the traditional cosmology to the new scientific knowledge. This adaptation takes several forms, no two of them mutually exclusive. Sometimes it is a kind of tacit avoidance of such topics for discussion. One university graduate put it that he avoided all discussions of religion and politics as equally dangerous; which, being interpreted, meant that he did not wish to speak out against any of the traditional religious beliefs (including cosmology) no matter how much he disbelieved in them. But there are other and more positive adaptations to the new situation. Some remind one of that kind of adaptation which goes on in conservative Christian circles with regard to the Genesis story of creation. Thus it is suggested that perhaps some 2500 years ago in the Buddha's day the continents on the earth were in different relation to each other, so that the traditional Buddhist cosmology might then have been quite correct. And again, sometimes by the same persons, it is suggested that the Buddha never said that there was a literal Mount Meru, but that these statements are to be taken in an "astral" sense. (An astral sense is presumably somewhere between the symbolical and the literal sense.) Mount Meru may not be physically perceptible to the eye of man, yet it is not thereby rendered completely non-existent. It is perhaps existent in another dimension or plane, perceptible only to the developed supramundane intelligence of the saint or the jhanic expert.[1]

There is also what we might call the practical solution to this problem. Cosmology is simply by-passed for the most part or left in the realm of optional interests, while the main emphasis is put upon the moral and meditational disciplines. "Let these matters be as they may; believe them or not, as you will. But the heart of Buddhism is moral purity and mind-training. Concentrate on these and the other will take care of itself". Sometimes this latter is said in full confidence that the meditation-practicer will come to full conviction in such matters at a higher stage of development; or again it may represent something of reservation or uncertainty in the believer's own mind. But practically speaking the immediate result is the same for both.

With regard to the dynamic phase of the universe, the Theravadin is in somewhat better position. He has no narrow three-tiered, six-thousand-year-old, earth-centred universe to discard or reinterpret as had the Christian. Or to put it better: He can discard or more easily modify his limited, static universe (Mount Meru type) by immersing it in the cyclic pattern of appearing and disappearing universes found in the dynamic interpretation of the universe, than can the Christian adapt Genesis to Einsteinian physics. When speaking in this context he may, and does, wax quite confident, even triumphant. Does not science, with its ever-expanding vision of illimitable worlds, many of which may be inhabited, and its ever-lengthening time-scale, accord with the Buddhist cyclic theory? Who can longer speak of our little earth as the one and

---

[1] Such is the standard answer to the non-Buddhist who asks for "evidence" of the reality of the various planes. They will become perceptible to him when he develops the proper insight through psychic training in meditational practice. If Christians would thus develop themselves, they might be able to communicate with Christ, who now doubtless inhabits one of the higher planes, and would confirm the truth of Buddhist teaching! This is somewhat in line with the classic teaching that those on the lower planes can perceive the reality of the higher plane only if they are receptive and if inhabitants of the higher planes so choose to reveal themselves. But, say contemporary Buddhists, this seldom happens now because of the spiritual degeneracy of our age.

only "world" that had an absolute beginning in time? Is it not far more likely that the history of the physical universe is endless, an infinitely long and beginningless process in which matter or energy forms achieve and lose a patterned existence over and over again; that worlds are born and die without cessation? Such a view, says the contemporary Buddhist, is both Buddhistically and scientifically true at the same time.

There is a further consideration: that of the governance of this whole process by the moral justice of kamma. This scarcely accords with the scientific interpretation of cosmic process. But the problem of the relationship of kammic and physical causality will be considered in detail at a later point. (See chapter on Buddhism and Science.) Here we may conclude our discussion of Buddhist cosmology by the following summary statements: (1) The traditional cosmology of the Mount Meru universe will hold its own in the Theravada world of Burma for perhaps another generation in almost its literal form. But it will be increasingly subject to modification or re-interpretation in a symbolic sense. If this modification is too slow, a generation of disbelievers may grow up, is perhaps now growing up, who will be unable to accept the Buddhist cosmology and with its rejection tend to reject Buddhist conviction *in toto*. (2) The dynamic interpretation of the universe will no doubt be increasingly emphasized and perhaps in the end submerge the "other" static universe concept entirely. What will then happen to the interpretation of the thirty-one planes is not clear. Will they too be engulfed by the dynamic forces of change, become subject, as are the universes, to impermanence and insubstantiality? Or will they remain above and beyond the tides of cosmic flux; or retain their place but in largely symbolic form? (3) The problem of readjustment faced by Theravada Buddhism here is surely no greater than that faced by Christianity two generations ago with the onset of the evolutionary theory. Perhaps indeed Buddhism is in a theoretically better situation. The major difficulty in the way of any readjustment is the great strength of the conservative tradition which has so insistently emphasized the literal inerrancy of its pristine purity and the infallibility of the transmission of its scriptures. And there is also the terrific suddenness with which cultural change is forcing itself upon Theravada countries today, a suddenness and totality of change that Christianity did not have to face in its readjustment. Undoubtedly there will be many types of response, but it is too early to predict which one will finally win the day in Buddhist cosmic theory.

THE THIRTY-ONE PLANES OF EXISTENCE
IN THE STABLE AND VERTICAL UNIVERSE
OF BUDDHIST TRADITION[1]

NIBBANA

No passage from Brahma Worlds to Nibbana
save for Anagamins

ARUPA-LOKA; IMMATERIAL SPHERES; REALM OF
FORMLESSNESS

No.	Name of Plane	Access by	Life-Span
31	Neither Perception nor Non-Perception	Formless Meditations	84,000 kappas
30	Nothingness	,, ,,	60,000 ,,
29	Infinity of Consciousness	,, ,,	40,000 ,,
28	Infinity of Space	,, ,,	20,000 ,,

RUPA-LOKA; REALM OF FORM; FINE MATERIAL SPHERE
(Planes 23–27 called Pure Abodes)

No.	Name		Access by	Life-Span
27	Sublime Gods		Fourth Jhana	16,000 kappas
26	Easily-Seeing Gods		,, ,,	8,000 ,,
25	Easily-Seen Gods		,, ,,	4,000 ,,
24	Untroubled Gods		,, ,,	2,000 ,,
23	Effortless Gods (Anagamins reborn here)		,, ,,	1,000 ,,
22	Gods without Perception		,, ,,	500 ,,
21	Richly-Rewarded Gods		,, ,,	200 ,,
20	Completely Lustrous Gods	(high)	Third Jhana	64 ,,
19	Immeasurably Lustrous Gods	(medium)	,, ,,	32 ,,
18	Limitedly Lustrous Gods	(low)	,, ,,	16 ,,
17	Radiant Gods	(high)	Second Jhana	8 ,,
16	Immeasurably Splendorous Gods	(medium)	,, ,,	4 ,,
15	Limitedly Splendorous Gods	(low)	,, ,,	2 ,,
14	Great Brahmas	(high)	First Jhana	1 ,,
13	Priests of Brahma	(medium)	,, ,,	1/2 ,,
12	Retinue of Brahma	(low)	,, ,,	1/3 ,,

High, medium, low refer to degrees of mastery
of the Jhanic meditative technique achieved on earth.

KAMA-LOKA; SENSUOUS WORLD; ELEVEN-FOLD REALM OF
PLEASURE

Seven-Fold Realm of Sensual Bliss

No.	Name	Kamma		Life-Span
11	Gods who control pleasure	Good Kamma		9,216 million yrs.
10	Gods who delight in fashioning	,,	,,	2,304 ,, ,,
9	Satisfied Gods (Tusita Heaven)	,,	,,	576 ,, ,,
8	Yama Gods	,,	,,	144 ,, ,,
7	Thirty-Three Gods (Top of Mt. Meru)	,,	,,	36 ,, ,,
6	Four Great Kings (Slope of Mt. Meru)	,,	,,	9 ,, ,,
5	Human plane of existence (earth)			84,000 yrs. on down

Four-Fold Realm of Punishment

No.	Name	Kamma	
4	Demon or Asura world	Bad Kamma	
3	Ghost or Peta World	,,	,,
2	Animal world	,,	,,
1	Hells or purgatories	,,	,,

[1] Partly taken from material in Warren's *Buddhism in Translations*.

IV

THERAVADA BUDDHISM ENCOUNTERS SCIENCE

IT IS NOT ONLY IN THE WEST THAT SCIENCE AND ITS TECH-
nologies have wrought a revolution that has touched every
phase of life from the strictly economic and practical to the
religious and philosophical. The same disturbing and transforming influences are at work all through the East. In some
cultures there is an ancient, even if temporarily outmoded,
scientific tradition to attach to; in others there is only a relatively primitive life and culture that have been innocent of
any kind of science or pre-science for centuries on end. When
science enters here it is a brusque and disturbing current that
unsettles all of the established ways of life and undermines the
ancient values and beliefs. It is in this connection that we
may inquire about the relations between Theravada Buddhism
and contemporary science.

The Dangers of Scientific Materialism

We may begin by saying that the reaction of Theravada
Buddhism to science is a mingled one. There is in it a considerable degree of anxious apprehension. For there is an
awareness of the manner in which scientific studies have undermined many Western-Christian religious beliefs and loosened
the hold of religious values and institutions upon life in general.
There is some comfort of a negative sort to be found in this
situation to be sure, in that the dissolution of the Western
religious fabric witnesses to the weakness and falsity of theistic
beliefs and constitutes a preparation for the universal triumph
of Buddhism. But in general among the educated Buddhists

there is also some distress at what appears to be a world-wide destruction of ancient ethical and religious values and their replacement by a new and aggressive materialism under the aegis of science. And however inferior those other religious values might be in Buddhist eyes, they are better than what has taken their place—a totally unspiritual view of life.

There is thus considerable apprehension about the materialism that the scientific revolution has produced. For the Buddhist this materialism takes two forms. One is the Marxist philosophy which proclaims itself to be thoroughly scientific in viewpoint and method, the first fully and completely scientific philosophy of society and history. And there has been some ideological flirtation between Buddhism and Marxism because both reject theism and eternal-soul beliefs.[1] But by and large this flirtation has been fruitless; Theravada Buddhism has been growing more and more distrustful of Marxism. For at least in its actual political expression in Communism, Marxism seems to be the apotheosis of Materialism. Material substance produces spirit or mind, says Marxism, a viewpoint emphatically denied by Buddhism. And the true hope of man, indeed his only hope, is to achieve complete happiness on this earth by the perfection of his material situation. This again is obviously completely at variance with the fundamental Buddhist tenet that only in Nibbana, beyond all time and space conditions, is man's salvation to be found.

The second form of materialism, though non-political, is fully as aggressive and dangerous in its way as Marxism. This form of materialism is not so much found in the materialistic statements of scientists and philosophers, though sometimes to be sure these are deplored by Buddhist writers as indicative of a short-sighted scientism that does not know its own limitations. (Yet on the other hand the "materialistic" scientist or philosopher is quoted with some enthusiasm and approval when he seems to be countering Western-Christian beliefs.) It is rather the practical multiplication of the material goods of life which scientific technology has produced that occasions the anxiety.

Now the grounds for this anxiety are quite obvious. The

---

[1] For a fuller discussion of this subject, and the related one of the Buddhistic socialism of Burmese premier U Nu, see the author's *In the Hope of Nibbana*.

Buddhist way of life has been traditionally a way of the passive
acceptance of one's economic and social situation as being
largely pre-determined by kamma. What one now is, he
deserves to be because of past good or evil deeds. And further,
and more fundamental, the good way of life according to
Buddhism, is one of the reduction of sense desires. The monk's
pattern of life in which Buddhism is to be ideally practised is
indeed the complete elimination of desire as far as is possible.
The holiest man is the one who has become desireless except
for Nibbana.[1] But even the good Buddhist layman is seeking
to free himself as much as possible from the clutch of rebirth-
producing desire by the simplification of his way of life and
the limitation of his sensual indulgences. For Buddhism's basic
assumption is that man has no real hope of enduring happiness
in the whole round of existence (*saṃsāra*) to which he is subjected, because it is impermanent, full of suffering, unreal, and
essentially unimprovable.

Such a view of life may well accord with the physical
realities of a situation in which the majority of people have no
visible prospects for the improvement of their earthly lot. But
now comes scientific technology with its exciting promises and
dazzling prospects. It says to the common man: "You may
change your lot. You need not passively yield to your fate.
Science offers to all men the prospect of powers and enjoy-
ments formerly undreamed of even by kings with the greatest
of wealth. And as a foretaste of such a glorious destiny, brand
new in this world, here are even now a thousand new inven-
tions, gadgets, and sensations within your grasp". Thus has
samsara been transformed in word at least from the home of
suffering and patient endurance of kammic destiny into a
realm full of glittering prizes, one indeed which might almost
be made into the likeness of a deva world. In any case
many devout Buddhists today speak with some concern about

---

[1] Or, perhaps more accurately, one must think of Nibbana as "desired"
either by the ignorant who do not understand its true nature even though they
strive for it; or as sought after, prior to its attainment or the vision of it, by a
motivational-force which should be given some other name than desire—for
"desire" as such is always evil, or non-Nibbanic, in Buddhist thinking. One who
has attained even to Nibbana-in-this-life is technically desireless in absolute
degree, because Nibbana is precisely the "going out" of all desire, known perhaps
in part even by the lack of desire for itself.

the worldly emphasis that science now brings and the alluring enticements of the new materialism. For what a stimulation to worldly greed all this is! What a multiplication of the forms of desire—that desire to be, to feel, to enjoy, which binds man ever more firmly to the wheel of rebirth!

So also this new materialism multiplies the occasions of sin. For when greed abounds then men strive ever more strenuously for what will minister to that greed. Thus in a world-order that emphasizes material possessions and prosperity, men set themselves against each other in competing groups— social classes, unfriendly nations and international blocs—all of them struggling for the materialistic prizes of life. And insofar as science multiplies the material goods to be obtained and the techniques of force by which to obtain them, to that extent it also threatens that life-pattern of contentment and peace that Buddhism considers to be life according to the Buddha's Dhamma.

Buddhism as Scientific

1. *General Statements*

What then is Buddhism to do with science? Deplore its fruits and oppose it? Such may be the tendency on the part of some, but far more often the opposite tack is taken: Buddhism is essentially scientific in its outlook. It has always welcomed investigation of its truths. Indeed long ago the Buddha himself specifically forbade the unquestioning acceptance even of his own teachings and encouraged his hearers first to doubt and investigate, and then only accept those teachings if they were personally satisfied as to their truth. The relevant passage, often quoted today as "the Buddha's Charter of Free Inquiry", is in part as follows:

> *Now, look you, Kalamas. Be ye not misled by report or tradition or hearsay. Be not misled by proficiency in the collections of traditional sayings, nor by mere logic or inference, nor after considering reasons, nor after reflection on the approval of some theory, nor because it fits becoming, nor out of respect for a recluse who holds it to be true. But, Kalamas, when you know for yourselves: These things are unprofitable, these things are blameworthy, these things are censured by*

the intelligent; these things, when performed and undertaken conduce to loss and sorrow—then indeed do ye reject them.[1]

A contemporary writer goes on to interpret this passage in the following words:

Buddha Dhamma is free from compulsion and coercion and does not demand of the follower blind faith. At the very outset the sceptic will be pleased to hear its call for investigation. The Buddha Dhamma from beginning to end, is open to all who have eyes to see and minds to understand. The Buddha never endeavoured to bring out of his followers blind and submissive faith in Him and His teaching. He tutors his disciples in the ways of discrimination and intelligent inquiry. To the inquiring Kalamas the Buddha answered: "Right is it to doubt, right is it to question what is doubtful and what is not clear".[2]

Thus it may be, and often is said, that Buddhism alone of all religions can accord with science, and can be called fully scientific in its spirit, methods, and teaching. Writes a European on this subject:

There can be no question that Buddhism is the one system, excepting perhaps science itself, which achieves an objective and detached view toward the nature and destiny of man. This striking objectivity divorces the Buddhist system from the realm of religion and allies it at once with the kind of scientific search for truth . . . which affords a major pre-occupation to most of the intellectual world—both East and West—today.
The Buddha experimented with ideas, not with things—he employed the crucible of life in which to measure human experience and he came up with a detached and tested answer.[3]

The author of the quotation goes on to classify Buddhism as "tough-minded" and completely "objective" in its view of the world; it has no preconceived ideas concerning reality, no emotionally dictated wishes that call for congenial solutions. If "faith in the unknown and unknowable" and "dogmatism" have obtruded themselves in Buddhist lands, they are not genuine Buddhism, he says. For genuine Buddhism is the "scientifically conceived Dharma of the Founder".

[1] *Anguttara-Nikāya* or *Gradual Sayings*, Book of Threes, Chapter VII, Section 65, Text i, 189. P.T.S. edition, 1951.
[2] "Seven Factors of Enlightenment", Piyadassi Thera, *Light of the Buddha*, Vol. IV, No. 2, February, 1959.
[3] "The Relation of Buddhism to Modern Science", Robert F. Spencer, in the *Buddhist Supplement*, of *The Burman*, April 13, 1959.

While the above was written by a Westerner in the general style of the "export Buddhism" described in our second chapter, it is echoed and re-echoed both in general and specific forms in the Theravada world today. Thus we read that "Buddha was the father of scientific thought and originator of philosophy, and Buddhism has been its promoter in several countries of Asia".[1] He might well have given his omniscient intelligence to scientific matters, but rather confined it to what he considered most important—man's salvation. Yet even here he was completely rational (and scientific) in his approach to truth. He and Buddhism after him completely dispense with that blind faith which is the core of all other religions. The Buddha Dhamma can be demonstrated as truth in a fully scientific and experiential manner.

Thus writes another contemporary author:

> *Buddha Dhamma will be found to be quite different from the blind faith of other religions or the uncertainties of speculative philosophies. It is the deepest science that should be studied in the light of facts of life with open minds, applying to it the highest attainable intellectual faculties. Analysis, tests, experiments, observations, logical thinking, reasoning and other methods used for all branches of study will be of great help to understand and appreciate the Buddha-Dhamma, which will give entire intellectual satisfaction to all thinking persons.*

To be sure there are bounds to science of the ordinary sort. It reaches up only to a limited extent toward those higher truths that the Buddha's "highest attainable intellectual faculties" were able to apprehend:

> *Supramundane knowledge or insight or enlightenment attained by the Buddhas and Arahats cannot by any means be realized by pure reason, imagination and logical thinking. It far transcends the realm of the mundane intellect and faculties.*

This highest knowledge is found in the Abhidhamma, third division of the Pali Canon, where the nature of the physical and psychical phenomena are "marvellously expounded with mathematical precision and expressed scientifically in unequivocal terms". And though they will be found to be "very logical and reasonable" it is

[1] "Buddhism's Contribution to World Culture", Umesh Chandra Mutsuddii, *Light of the Buddha*, Vol. IV, February 29, 1960, p. 25.

Essential to realize that they were discovered in the light of His [the Buddha's] supramundane knowledge and not as inferences deduced from logical thinking and reasoning.

In conclusion the author urges scientifically-minded materialists to study the "super-science" of the Buddha. For

if they will only try and understand this super-science thoroughly, they will be able to serve humanity in a much better way . . . than ordinary materialistic thinkers and ardent social workers.[1]

Elsewhere he also notes that the highly developed scientific knowledge of the scientists will "help them to understand the *Buddha Dhamma* thoroughly and to take up a course of *Vipassanā meditation* successfully.[2]

And as a final example of this so-frequently expressed confidence in the scientific nature of Buddhism, we have the following, by a Western convert to Buddhism:

without being aware of it the modern scientist and philosopher are being propelled irresistibly in the direction of Buddhism. Their uncertainties and doubts are spiritual "growing pains"; but a time will come when they will realize . . . there is a higher religion— one based upon systematic investigation and the sincere search for truth.[3]

2. *Some Popular Expressions*

Such then is the contemporary invitation of Theravada Buddhism to science to investigate its truth to the fullest extent, with the sole proviso that the scientist must not expect to attain to the highest truths except by means of the Buddha's insight and method. The philosophic implications of this proviso must be examined later, but for the moment we are concerned to observe some of the more specific expressions of this unbounded confidence in the fully scientific nature of Buddhist truth. Naturally there are various types of such statements. We shall begin with the rather crude and popularized forms in which the scientific nature of Buddhist truth is held to confirm the literal truth of all the statements attributed to the

[1] "What is Buddha Dhamma?", Khin Moung, *Light of the Dhamma*, Vol. IV, No. 2, April, 1957, pp. 53–6.
[2] "Buddha Dhamma and Modern Science", U Khin Moung, *Light of the Buddha*, Vol. I, No. 9, December, 1956, p. 40.
[3] "The Scientific Approach to Buddhism", Francis Story, *Light of the Dhamma*, Vol. I, No. 4, January, 1953, p. 9.

Buddha—and that includes all of the Pali Canon! Thus there is a story in the *Majjhima-Nikāya* (*Middle Length Sayings*) of some monks who "borrowed" the roof of a potter's house for the repair of their monastery. But rather than being angry at this appropriation of their roof, the potter and his blind parents

> *were suffused with ineffable joy for 7 days. Then in accordance with the law of Cause and Effect a strange phenomenon comes into being. Drench the whole village or the whole country by immense rainfall, but not a single drop of rain falls into this roofless house. The sun's rays too do not penetrate into this roofless house. And it is ordained that this site of Gati Kara's house be in such state as long as the world lasts.*

The author goes on to make a contemporary application of the above account:

> *This place must be somewhere in the vicinity of the eternal town of Benares. The Indian Government should find out, especially Mr. Nehru who seems to venerate Buddhism. It is an easy task. Within a radius say of a hundred miles around Benares each and every headman of the village tracts can enquire minutely and try to seek for this marvellous place. Once it is found the impact of Buddhism upon humanity will be enormous and the tourist income of India will be magnificent.*[1]

We also find the position taken that though the Buddha did not turn his full attention to scientific matters, when he has made a statement about the physical facts in the universe his inerrant word is to be trusted over against contemporary scientific statements on the same matter. Thus, under the caption "Buddhism Challenges Western Scientists" we read the following:

> *The Buddha said, "The diameter of the Sun, is Fifty Yojanas and that of the Moon Forty-nine Yojanas." Now one Yojana is equal to 13½ miles. So by such calculation the Sun has the diameter of 672½ miles and the moon 661½ miles. It is a very important and far-reaching point. By this Buddhism challenges the Western scientists. . . .*
> *The Western scientist computed that the diameters of moon and sun are 2,160 miles and 865,400 miles respectively. Once men land on the moon and find the lunar diameter to be 661½ miles as explained by*

[1] "The Most Unique and Marvellous Place in this World", Kyaiklat Ohn, *Buddhist Supplement, The Burman,* July 13, 1959.

For scripture reference see the *Ghati-Kara Sutta,* No. 81, of the *Majjhima-Nikāya* or *Middle Length Sayings.*

Buddha, then it is a truth that the Buddha is Ominscient. Let us wait and see which Religion is the True One.[1]

We shall give one more example of the confident expectation that scientific findings of the future will confirm the Buddha's statements about matters that science has not yet penetrated, that indeed the Buddha has often provided science with a valuable clue in his sayings. A Thai doctor writes as follows:

> *The Embryonal stage immediately after conception (Rebirth) is called by the Buddha, Kalala-Rupa. It is a minute speck of proto-plasma resembling a round and transparent drop of caraway-seed oil. After one week it develops into the Ambudda-rupa which is more dense and slightly bigger. Its colour resembles that of reddish meat juice diluted in water . . . (and so on through the 63rd day after conception).*
>
> *The Buddha did not disclose the later stages of the infant's growth in the womb, obviously because they could be seen with the naked eye, whereas the earliest stages could not be seen. Even today, in spite of all medical appliances, we are ignorant of the human fertilized ovum immediately after conception, and the earliest ovum found in recent years was seven and a half days old. What the Buddha taught of human embryology is still valid today. It cannot be contradicted. He was omniscient.*[2]

3. *Philosophical Reconciliations*

No doubt some such attempts as these will persist for some time to come. They are analogous to a certain type of attempt to conform the statements made in Genesis to modern scientific doctrines; or to see in certain Biblical passages "predictions" of the aeroplane, the automobile, and the submarine. However, there are other and more intellectually sophisticated reconciliations between science and Buddhism to be found in contemporary Theravada Buddhism. These in general move on a more fundamental level than the above and need to be taken more seriously. We may note several expressions of this scientific interpretation of the Buddhist position in the follow-

[1] Letter to the Editor of *The Burman*, Rangoon, May 22, 1959.
[2] "The Buddhist Conception of Man", Luang Suriyabongs, M.D., in a pamphlet entitled *Visakapuja B. E. 2501*, published by the Buddhist Association of Thailand, p. 16. Compare with the *Samyutta-Nikāya, Mahā-Vagga* division, *Indriya-Sutta*, (Vol. V of *Kindred Sayings*).

ing order: 1. a general conviction that the new relativistic
science of the last few decades is both less materialistic (hence
more friendly to religion in general) and that it tends to confirm the basic Buddhist doctrines of the primacy of the mental
category and the composite changing nature of all reality;
2. an assertion that the law of kamma is a completely
scientific rationale of man's moral life and present existence;
and 3. the contention that the Buddhist discipline of meditation is first-hand proof of the truth of Buddhist doctrine.

a) *The Spiritual Character of the New Science.*

There has been fully as much rejoicing in Buddhist as in
some Christian circles at the "reformation" of science in the
late-nineteenth and early-twentieth century. From a blatantly
materialistic approach to "reality", and the confident assurance that the hard-particle molecularism of earlier science was
the final formulation of physical theory, science has moved to
the "dissolution" of hard matter into electro-magnetic fields
of energy or force in which certain types of vibrational eddies
form what we call matter or solid substance. And there has
also been the growth of new psychic interests in the West:
experimental psychology, para-psychology, psychic-research
societies, psycho-somatic medicine, and the use of hypnotism
in physical therapy. All this has meant to the Buddhist a
"friendlier" attitude on the part of science to religion and
even a confirmation of long-held Buddhist principles.

We shall notice first of all the Buddhist interest in the new
psychic climate in the West. This interest takes several forms.
The "stream of consciousness" psychology of William James is
often noted with approval. To be sure its value for the Buddhist is chiefly negative, i.e. it disproves Western Christian
soul theories and accords with the Buddhist idea of no-self or
no-soul in its resolution of the mind into a set of mental items,
or into its content, without any remaining mind or soul which
possesses or 'thinks its ideas. Here, says the Buddhist, is a prime
instance of the "new" psychology confirming what the Buddha
said 2500 years ago, and said much more profoundly and
exhaustively in the Abhidhamma!

But the deeper note of approval is reserved for the newly
"mentalistic" outlook of Western science. For example,

Western medicine is at last realizing that the body is no mere set of material particles that can be treated by physical means (drugs and surgery) alone, but has a mental aspect as well. It is using psycho-theraphy, psycho-analysis, and hypnotic techniques to treat not only mental derangements, but organic diseases too, or at least some aspects of them. This is what we have been doing for centuries, says the Buddhist. The Buddha's meditational discipline is a complete self-administering course in psycho-analysis which every Buddhist has directly at hand in his own tradition. And Buddhists remind the West of their ancient doctrine that it is mind-states that determine and produce physical states, not only in the individual physical organism but in the world at large, for that matter.

Of especial interest to the contemporary Buddhist is the area of psychic research and para-psychology. There is a general tendency to take these research efforts as fully scientific and to interpret the interest shown by a fringe of scientists in such matters as a turning of all science in this direction. Or at the very least there is a tendency to regard the findings in these areas as fully accepted scientific proofs, now beyond question. But perhaps of more interest than the possible over-estimation of the importance and scientific recognition given such researches, is the manner in which they are related to Buddhist doctrines. The reports of psychic researchers indicating communication with the spirits of the dead is held to confirm, though in a feeble and inferior way, that insight which the developed Buddhist meditator may enjoy with regard to the thirty-one planes of existence: communication with supermundane beings. But it does not prove that men have immortal souls, says the Buddhist. Para-psychology, particularly as developed in the Duke University experiments by Professor Rhine, is considered to confirm the general truth of telepathic communication and in particular to accord with the Buddhist tradition that mental waves of force can have direct physical effects. Thus under the title of "Historicity and Super-Normal Powers of the Buddha", Mr Arthur de Silva of Ceylon suggests that the ability of a concentrating mind to influence the fall of dice at a distance is a confirmatory though meagre example of the way in which the Buddha mentally projected a big rock into countermotion against one sent plunging down by Devadatta to destroy him.[1]

This leads us to a consideration of the friendliness that Buddhism feels toward the new dynamic physics of the Einsteinian epoch. Like some of their Christian counterparts in the West, Buddhists find in the principle of indeterminacy in the behaviour of atomic particles (Heisenberg principle) room for free will. Francis Story writes:

> *From the philosophic viewpoint, which is, strictly speaking, no concern of the pure scientist . . . this "uncertainty principle" made room for the idea of free will, which had necessarily been absent from the idea of a universe entirely determined by causal principles that admitted of no variation.*[2]

And on an even more basic level the "spiritualization" of matter into energy, fields of force, and vibrations, is held to be a victory for religion in general and Buddhism in particular. The reasons for this are easily seen. "Energy" sounds far less materialistic and far more mentalistic than "matter". Energy is such an elastic concept that it can be used to indicate many sorts of force and thus apparently link together as one in kind the physical and the psychical. And this is most congenial to the latent philosophical idealism of Theravada Buddhism, which is usually held in abeyance as an explicit philosophical doctrine but is genuinely present as an implicit bias toward a mentalistic interpretation of physical reality. As noted elsewhere, mind states determine physical states and when highly developed may dissolve and reform the physical particles of the body. Indeed (cf. chapter III), it is the strength or weakness of the mental-moral force of its inhabitants that makes even a physical universe to rise or fall. Besides this general consonance of the new physics with its latent idealism, there is the very specific usefulness of the concepts of energy and vibration with regard to some essential Theravada doctrines. How shall that which passes from birth

---

[1] *Light of the Buddha*, Vol. II, No. 8, August, 1957, p. 12. In the same article it is suggested that the Buddha foresaw the germ theory as indicated by his prescribing water-strainers for the monks; that he chose one of the two colours that science has shown do not attract mosquitoes for the monk's robes; and that perhaps he foreknew the atom bomb. See also author's discussion of "televolition" in *In the Hope of Nibbana*.

[2] Op. Cit., p. 9.

to birth be understood if not as an immaterial soul? It may be understood as a form of (personality-producing) energy. "Energy" may be thought of as combining both the mental and physical characteristics in one unit especially in this re-birth context; the use of the word does not commit the user to a specific form of the element which is carried over to the new existence. Likewise the concept of energy in the form of vibrations whose nature again may be psycho-physical, encourages the Buddhist in the use of his basic spiritual category of radiation, i.e. the sending out of waves of mental-moral influence throughout the universe. Is not the potency of such methods, which the older hard-headed materialistic scientist treated as merest superstition, now allowed and perhaps even proved by the new physics? At the very least, the Buddhist would say, the new science must make much more generous room for such possibilities than it has in the past. And he cherishes the very hopeful suspicion that the newly spiritual science will in the end prove the validity of most or all of the Buddhist teachings about the higher psychic powers attainable by the saint.

b) *Kamma, the Law of Causality in the Moral Sphere.*

A second area in which Buddhism emphasizes its genuinely scientific character is that involved in its conception of the operation of law of kamma. It maintains that the same sort of causal succession rules the moral sphere, and the lives of sentient beings, as rules the physical world at large. We shall first begin with a general consideration of causality before proceeding to this particular Buddhist application of the principle, however.

Generally speaking Buddhism understands causality in terms of the traditional Western doctrine. A "cause" is an event or state which precedes another event or state in time, and without which the latter would not occur. Or to reverse it: Whenever the first state or event occurs, the second invariably comes into existence. The same general and specific aspects of causality are also recognized. In the wide sense each event, however great or small, is the product of the state of the total universe at the moment of its occurrence, whether the shifting of a grain of sand, or a word spoken by a human being, or the flaming death of a world system. Especially does

Buddhism emphasize the organic and interrelated situation of everything with everything else. But, on the other hand, it is also sharply aware of the specific causal linkages, particularly those involving sentient beings, in which one series of events, i.e. a sentient being, is separated from all others and considered as a single-line succession of states in which each is the cause of the one following it and the result of the one preceding it.

We may note, however, that in the Buddhist interpretation of causality, there are distinctive emphases. For while Buddhist theory agrees with science that the total cosmos is an infinitely intricate and interrelated series of causal linkages throughout—and sometimes gives the same name to this as to the Buddha's teaching, namely Dhamma—yet it is almost exclusively interested in that Dhamma or law which specifically governs the birth, nature, course, and death of sentient beings. And, secondly, the Buddhist interpretation of causality is distinctive in its selection of those elements which it places at the heart of its causal series.

The distinctive Buddhist type of causal interpretation is most clearly evident in its formulation of its doctrine of *Dependent Origination* (Pali *paticcasamuppada*). Briefly stated it represents a rigorous extension of the principle of causality to the total life and being of every sentient individual. It "shows the conditionality and dependent nature of that uninterrupted flux of manifold physical and psychical phenomena of existence conventionally called the Ego, or Man, or Animal".[1] Each sentient individual, that is to say, is integrally and completely included in the universal causal series. He is a compounded article throughout, a "confection". Every part of his being from the inmost private thought to the outermost physical appearance or public action is a composite of many elements, sub-linkages of causal chains, temporarily met in his present being. There is no pure, self-subsistent, or enduring element within him that is above or beyond this causal nexus or safe from its continually perishing flux.

So far we are still within the realm of the generally causative without any distinctive Buddhist emphasis apparent, save perhaps the rigorous insistence upon applying causal categories exhaustively to the total human being—though even

[1] *Buddhist Dictionary*, Nyanatiloka, Frewin and Co., Colombo, 1956, p. 119.

this might be paralleled in Western bio-chemistry and psychology. But when we come to the terms of this causal series, then we realize that we are on distinctively Buddhist ground. For here we have the famous 12-fold linkage or series of events that produce, determine, and destroy the sentient being, represented in circular succession as the Wheel of Life.

Into a detailed discussion of this series we cannot enter here, for its exact interpretation is much disputed.[1] But we must notice its cyclic and repetitive form. With whatever step we start in the series, that step leads forward inevitably and irreversibly in the direction indicated by the numbers, yet always and inevitably comes back upon itself again with step 12 producing step 1 and so on through the series. And we may also observe the almost completely psychic—or at the very least the psycho-somatic—nature of nearly all the steps. They are as follows: 1. Ignorance; 2. Kamma-formations; 3. Consciousness; 4. Corporality and mentality; 5. Six bases (or sense-powers, including consciousness as a sixth sense); 6. Impressions or sense-contact with the object; 7. Feeling; 8. Craving; 9. Clinging or mental-emotional attachment; 10. Becoming (again); 11. Rebirth (actual); 12. Old Age and Death. So it is that Buddhism views the life of all sentient beings, including man. Or we should actually say the "lives" of sentient beings, since we have here an all-embracing formula for the infinite series of re-births to which all sentient beings are subjected.

Now it is here in the context of life-production considered as a series of linked steps that we come to the core of the Buddhist interest in, and the distinctive Buddhist interpretation of, causality, namely kamma. For this series of twelve steps, however we may regard it, is governed by the inexorable law of kamma in all its parts. And in the working of the law of kamma the Buddhist finds the supreme example of the

---

[1] Thus some Western interpreters consider the series simultaneous, the constituents of one moment of human experience considered in kammic terms. Others see both a non-temporal vertical (simultaneous?) aspect and a horizontal temporal succession involved. Still others consider it a generalized statement of the factors of all sentient existence, loosely and partially chronological, but not narrowly so in terms of any one being. And the author of the *Buddhist Dictionary* flatly states that the true interpretation is in terms of three lives; past, links 1 and 2; present, links 3 to 7; future, links 11 and 12. See article on *Paticcasamuppada*.

scientific character of Buddhism: for it takes the moral and spiritual life of man out of the vague and imprecise, even chaotic, realm of inspiration, prayer, Divine favour and disfavour, sin, repentance and forgiveness, grace and the salvation of the unworthy, and subjects it to the reign of predictable cause and effect.

We may very briefly reiterate the often-stated doctrine of kamma: kamma is the cosmic law of the inescapable reaping of the morally-deserved results of one's own deeds. Just as every physical event is the result of a preceding event or set of circumstances, and in turn acts as the cause of another event, so every deed of every sentient being produces its consequences; and the nature of those consequences is in ethical accord with the nature of the antecedent deed. Thus the good deed of mercy, kindness, or generosity will inevitably yield its benefits of long life, health, or wealth in this existence in part, but most importantly in one's next existence. And precisely the reverse occurs with evil deeds. Thus step 2 in the 12-fold series is kamma-formations, or the power of one's past accumulation of good or bad thoughts, words, and deeds, to determine the nature of his next birth. Not by blind chance, says the Buddhist, is one man born happy, rich, handsome, and long-lived, and another poverty-stricken, miserable, and ugly; not by chance are some born as animals or in the hells and some in the glorious company of the devas or gods; all these circumstances, and the very nature of the man himself, are the result of the absolutely just and impartial law of kamma. Always, world without end, a being reaps the morally deserved results of every word, thought, or deed he has ever been responsible for in every one of his innumerable past lives. And is not this the essence of scientifically conceived causality, penetrating to the very heart of man's inmost being? Writes a contemporary Buddhist author:

> It is the twin doctrines or fundamental principles of Kamma and rebirth together with the doctrine of Anatta which distinguish Buddhism as the foremost and peerless of the world religions. . . . Buddhism stands pre-eminent over all other teachings in its unrivalled ethics and its sane rational scientific philosophy or exposition of the natural laws and causes of life and all phenomena. The cause of rebirth, according to the law of physics, is the Con-

I

servation of Energy. Force is indestructible or is never lost or destroyed, but only changes or passes through various forms or phases. . . .

Thus, so long as the psychic force of cravings inherent in and generated by all conscious beings is not exhausted, so long will it manifest itself repeatedly and endlessly through successive forms . . . the nature of which is determined in accordance with the preponderating purity or impurity of the Kamma.[1]

c) *Experiential (Scientific) Verification of Buddhist Truth*

We will deal with this Buddhist contention in the chapter on Buddhist Meditation in connection with the "practice" of the Buddhist way. It will be observed in that connection that Buddhism holds that its basic and deeper truths can only be known at first-hand through meditative experience. Only as we experience certain truths in our own being can we truly know them, or in the better term fully "realize" them.

That discussion need not be duplicated here. But some further attention must be given to this experiential note because Theravada Buddhism is today sounding it so insistently, and so directly equating it with the "scientific proof" of its teachings. In a 1956 speech in New York City, then (and once-again) Burmese Premier U Nu invited any serious students, who desired to learn the truth of Buddhist doctrine at first-hand by a truly scientific experimental method, to come to Burma and live for two or three months at the government's expense in a meditation centre. Nor is this an isolated statement. Both in particular reference to meditation and in general reference to the doctrines of Buddhism, it is asserted that Buddhist truth is provable in the scientific manner, i.e. by experience, not by theory. What we shall note briefly here is that particular area to which this is applied and its correlation with scientific truth.

The three basic characteristics of all tangible experience, or tangibly experienced reality, are impermanence (*anicca*), unsatisfactoriness (*dukkha*), and insubstantiality (*anattā*). This

[1] "The Nature and Cause of Rebirth", Samanera Pandita, *Light of the Buddha*, Vol. IV, No. 9, September, 1959, p. 38. It is interesting to speculate whether the attainment of Nibbana represents the final *destruction* of the energy-components of the individual. The answer is, logically speaking, yes; but I am uncertain of the Buddhist answer.

was the negative essence of the Buddha's Enlightenment. It is the core of his knowledge of "things as they are"—a realistic picture of the essence of that existence we experience. Buddhism finds this, its pristine realism, confirmed at every point by modern science and philosophy. Reality is not hard permanent substance, as we have observed, but infinitely variable and always perishing forms of energy. Selves are not immaterial, imperishable, immutable, spiritual units nor unchanging minds that perceive, but simply psycho-physical series of events, *à la* Jamesian psychology and Whiteheadian philosophy. They are quicksilverish in their moment by moment changeability and quite altered even in their totality after the passage of some years. To this may be added that restless blind craving for existence that characterizes the total scale of biological evolutionary "progress"—the veritable incarnation at all levels of what the Buddhist calls suffering.

Now, as we shall observe in the description of the meditational discipline, particularly at the Vipassana stage, these are precisely the characteristics of reality that the meditator comes to experience vividly and at first-hand in his own body, or, in the case of some variant methods, in other entities as well. He directly experiences the emptiness and the changeability of matter itself, thus confirming, or better, being confirmed by, the latest discoveries of modern physics itself. So it is that we read, for example, of a Mr M. who was telling a meditator:

> *The West is aware of the fact that all matter is full of holes, so to speak, even the most solid-seeming forms of so-called solid matter. It knows that the atoms which compose any piece of matter do not touch one another. . . .*
> *"Yes," said U Tiloka, the meditator, "I was meditating before a pagoda, and I saw right through it. The bricks were full of little holes. Everything must be full of holes . . . even hard iron. Else how could the heat of the fire below . . . cook the rice inside it."*[1]

Sometimes, it is true, the theme of "confirmation by experience" is rather vaguely extended to the whole of the traditional Buddhist structure of doctrine and practice. But more usually it is this heart of Buddhist teaching (the above three character-

[1] "Buddhism and Western Philosophy, *Buddhist Supplement, The Burman*, July 27, 1959.

istics of "reality") that the Buddhist believes can be experientially (scientifically) proved. And with these central doctrines of impermanence and insubstantiality thus confirmed by modern physics, as well as being directly experienceable through meditation, the Buddhist sees no cause to worry about the inroads of scientific unbelief. Indeed science is just now catching up with the Buddha's vision of things as they are; and no doubt it will need to catch up with him at still other points in the future! Such is the mood of a newspaper editorial entitled "Buddha, The Greatest Scientist":

> *It can be said that the Buddha was the greatest discoverer and scientist of all times. He devoted His whole life to the noblest of all sciences, the study of human nature. His greatest contributions to mankind were His discoveries of the Law of Change and Law of Kamma and Rebirth. . . .*
> *Science has by its latest discovery of atomic energy proved the Buddhist Law of Change (anicca, dukkha, anatta) to be a reality. And psychology has already proved the existence of an unconscious mind, has admitted that there is some sort of survival after death and that para-psychologists may well one day, through age-regression experiments, prove Rebirth to be a reality. The scientific proof of rebirth would remove the last stumbling block that stands in the way of world-wide recognition of the Teaching of the Buddha. . . .*
> *Telepathy, clairvoyance, precognition, psycho-kinesis—all these have now been acknowledged by the scientists to belong to the class of E. S. P. (extra-sensory perception). But the Omniscient Buddha has taught us all these things more than 2500 years ago.*[1]

Critical Evaluation of Scientific Buddhism

Such is the case then that modern Theravada Buddhism makes for itself in relation to science. What can be said in evaluation?

One recognizes of course to begin with that much of the popular belief and practice of Theravada Buddhists does not square with what the West understands as scientific. Popular practice represents the realm of credulity and superstition, of nat-propitiation and protective charms, or wonder-working images and prayers—all a part of primitive folk-lore the world

[1] *The Burman*, June 15, 1959.

over. This total structure is not scientifically verified or verifiable. And many Theravada Buddhists would agree with this stricture themselves, though as we shall note at the chapter's end, the precise line where "superstition" ends and "higher knowledge" begins is often hard to define. We may note also a certain resistance in the Theravada tradition to a line of scientific investigation to which Christianity has now been subject for more than a century, namely the historical-critical study of its scriptures. This extreme reluctance to embark on the historical and literary study of its own scriptural Canon is understandable, for as before noted, a basic Theravada attitude is that the Pali Canon as it now stands is the *ipsimum verbum* of the Buddha handed down to the present by an inerrant process of recitation by succeeding generations of monks met periodically in great confirmatory councils. The latest of these, met in Rangoon in 1954, continued the tradition with a newly edited and approved edition of the Canon and Commentaries, as authoritative as anything Buddhist can be for all Theravada countries. But no significant critical analysis of this Canon or the process of its formation has been done within the Theravada tradition, nor seems to be in process of accomplishment. The most that one meets with is a guarded admission that some elements of the *Jātaka Tales* are later than others; or that such investigation perhaps "ought" to take place, but is now impossible.

There is still another facet of the textual problem that is worthy of mentioning here, though it is somewhat different in nature. I am speaking of the *Abhidhamma*, or the third division of the Pali Canon. The *Abhidhamma* is an extensive and elaborate treatment of ethical-psychological-philosophical-cosmological questions that is regarded by Theravadins as the summit of Buddhist intellectual attainment and perhaps a statement of absolute truths themselves, far beyond and above the pictorial level of the Suttas or discourses of the Buddha to common folk. Of course, the text of the *Abhidhamma*, first delivered in one of the heavens to the Buddha's former or human mother, is sacrosanct along with the rest of the canon. But the point here is that the term "scientific", or even "super-scientific", is often and most specifically applied to the whole elaborate set of Abhidhammic categories. The almost endless structure of classification, division, and sub-division of the categories of the constituent elements of matter, of mind-states, of emotions, and the like is considered to be of the very essence of scientific procedure, out-sciencing the scientist himself, perchance.[1]

But there seems to be a confusion of terms in this context. The Abhidhammic vocabulary, for example, is clearly pre-scientific in nature. Earth, air, fire, and water, even when contemporarily explained as the principles of extension, mobility, heat, and cohesiveness, take one's thought back to the days of the pre-Socratic Greek philosophers. And the same might be said with regard to the psychic categories. They contain pre-scientific premonitions of later discoveries and represent a psychological analysis in terms of the then (500 B.C.) contemporary culture.

But leaving aside the question of the scientific value of such terms, we may note also the manner of the development of the Abhidhammic tradition and the contemporary attitude toward it. The manner of the "development" is this: for at least 2000 years there has been no development or change; and if

---

[1] As an example of the type of elaboration found here there is the following list of Material Qualities:

Primary Qualities (earth, air, fire, water)	..		..	4
Sensitive Qualities (five senses)	..	..	..	5
Sensible Qualities (form, sound, smell, taste)	..		..	4
Sex Qualities (male and female)	..	..	..	2
Seat of consciousness (heart)	..	..	..	1
Life-principle or vital force ..	..	..	..	1
Food value or nutriment	..	..	..	..	1
Relative limitation ..	..	..	..	..	1
Expression, bodily and vocal	..	..	..	2
Conditions of matter (lightness, pliability and adaptibility				3
Essential characteristics (growth, continuity, oldness and death)				4

28

(From *The Abhidhamma Philosophy*, Bhikkhu J. Kashyap, Buddha Vihara (Patna, India). p. 171.)

Or again one may divide consciousness into a total of 89 varieties. There are the kammically wholesome varieties; joyful, with knowledge, unprepared; joyful, with knowledge, prepared; joyful, without knowledge, unprepared; joyful, without knowledge, prepared, etc. There are kammically unwholesome varieties: joyful, with evil view, unprepared; joyful, with evil view, prepared ... indifferent, with evil view, unprepared; indifferent, with evil view, prepared; etc. etc., through all 89, plus 50 more "mental formations". *Buddhist Dictionary*, Appendix.

we accept orthodox tradition, not for 2500 years in fact, i.e. since the Buddha's death. The vocabulary and the essential concepts have remained entirely static. The tradition has been studied and developed solely within its own context. There has been no synthesis with other or outside viewpoints; no critical or objective analysis from without. There has been only pious, believing, elaboration of the original themes. Resultingly there have never been any disturbing or contradictory novelties discovered, no felt need to change, expand, or discard parts of the apparatus.

Thus the West may and should generously recognize the considerable intellectual effort that has gone into Abhidhammic analysis, but it cannot be called scientific. Indeed its quality as "super-science" indicates its non-scientific character. For the *Abhidhamma* is not a scientific but a religious document, not a formula but a scripture. It is the revelation of absolute truths by the Omniscient One, and its terms are to be received with reverence and veneration. One can only investigate within their bounds; he cannot sceptically doubt them or alter them. It may well be a charter for religious experience but it is scarcely a scientific blueprint of the universe.

But if we may not, at least in Western opinion, extend the mantle of a truly scientific character over popular Buddhism or give the name of scientific method to the orthodox Abhidhammic exposition, there are some basic Buddhist beliefs and attitudes within this total structure that must be examined more seriously in the context of our present discussion. And if we shall hold, as some do, that these beliefs represent the "essence" of Buddhism, then the claim that Buddhism is in accord with the spirit of modern science will bear more weight. Whether such a revised version of Buddhism will be considered Buddhism by the Theravadin, or only the mangled fragments of it, is a debatable question; his tendency is to call every item of the total traditional structure "essential" Buddhism and to believe that it is all scientifically verifiable. However we must turn to the examination of this possibly truncated form of the faith in its relation to science. And we may distinguish three general areas for the purpose of discussion: (1) Cosmological; (2) Causal flux and kamma; (3) Experiential confirmation of the higher truths.

1. *Buddhist Cosmology and Science*

The Buddhist cosmological ideas have already been detailed at some length in a previous chapter. We need not repeat them here to any considerable extent. What may be said is this. With regard to the vertical and static universe with its thirty-one planes we must say that this clearly comes from primitive folk-lore. It is on the level of the Genesis and Babylonian versions of the three-tiered universe of heavens above, the earth between, and the infernal regions below. None have meaning in the world revealed by modern astronomy, not even though the physical dimensions of the Buddhist version are tremendously large. It may be that the thirty-one planes of existence, which are directly correlated with certain meditational attainments (see below) will retain their status as meditational entities or experiential levels, but they can no longer be thought of as physical levels beginning on the summit of Mount Meru.

With regard to the dynamic cyclic concept of the universe, the case is quite different. To be sure one can scarcely call this a scientific concept in the narrow sense of the word. The picture of the rise and fall of endless world systems through infinitely long periods of time is a typical product of Indian philosophical imagination for which human history (and historical sequence) meant little, and of the Indian religious perspective that was concerned primarily with the relation of the individual to the Absolute, and not with the value of the social and temporal. Indeed in the Brahmanic-Hindu tradition the eternalities and absolutes almost swallowed up the temporalities and relativities of the space-time order. Yet, unscientific and fantastically loose-jointed as this may all be, it has the benefit of that roominess of conception which modern physics and astronomy need, and which the one-world, one-directional view of Western man could not accommodate unchanged. Here in the cyclic concept there will be no world-view bursting at the seams for want of adequate space and time for the new conception of world ages. Here will be no embarrassment by the concept of the existence of yet other worlds and other intelligent beings—for such is the Indian-Buddhist concept also. And the prospect of the birth and death of astral systems is faced with equanimity, for this again is integral to the Buddhist scheme. Whether the new astronomy and new physics will go on to support the total cyclic view of repeated progress and deterioration remains to be seen.

2. *The Causal Flux and the Kammic Law*

A basic doctrine of Buddhism, perhaps the basic one according to some Theravadins, is that of Dependent Origination, or as we may call it, the causally-conditioned flux of events. We have already noted how Buddhism rigorously extends this interpretation to absolutely all phenomena save Nibbana itself. Gods, spirits, sentient beings in both their physical being and mental powers, and the inorganic universe of matter about us, are all instances or products of this process. Each is a "confection" or composite group of elements of greater or lesser extent and duration but essentially of the same impermanent and insubstantial quality in the final analysis. And each is governed by the same inevitable and inexorable causal relationship.

Now it is at this point that Buddhism believes itself to be most importantly and most fundamentally at one with science. Its structural scheme of pervasive causal relations, its insistence upon the fluidity of all distinctions of time and space and individuality of being, and upon the almost insuperable difficulty of dealing empirically with such entities as God, soul, or mind, are negatively in deep accord with science. For science, *per se*, cannot find a soul or a God either, and more and more tends to think of any individual, body and mind, as a kind of vortex of psycho-physical events in space-time, rather than a sharply defined and separate self. Nor does science exempt from its category of causality—though that category is undergoing drastic revision—any of the phenomena of experience, be they mental or physical, organic or inorganic. In this vein T. Stcherbatsky, in his volumes on *Buddhist Logic*, remarks somewhere how marvellously the Buddhist theory of relations anticipated modern physics.

If this then were all, we might say that whatever the superficialities of practice and accumulated doctrines in the total Buddhist structure, at heart Buddhism and science are one;

and that Buddhism has absolutely no readjustments to make with regard to science. But this is not all and in the moreness of Buddhism lies the problem. For after we have sketched out the world in terms of Dependent Origination and included absolutely all phenomena within its scope we must note that it is governed by the law of kamma, the distinctive Hindu-Buddhist version of causality. For Dependent Origination does not represent the working of chance, nor does it represent a merely mechanical interaction of the physical factors of the universe. The whole process, from the individual's private thoughts up to and including the dissolution and re-formation of worlds, is basically governed by ethical forces. For the law of kamma is an ethical one, through and through.

We need only recapitulate the theory of kamma here for it has been discussed in detail before. Kamma is the absolutely inexorable and uniform tendency in the action of sentient creatures, particularly man, to produce like results sooner or later in the life and being of the same individual. Thus is the "iron law" of causality honoured in word and thus far we remain "scientific" in the interpretation of causality. But the word "like" needs further interpretation. First of all it means moral likeness. Evil deeds, morally speaking, produce evil results; and good deeds produce good results. And, secondly, the "likeness" of deed and result suffers a sea change on the way between the causal deed and the resulting condition. A morally good deed produces a pleasant result, i.e. a "better" rebirth in terms of greater material prosperity, more physical beauty, happier disposition, or even of age-long life in a deva-world. The likeness of kammic law to providential reward and punishment is so great as to make any difference between them negligible, practically speaking.

To be sure many attempts are made to keep the strictly "scientific" character of the kammic process intact. It is stressed that one reaps only his own deeds' consequences; that is, there are no interventions in the causal process by supernatural forces. It is emphasized that the kammic law is absolutely "just", i.e. impartial, and absolutely certain in its results, causally inviolate—even though the causation may skip many incarnations before it is effective. It is maintained that the law of kamma "explains" all human inequalities—

an explanation that is necessary, of course, only if one believes that the total order of things is just. (Why it *must* be so is never explained.) And the kammic process that governs rebirth and the rewards and punishments inherent therein is explained as being nothing more than a purely impersonal process of the addition of good and bad, or the mechanical succession of states and conditions exactly similar to any other causal order.[1]

But obviously the kammic order is not a scientifically conceived causal order. "Justice" is not a scientific category; it involves a moral judgement and, in the case of kamma, a Power that rewards and punishes in terms of physical-mental pleasures or pains added to moral deserts. The comment made by Professor Hocking some years ago is undoubtedly correct:

> *Modern Buddhism has sometimes tried to recommend itself to the scientifically minded by pointing out that its view of the universe is one of law, that it denies the personal God professed by most religions, but asserts that the universe does impersonally (and therefore justly) what the personal gods were supposed to do on sporadic volition. It teaches that there are unchangeable principles such as Karma and the four-fold Truth upon which the human being can absolutely rely.*
>
> *This is the law, and the view is on the whole well reasoned; but here its affiliation with science comes to an end. The whole genius of the "laws of Nature" as science finds them is that they are indifferent to the ethical quality of what they regulate, whereas the law proclaimed by Buddhism is, after all, a moral law.*[2]

3. *Experiential Confirmation of Buddhist Truths*

We have already referred to the Buddhist invitation to test Buddhist truth and personally experience its self-validating power. It may be repeated here that not only has Buddhism, but almost every other religion in the world, from primitively magical superstition to post-Schleiermachian Protestant Christianity, believed that anyone who cared to try could prove its truths by experience. And particularly since the rise of science in the Western World, many there have made the

[1] For a more extensive discussion of the same matter, see author's *In the Hope of Nibbana*.

[2] *Science and the Idea of God*, University of North Carolina Press, 1944, pp. 16–17.

same claim that Buddhism today makes: The religious invitation to "come and experience" is the same in nature and in the verification of its results as the scientific call to "come and experiment". That is, experiential religious verification is scientific in quality. This proposition is therefore worth examination, especially since Buddhism believes that such experience is beyond and above all faith-elements, as absolutely objective in quality as is the scientific experiment itself; and though our concern will be specifically with Buddhism, the discussion has a general relevance for all such religious claims in whatever context.

What then are the likenesses between experience and experiment that make religionists of all varieties insist that the two are identical in nature? One likeness is that of first-handedness. In each case there is a direct personal experience. Of course, in these days of massive scientific experiment much routine testing is done by teams of assistants, not by the directing scientist himself. So also scientists depend much upon each other's published works without new experimental testing. Yet essentially the flavour of experiment is that each experimenter see for himself, not depending upon the word or experiences of another. Obviously in the religious sphere this is even more radically so. In a much more intimate and personal way, within his own being, the religious experiencer knows in and for himself alone. It may even be that he cannot express what he has found to another, except indirectly. That is, religious experience may be so completely personal that it is completely ineffable.

There is also a degree of faith-commitment in both science and religion. Both follow certain assurances and intuitions which are not fully provable, in a spirit of adventure. In the case of religion there is no doubt about this; commitment in faith (not knowledge) would seem to be its hallmark and in this respect it is sometimes diametrically opposed to science. But from the Buddhist viewpoint two things must be said. In the early stages of religious seeking—such as a non-Buddhist trying to sample Buddhist truth through meditation, for example—this faith is only provisional. George Grimm says somewhere in his *Buddhism: The Religion of Reason* that the only "faith" needed in Buddhism is the confidence one must show in the guide he is following at least temporarily. It is not, therefore, blind or absolute faith in the unproved or unprovable.

With regard to faith in science we may observe that this also has its absolute quality—faith in scientific methodology in general as the best means for discovering at least one class of truths. It has also a very solid variety of confidence in some of the laws that have been established by repeated experiments. There is further a provisional faith-commitment to the hypothesis currently being pursued. It appears to be true, and a scientist will commit his time, money, and efforts to following its lead—until it is proven true, qualifiedly true, or completely false. The Buddhist who invited one to test Buddhist truth "experimentally" says that it is precisely this latter variety of willing-to-try faith, and this only, that is needed in Buddhist experiential efforts.

Buddhism would also claim a third likeness, especially with regard to its meditational method: a systematic technique. This is obvious in science. What is science but technique? A vast body of specialized techniques has now been worked out in almost every major scientific field; it is being added to constantly and being incarnated in every new instrument. Or to put it in other words: a technique is an ordered procedure of investigation—which is simply another name for science. What then of Buddhist meditation? Here, too, is an ordered, systematic, time-proven system for achieving results, the Buddhist would say. Most other religions have only hit-or-miss methods of cultivating the spiritual life by prayer and religious exercises. But in Buddhism there is a complete system of varied techniques suited to all types of personality, which is available to any meditator who wishes to avail himself of it. In other words meditation is a scientific approach to religious truth.

Finally we may note a fourth likeness between religious experience and scientific experiment: The scientist can say: This is true because I have proved it so in my laboratory. Here are the steps taken, and here is the actual result achieved— some new chemical compound, some micro-photographs of the course of atomic particles, some new equation that brings discordant truths into harmony. So, too, the successful meditator, or religious experiencer, can say: I have seen, or felt, or realized this truth. And it makes a difference. Behold the difference in my life! Thus it is, says Buddhism, that one can point to the Buddha who actually achieved detachment and Nibbana as concrete proof of the truth of the results of meditation. And to thousands of arahats since his day. And so also can one himself prove something of that truth which these have experienced.

But having said these things we must go on to raise some questions, not only in the case of Buddhism, but for all religious experiencers. What about the quality and degree of commitment found in religious experience and scientific experiment? Despite superficial similarities, there seems to be a radical difference. There is indeed a kind of absolute commitment in science to the proposition that truth is discoverable, which is analogous to the religions faith that truth is experienceable. But with regard to the hypothesis to which a scientist commits himself, the quality of commitment seems quite other than the religious one. His commitment is merely provisional. He may harbour sceptical doubts about its results; and it is not usually a matter of life or death to him as to whether it proves to be true or not. But it is hard to think that one can as lightly commit himself to religious experience as to scientific experiment. This is why the word "experiment" is so seldom used with regard to religion—Gandhi's *My Experiments with Truth* being an exception. For the cold-blooded, deliberate, it-may-or-may-not-be-true mood of experiment is scarcely likely to succeed, even in trying out Buddhist meditation. One must first be an earnest seeker after religious truth, which is a matter of life and death, before he can succeed. His use of meditation may be provisional, but not his search for that life-or-death truth that he believes exists somewhere—else it will be a fruitless exercise. In religion it is always and only true that "If with all your heart ye truly seek me, ye shall ever surely find me".

And this leads to a second consideration: The meaning of truth for science and religion; or the class of truth which they respectively seek. Science is in search of particular items not yet known; its curiosity is insatiable. It will, of course, grind up all the particular colourful facts that it collects into the colourless principle or law. But this law will in turn guide it again in the search for more particular facts. Thus science is ever avid for the absolutely new item. But religion's pursuit of truth is quite other. It assumes that there is some final or absolute truth or experience beyond which one cannot go. This is One in nature and eternally existent. The goal of the religious seeker is therefore not to discover some new item of informational knowledge or particular new fact; nor can he go beyond the One in his search. His goal is already set. The essential newness of religious knowledge therefore is that of personal relation to truth; it is the new appropriation of the eternal Truth to oneself; the basic discovery is the way in which it is true for me. If this were to be applied to the scientific search for knowledge it would place the centre of interest in the researcher's discovery of some old truth—say, the second law of thermodynamics—for himself and by his own instruments, rather than in the acquisition of new facts or the addition of new principles of interpretation. These latter, however, not the former, are clearly what interests science.

Or we may put the matter in a related context. Science is interested to discover tangible, objective, public truth. Even when it studies man, as in the case of experimental psychology, it approaches its materials objectively and impersonally from the "outside". It hopes to make its results fully communicable to others. Indeed, maximum communicability is the hallmark of scientific truth. While some of the higher ranges of its calculations may be known only to the few (only a dozen men can understand Einstein, says someone) the basic effort here is to make it as public as possible. If one has a strictly private experiment or type of calculation that no one else can be made to understand, then it is suspect scientifically. Science consists in great part in the effort to communicate by means of an impersonal apparatus or medium, such as mathematics, which is fully open to the inspection of any mathematically trained person.

But religious truths are again quite other. They are deeply and radically personal and subjective. Even if we consider a "person" only a set of kammically conditioned factors, it is the purely private inside of these factors that is seen in meditation. One is here dealing with attitudes, emotions, and all the intangibles of personal adjustments; and most especially he is dealing with his materials in a context completely meaningless to science—the desire for personal salvation. Such truth as he will discover will be true primarily for him, i.e. will be truths of satisfactory personal states of mind, of the new relevance of some old moral standard to the new circumstances of one's own life, or the suddenly perceived personal significance of a general truth. And these "truths" are not fundamentally communicable; the attempt to state them may indeed distort or destroy them.

That such truths cannot ever be fully public, Buddhism recognizes in another context in a double way. It proclaims that the higher truths, particularly the Supreme Truth of Nibbana, are not describable or stateable in words. The Highest Truth is ineffable; it can only be indicated and manifested, not expressed. Secondly, such truths are not open to the ordinary type of reasoning, but are Higher Truths discoverable only by a Buddha or one possessing superior (supra-normal) powers. Both of these factors put such truths far beyond the scientific realm into a super-scientific area where scientific canons no longer apply. This, of course, is the Buddhist form of the Thomistic doctrine of two kinds of truth: a first storey of those rationally perceived truths that can be attained by ordinary (scientific and philosophical) reason; a second storey of truths that can only come by divine revelation. Here, as there, is then a barrier beyond which "scientific method" cannot pass, and beyond which truths are "super-scientifically", i.e. non-scientifically, perceived and proven. And for "super-scientific" personal truth there is ultimately only one test: subjective satisfaction.

Thus, in the final analysis, it seems that religious experience and scientific experiment move on different levels and are only most superficially to be called equivalent. In terms of basic attitudes, of the type of truth known, and of the materials involved there is radical divergence. And it is better for both science and religion of whatever tradition to recognize this divergence. For the attempt to equate the two leads only to confusion.

This confusion is obvious in some of the contemporary attempts to make Buddhism scientific throughout. Two or three summary instances of this may be given. We have noted, for example, the tendency to make Buddha into a great scientist, who latently or potentially had an infinite scientific knowledge within him. His intuitive insight into the insubstantiality and impermanence of all natural processes is thus taken to indicate his complete mastery of the principles of modern physics. And sometimes he is spoken of as having specified the actual physical dimensions of the atom. This is clearly a confusion of an intuitive, qualitative sense of the flux of nature, with the itemized, fully specific determination of physical dimensions and relationships within that nature, which is the material of science. This is on a par with the attempt to equate "Vanity, Vanity, all is Vanity" of Ecclesiastic with the Einsteinian formulae of relativity, and call both scientific.

Again this confusion is evident in such reports as that above, in which a meditator, who has observed that during meditation solid objects like pagoda-walls appear "full of holes", equates his vision of the "emptiness" of matter with that of the scientist. The first represents a fully subjective experience in which one had withdrawn his attention from outward stimuli and knows only the simplified materials of his own state of mind; and the other is the constantly checked and rigorously inferred consequence of many systematized observations. But the two categories should not be confused. Nor should those "personality-producing energies" transferred from one life to another—a transfer which is completely unverified by science and hence becomes a matter of faith[1]—or the radiations of goodwill throughout the universe be confused with that energy and radiation that science deals with. One is a religious symbol and the other a physical dimension.

Finally we may note that often the sometimes-erected barrier between the Higher Truths, super-normally perceived, and the ordinary truths, perceptible by science and phil-

---

[1] It was Rhys Davids who wrote in his *Buddhism*, pp. 105–6, with regard to the Buddhist "arch over sorrow":

"On one side of the keystone is the necessity of justice, on the other the law of causality. But they have failed to see that the very keystone itself, the link between one life and another, is a mere word—this wonderful hypothesis, this airy nothing, this imaginary cause beyond the reach of reason—the individualized and individualizing force of Karma."

K

osophy, is forgotten in the enthusiasm to conceive of Buddhism as fully scientific in nature throughout its length and breadth. It is implied that both beginning and continuing with a purely scientific methodology one discovers not only that all reality is a flux, but that there are a full thirty-one planes of existence, just as the popular tradition has it. And the pilgrim along the scientific way to truth asks himself amazedly: When did we turn the corner from purely psychological analysis and discipline, perhaps semi-scientific in nature, into the realms of woe and blessedness that cluster below and above Mount Meru? Does science prove these too? The answer that is given is that if only one will train his mind powers properly, then he can perceive those planes, just as the highly trained scientist can perceive the higher scientific truths.

How then can one tell the difference between scientifically proved truth and the elaborate fantasies of traditional folklore? or between the objectively true and the subjectively satisfying? or the physical fact and an hallucination? The whole structure of distinctions between fact and fiction, dreams and reality, elaborately and painstakingly built up by modern science and necessary to its on-going life, seems here threatened. Clearly the line between the lower and the higher truths, or the distinction between scientific fact and religious symbol (or subjective experience) has been unheedingly crossed, to the detriment of both.

In conclusion it may be pointed out that it is not only Buddhism that has been guilty of such confusion between its worlds of experience. It has happened often enough in Christianity. And the recipe is the same for both. Science and religion should be clearly distinguished from each other, and their respective truths distinguished. When religion, which deals with man's inner vision of good and with the truths of his adjustment to that vision, tries to ape science and its cold impersonal view of the objective world in order to prove itself true, it has lost its way. Thus even in a scientific age Buddhism must recognize that it is religious and not scientific in nature.

V

TEACHER OF GODS AND MEN

IT IS VERY DIFFICULT, INDEED ALMOST IMPOSSIBLE, FOR A a member of one religious community to describe truly how a member of another religious fellowship and faith views the founder of his faith. The attitude of a devotee is a compound of thought and emotion, a result of doctrine, traditional practice, and contemporary culture, whose inwardness or essential nature the devotee himself may be unable to describe. That his faith is both true and meaningful for him there can be no doubt; but to *state* that truth and meaning is quite another thing—and the more intense his devotion, the more spontaneous his expressions of reverence for the object of his devotion, the more difficult such description. And there is the further matter of a variety of attitude and viewpoint to be found in any religious tradition, Theravada Buddhism no less than the rest.

Still further one must always be on guard against the betrayal inherent in communication itself, especially when an attempt is made to cross cultural and religious lines. An Eastern Buddhist and a Western Christian, having in common the strongest desire to understand each other religiously, may agree to use certain words for given meanings or to indicate a specific quality of religious experience and sincerely believe that they are in genuine communication; but actually the connotation each gives those words may unconsciously, even inevitably, be quite different. And sometimes there occurs a situation in which there is neither specific agreement or disagreement, but rather sheer bafflement or an uneasy sense that somehow something is wrong and no communication of meaning is really taking place behind the screen of words.[1]

[1] As an illustration of the more obvious sort of connotative dislocation: the author once tried, in conversation, to state his conception of the Buddhist

Notwithstanding these inherently serious difficulties, inter-religious communication must be attempted, even in those difficult areas of devotional feeling and half-verbalized emotion. And in defence of the attempt it may be said that religious traditions do make statements of a devotional nature and individual devotees are continually expressing their own religious attitudes in a variety of ways. Thus it is not impossible for an observer to gather some fundamental impressions of the quality and significance of the attitude of those belonging to another faith than one's own to the supreme object or objects of their faith and devotion—though he must not expect to perceive the fine shades of meaning or emotional flavours.

In this spirit we shall endeavour in this chapter to deal with the place that the Buddha occupies in the thought and feeling of the contemporary Theravada Buddhist. For the Theravada Buddhist yields to none in the depth of his devotion to the Founder of his faith; and thus his attitude to the Buddha is a key point for the proper understanding of the structure and quality of the Theravada tradition itself.

Buddha: The Ideal Man

It is not important to recount in detail the life of Gotama, the man, for our purposes here. This life is, of course, well-known and significant for the devout Buddhist; and every step of it, from birth to death, has been recounted and elaborately embellished with miracle and splendour by the loving piety of generations of believers. Yet just as Jesus becomes of significance for the Christian primarily when he is thought of as the Christ, so Gotama is significant for the Buddhist only because he attained enlightenment and became a Buddha. It is this event that gives importance to all the rest of what he said or did; those other events are of interest only because of this

---

doctrine of the momentariness and insubstantiality of individual being, to the Venerable U Thittila. After half an hour of futile effort, the latter suddenly exclaimed: "Are you speaking of one existence or many?" And it developed that I had been speaking (Western style) in a one-life context, while he had been speaking (Eastern-Buddhist style) in terms of a many-life view.

supreme insight, and are only recorded as a result of its occurrence.[1]

But while the life of Gotama the man may be of secondary religious importance, the fact that he was a living person and not a disembodied spirit or supreme ideal, is important. And the Buddhist, like the Christian, instinctively defends the historical existence of the founder of his faith against those who may assert that "The Buddha" is only a fabrication of the myth-makers. For herein lies the basic conviction of the Buddhist about the Buddha: He was a man. Indeed, he was only a man. To be sure he was a ideal man, The Ideal Man of our world-age; and this has important consequences and extensive ramifications, as we shall observe later. Yet the Buddha, even in his Buddhahood, represents what is in man, as man, to become—in all his human fullness.

This is how we must understand that supreme event in Gotama's life, the Enlightenment by which he became a Buddha. Indeed a Buddha is just that, an Enlightened One. And though the Enlightenment is possible only to one of immense and age-long spiritual attainments, hence rare in the history of the universe, yet Buddhists maintain that it was a self-enlightenment, not a revelation. It was by virtue of his own super-normal, but fully natural and human powers, powers developed by continued spiritual discipline through many existences, that he pierced through to a realization of the one way to end suffering, now set forth in the form of the Four Noble Truths. The essence of this enlightenment is open to all men, even though its fullness in Buddhahood is limited by Theravadins to only one individual in millions of years. But all men, by following the Buddha's way, may attain equally with him to his goal, Nibbana. Hence the actual historical human existence of the Buddha is a ground of hope to every man. No mysterious or arbitrary Higher Power can

---

[1] "Buddhists" and "Christians" are to some extent misnomers, literally meaning "enlightenists" and "Messiahists". They were affixed by outsiders who mistakenly thought that Buddha and Christ were personal names. Yet they are better, no doubt, than "Gotamist' or "Jesusite" would have been, for they locate the religious significance at the proper place—Jesus' Messiahship and Gotama's Enlightenment. It may be further noted that Gotama is probably a family or surname, and Siddharta the truly personal name of the Buddha, though it is seldom used nowadays.

withhold from the determined man the privilege of his own enlightenment and his consequent liberation from birth and death. Enlightenment is not the gift of unpredictable grace, but the result of freely-willed, energetic self-effort.

We must then say that Buddha is not a god, according to the Buddhists, nor the Supreme God. There are indeed many gods or devas, more powerful and longer-lived than human beings, who live in the celestial realms; and they have considerable control over the events of the natural world and over ordinary human fortunes. Yet it must be remembered that a "god" is neither intrinsically or permanently divine; he (or she) is only an ex-human being or ex-animal, temporarily for a few million years raised to higher-than-human level by his past good deeds. When his merit or good kamma is exhausted, he will sink to human or animal level again.[1]

And indeed the status of the gods is, religiously speaking, less fortunate than that of men. For, as noted in the previous chapter, only on the human level can one attain to that insight capable of achieving salvation. The gods, when not debauched by pleasure, yearn for such opportunity and in the scriptures are pictured as paying continual attendance on holy men, especially the Buddha himself. For it goes without saying that gods are far, far below a Buddha, mere ignorant laymen, inferior in intelligence, goodness and even in power to him. (At least the Buddha can always out-miracle any god, if it comes to a contest.) And it is they who humbly beseech him, when he is a Bodhisatta in Tusita heaven, to allow himself to be born on earth, and when he has been enlightened, to remain on earth and share his liberating insight with men.

In this arrangement of things we can observe the manner in which Buddhism disposed of the Brahmanical gods who might

[1] This implies that any given god, say Sakka, Lord of the Thirty-Three, is not the "same" god as he was some thousands of millions of years ago. That Sakka was another ex-human who has since descended to the human level because his good kamma has been exhausted. Thus there is now a different Sakka, and there will be many more in the future.

There is some inconsistence here, of course, due to the origin of the Buddhist "pantheon" in Indian polytheism. For many of the gods are thought of in one context as "permanent" individuals, and in another as passing phenomena. Mara, the-evil spirit, lives as previously noted in one of the heavens because of his past good deeds. Yet theoretically there must have been several million Maras already.

in time have rivalled the Buddha in importance, and included him as one of their number—as indeed later Hinduism has done in making the Buddha an avatar of Vishnu. The existence of the gods is not denied but they are down-graded and mingled with nature spirits (cf. Chapter II) even though they still keep their names and to some extent their identity. In the Buddhist scheme they are also denied any creative function of real stature and especially any competence in effectuating man's final salvation.[1] Therefore almost inevitably, as we shall observe in more detail later, most of the powers and super-human qualities which are subtracted from the devas (earth-creative power excepted) are transferred to the Buddha.

That is to say, it is incorrect to speak of Buddhism as an atheism in the Western sense. Nor is it the same as modern Western humanism, which ordinarily pictures weak and mortal man defying the impersonal universe about him and making his way the best he can through overwhelming odds toward some feeble sort of dignity and meagre accomplishment. That is the negative humanism of totally rejected theism. But in Buddhism we find the positive humanism of the deified man. It holds that man is indeed the master of his fate and that the universe is full of spiritual beings and forces who will, indeed who must, assist him in his drive toward ultimate liberation. The good man is superior to the gods except in power and length of life—and even those superiorities will soon pass away. And Buddhas, or Ideal Men, are lords and teachers of even the mightiest gods.

A passing comment on the use of the words "supernormal", "supernatural" and "superhuman" is in place here. The latter two are not in favour with Buddhism when describing the saints or Buddhas, because of their theistic connotations. They suggest the illusion of arbitrary Higher Powers or Beings who control human life and are not subject to the law of kamma, or morally governed cause and effect, and upon whose whims or "grace" man is dependent for his salvation. All this the Buddhist steadfastly denies. But the term "super-

---

[1] This is not unconditionally true. Though a deva cannot actually bring a man to enlightenment, now and then he can render valuable assistance. And some contemporary Buddhist tracts promise such assistance to the faithfully striving Buddhist as a matter of great encouragement.

normal" he accepts. The supernormal may be far above the power of the average man to perform, to understand, or even to perceive. But it is not beyond the capacity of human nature as such. The difference between a supernormal state, or supernormally developed person, is held to be one of degree, not of kind. Theoretically every man, in some future existence if not this one, can develop the psychic powers of knowing the thoughts of others, remembering his own past existences, changing his physical form at will, and flying through space in his astral body. Thus writes Christmas Humphreys from a European view point, yet in this case harmoniously with the Theravada conception of miracle:

> *In the sense of happenings resulting from the violation of natural law by an extra-cosmic being, miracles are unknown in Buddhism. Control of nature by super-physical methods through the development of the individual is possible to a much greater extent, but those methods are not supernatural and therefore not miraculous.'*[1]

Thus, at least verbally, is miracle avoided in Buddhism, though, as we shall note later, the distinction between supernatural and supernormal miracles is of little practical significance. However, it is this insistence that the Buddha is only a Man and his deeds supernormal rather than supernatural that determines the basic doctrinal statement of the proper attitude of a Buddhist toward a Buddha, be he past, present, or future Buddha. We may put this attitude in terms of those negatives that Theravada Buddhism so dearly loves, three in number.

Firstly, *the Buddha is not to be revered personally.* According to some of the scriptures the Buddha, much like Jesus, discouraged emotional attachment to his person. (It will be remembered that when an adoring woman exclaims, "Blessed is the womb that bore you, and the breasts that gave you suck", Jesus replies: "Yes, rather, blessed are they that hear the word of God and do it.") So we read of the Buddha and a certain disciple named Vakkali. The latter was "never sated by looking at the perfection of the Master's visible body" and followed him everywhere like his shadow. He entered the Order to be with him and "spent all his time, save at meals and toilet, doing nothing else but contemplating the Exalted One".

---

[1] *A Buddhist Students' Manual*, Buddhist Society, London, 1956, p. 157.

After a time the Buddha gently said to him:

What is to thee, Vakkali, this foul body that thou seest? He who seeth the Norm [Law or Buddhist Truth] he it is that seeth me. For seeing the Norm he seeth me, and seeing me he seeth the Norm.

But though ceasing to stare at the Buddha, Vakkali would not go away until the Buddha expressly commanded him to leave. Thereat Vakkali was so dejected that he went to a steep precipice with the purpose of committing suicide. Then the Buddha appeared to him in a kind of (supernormal) transfiguration body, and said, "Come, bhikkhu"—words often used in primitive ordination. Vakkali then realized that the true nearness to the Buddha was spiritual, not physical, in nature.[1] This passage, incidentally, is much quoted in Burma today. It agrees also with the Buddha's consolation of his disciples just before his death, when they bewailed their approaching loneliness: He would continue to be present with them in his Teaching (Dhamma).

The second negation is this: *The Buddha is not actually living now and hence cannot be prayed to.* Nibbana, into which he entered upon physical death (his *pari-nibbāna*) is not a heavenly realm from which he can hear and answer petitions. It is absolutely beyond space-time existence and whatever the Buddha's "condition" therein, it is not one that allows for an inter-communication or radiation of beneficent influences. The half-closed eyes of the image before which the Buddhist bows will never open; its gently smiling lips will never answer his petitions. That meditative absorption which the statue represents is qualitatively the same as Nibbana itself. No one can penetrate its calm. The Buddha is "dead" for all practical purposes of worship.

The third negation is corollary to the second: *The Buddha is not a saviour in the religious sense.* For one cannot address a

---

[1] *Psalms of the Buddhists,* tr. C. A. F. Rhys-Davids, Luzac, 1951, p. 197ff. (*Theragata,* 205). These same words are recorded as spoken by Buddha to a similarly named monk, in another passage and perhaps represent two variations on the same story. The similarity to Jesus' "He that seeth me seeth the Father" and his promise to send the Holy Spirit as his (Jesus') presence among them after his death, is striking. Of course it should be noted that there is some difference between the presence of a living spiritual power (Holy Spirit) and the continuation of a memory by its embodiment in a written scripture, though actual Buddhist devotion repersonalizes the Buddha.

prayer to him, saying, "Save me!" Nor make an offering to him to "please" him. Nor expect acts of grace to emanate from him nor experience his love. One reveres the memory of the Buddha as a supreme teacher and example. When the Burmese Buddhist bows before the image of the Buddha in "worship" this is not to be translated as "adoration" or personal "self-surrender" to His will and power, but understood only as the highest level of honour and esteem that he can render. It is the same in kind, the Buddhist insists, as that sort of reverence which he shows to parent, elder person, worthy teacher or to a monk.

A contemporary monk, the Venerable U Pyinnya Dipa, writes in an unpublished address the following words, often heard in Burma, about the nature of the "worship" of the Buddha images:

> *Here you may ask a question as to whether Buddhists worship images or statues or idols in a religious sense. Yes, you can see the Buddhists bow their heads down before the images and putting their hands together above their heads. But actually, true Buddhists do not worship the image and pray for worldly boons and sensual pleasures. They know, in a real sense, what and who the Buddha is. Whether they pay homage to the images of the Buddha, the pagodas, the sacred relics, or the sacred bodhi tree, they are venerating them in an attitude of reminding themselves and concentrating their minds only on the Gotama Buddha and His noblest attributes.*
>
> *The images are only symbolic representations of the Buddha, but not actual statues in the sense of a personal likeness. It was hundreds of years after the Buddha's death that these images began to appear. . . . Just as people love to see the portrait or photograph of dear and near ones from whom they are separated by departure or death, so also the Buddhists pay homage and respect to the image of the Buddha as a gesture of symbolic veneration to His greatness and nobleness.*

He goes on to express the Buddhist apologetic for physical symbolism: "Simple or average people require simple doctrines and are able to conceive an idea only through a symbolic image or ceremony."

To sum up: The Buddha represents the ideal limit of manhood. What he was it is possible (theoretically) for any or every man to become; for Gotama achieved Buddhahood by his own unaided human efforts. He is not to be worshipped as a superhuman god or saviour, or personally adored, but to be reverenced as the supreme Way-shower. Truest reverence to him is to be expressed by following his way to salvation. Indeed, though not all men may become Buddhas in actuality, all may reach Nibbana where they become "equal" to the Buddha—for Nibbana is one. Yet functionally, if not conceptually, the Buddha is more and somewhat other than an Ideal Man in actual Buddhist thought and practice. It may be more a matter of emphasis and attitude than of doctrine, yet this functional plus-value of the Buddha is important for our understanding of actual Buddhist religion. To this further aspect we now turn.

Buddha: The Supernormal Man

Though Theravada Buddhism asserts that the Buddha was essentially only a man, applying the term supernormal rather than supernatural to his Enlightenment and to his deeds, it must now be observed that he is conceived to have been markedly supernormal. Indeed it can be said that when speaking to theists, Buddhists emphasize that humanity of the Buddha which he had in common with all men; but when thinking of him as the object of their reverence and when speaking as Buddhists among Buddhists, they emphasize the supernormal aspects of his humanity.

We must note in some detail the significance of the term "Buddha". We need remind ourselves again that it is not a personal name, nor indeed the name given to Gotama alone—though for Theravada devotional purposes "the Buddha" is equivalent to Gotama Buddha alone. "Buddha" or Enlightened One represents a category of being, or better, a level of psycho-moral attainment which, while truly rare, has been achieved a multitude of times during a multitude of ages. The difference between Mahayana Buddhism, that is often thought of as a multiplier of Buddhas, and Theravada Buddhism, that is often considered to be a One-Buddha Faith, is only one of degree and of usual emphasis. For though Gotama Buddha is the pre-eminent one for the latter, and while the attainment of Buddhahood is not precisely the goal of Everyman as it is in Mahayana, yet here too many Buddhas are theoretically recognized.

The number of recognized Buddhas varies according to the context. In this world-age it is held that there have been three predecessors to Gotama, namely Kakusandha, Konagamana, and Kassapa,[1] though of course there are no historical records of their existence or activities. And in the *Dīgha-Nikāya* there is a classic passage that speaks of one more Buddha to come in this world-epoch under whom a kind of revival of the faith will take place and perhaps an upward turn of the world cycle. Thus, in words attributed to Gotama Buddha:

He will be accompanied by a congregation of thousands of brethren, even as I now am accompanied by a congregation of some hundreds of brethren.[2]

But there have been other world ages, and among Burmese Buddhists some twenty-eight Buddhas, including Gotama as the twenty-eighth, are considered to be known by name. (See Warren, op. cit. for the list.) It was under the fourth of these, Dipamkara, that the being (or should we say stream-of-kammic-continuity?) who was to become Gotama Buddha in our world-epoch, took a vow to become a Buddha like Dipamkara then was. He was then one Sumedha, a Brahman. And in successive world ages since, under each succeeding Buddha, he renewed his vow.

But the matter of Buddhas does not end here. There have been thousands of them, perhaps millions, perhaps an infinite number in a world-process that is infinitely long. These are recognized in popular devotion in the following "prayer" which is used by many a Burmese Buddhist upon arising and before retiring, and on special occasions of crisis or danger:

In the three worlds twenty-eight Buddhas shone with Enlightenment. There were also twelve thousand Buddhas who illumined the worlds with the Four Noble Truths like the moon. There were also five million Buddhas who shone like the sun. Innumerable Buddhas, uncountable like the sands of the River Ganges, have destroyed their khandas [constituents of personal being] and won Peace. To these Buddhas, I with humble head, give worship. I worship also with my head [bowed in submission] the Dhammas composed of ten factors and the noble Sangha [Order of monks].

[1] Cf. *Buddhism in Translation*, H. C. Warren, Harvard University Press, Students' Edition, 1953, p. 5 ff.

[2] *Cakkavatti-Sihananda Suttanta*, in *Dialogues of the Buddha*, S.B.B., Vol. IV, Sutta XXVI, Section 25.

By the power of this worship of the Three Gems may all dangers and hardships be averted from me. May all evils be banished forever.[1]

Thus Buddhahood is a category of infinite proportions. But one may say that the process of producing a Buddha is also of infinite extent—so that one infinite cancels out the other so to speak. That is to say: Though there have been an infinite number of Buddhas in the infinite ages of existence, they represent only an infinitesmally small number of those beings in existence at any one time or in all times together. A Buddha comes to a universe only once in ages; the number of other beings that have existed during those ages is beyond calculation. For it takes ages of consistent effort to bring a sentient being to Buddhahood. As noted above, Gotama came to be a Buddha only after he had made and successively repeated his Buddha-vow under twenty-four successive Buddhas, each countless ages apart. In popular form the *Jātaka Tales* portray the process of Buddha-becoming, showing the Buddha-to-be as king, commoner, priest, merchant, counsellor, bird, animal, building up his virtues to full perfection through many successive existences.[2] By age-long endeavour this being at last arrives at that height of mental-moral attainment whereby he can push on to the final insight that will make him a Buddha. The practical consequences of this conception of the Buddha-producing process upon the Buddhist attitude toward the Buddha will be noted later.

It should be observed in passing that there are several types

[1] Words in brackets are explanatory additions, not parts of the prayer. The Three Gems, of course, refer to the Buddha, the Dhamma or Teaching, and the Sangha or ideal order of monks. The passage is a Burmese adaptation of a Burmese-Pali original whose actual origin is unknown.

[2] Some ethical problems are raised by some of the *Jātaka Tales*. The Bodhisatta, or Buddha-to-be, sometimes indulges in actions which could scarcely be considered as meeting even minimal Buddhist ethical standards. Thus in Jataka 193 he connives with his six brothers in cannibalism, eating the wives of the six successively to keep from starvation, but shrewdly managing to save his own wife in the end. In another case, as a treasurer, he receives the revenues from the sale of liquor, etc. But one can scarcely expect these pre-Buddhist folk-tales to be rigidly consistent with later Buddhist principles. And on the whole the Bodhisatta is a noble character who, though always the cleverest, strongest, or wisest, yet nearly always shows moderation and kindness, or even gives his life for his fellow animals or humans. Some in Burma say that a Buddha-to-be, whatever other mistakes he makes, never deviates from the truth in any of his deeds in any of his existences. In any case, until he becomes a Buddha, full perfection of behaviour cannot be expected.

of Buddhahood. There is the *Pacceka* or Silent Buddha, or as he is popularly termed, a little Buddha. He is a sort of super-saint, who has achieved liberation without ever hearing the word of the Buddha, in his last life at least. But he has no capacity for bringing others to salvation as do the Universal Buddhas. Among the Universal or Teaching Buddhas there are three types, each of which represents a given period of perparation for Buddhahood. There is the *Wisdom*-Buddha (*paññādhika* Buddha) who in four periods of 1000 world-cycles (*kappas*) each attains Buddahood. Such was Gotama Buddha. There is the *Will-force* Buddha (*Viriyadhika* Buddha) who by virtue of unflagging will-force exerted for eight periods of world-cycles becomes a Buddha. And, thirdly, there is that product of sixteen periods of world-cycles of devotion, a *devotional* (*suddhadhika*) Buddha. There is perhaps a suggestion here of the superiority of the wisdom way to Buddhahood (and to Nibbana) since it takes the least time of any of the methods.

The Perfections and Powers of the Buddha

What then are the intrinsic qualities of the final result of this age-long process of Buddha-making? They are four in number: (1) absoluteness of moral-mental perfection; (2) possession of super-normal powers; (3) omniscience; (4) a capacity to reveal Nibbana-bringing truth to men. We shall deal with each of these in turn.

1. *The Buddha's Perfections*

As a result of his ages-long efforts, a Buddha has achieved a kind of personal development that may be expressed in terms of paramis (*paramitas*), i.e. perfections, or *guṇas*, i.e. virtues. The paramis are ten in number in contemporary Theravada tradition, though most scholars believe that the ten-fold enumeration does not come from Gotama Buddha himself, but represents a later development. In general these perfections have something of a social character. They are attained only by exercising loving-kindness (*mettā*), compassion (*karuna*), altruistic joy (*mudita*) and equanimity (*upekkha*). They express a disposition of concern "about the welfare of living beings, not tolerating the sufferings of beings, wishing long duration to the higher states of being and being impartial and just to all beings".[1] The ten qualities which are thus brought to perfection are these:

(1) Almsgiving—to all beings impartially, whether good, bad, or indifferent;
(2) Morality especially as regards harmlessness to all other beings;
(3) Renunciation, or freedom from sensual lust;
(4) Wisdom constantly purified in each existence;
(5) Energy exerted for the Bodhisatta's own perfection and the welfare of others;
(6) Forbearance, which tempers the exercise of energy;
(7) Truth-telling, or act of truth, i.e. never breaking a promise;
(8) Resolution in working for the welfare of others;
(9) Loving-kindness for all;
(10) Equanimity, which expects nothing in return for any of its love or efforts.

This is one very popular form of expressing the Buddha's perfection and of setting a standard for one's own moral efforts. But sometimes also the Buddha is said to be possessed of ten virtues or gunas—perhaps better, qualities or attributes —that are unique with the Buddhas. This occurs in a formula found in the Pali Canon and is frequently used in contemporary Buddhist devotions where the Buddha is hailed as "Arahat, The Fully Enlightened One, perfected in wisdom and conduct, well-farer (i.e. farer to ultimate salvation), knower of the world, supreme, unrivalled trainer of men to be tamed, teacher of devas and men, enlightened one, and Lord or Exalted One". These gunas are the crown of the full development of the paramis, representing qualities which are achieved only upon Enlightenment, i.e Buddhahood.

2. *The Buddha's Super-normal Powers*

A second notable feature of all Buddhas is their perfection of super-normal powers. And before describing them we need to emphasize, in partial repetition, the following points: First,

---

[2] Quoted from Buddhaghosa's *Path of Purification*, Chapter IX, in *Buddhist Dictionary*, Nyanatiloka, Frewin and Co. (Colombo), 1956, definition of Parami.

Buddhism looks upon such powers as super-normal, not super-natural. They come as the result of increasing moral purification and mental concentration. A highly developed mind is able to control the physical components of self and environment to a remarkable degree. Secondly, such powers are possessed by saints as well as Buddhas, though in lesser degree. Thirdly, their possession is a mixed blessing because one may be tempted to use them in vain display or for evil purposes. And their possession may distract one from that higher quest for Nibbana itself. The Buddha is sometimes (*Dīgha-Nikāya* or *Dialogues of the Buddha*, Text i, 212), represented as deprecating such powers and warning his disciples not to use them to make converts.

Having said this we must note, however, that the super-normal element is quite prominent in the Buddhist scriptures. Because of the uncertain process of Buddhist scripture-formation one cannot attribute the miraculously supernormal descriptions of the Buddha's actions exclusively to "later" strata in the Pali Canon and rule them completely out of the "earlier" books, *for they are found throughout the scriptures.* No doubt supernormal deeds were attributed to the Buddha by his contemporaries, just as miracles are an essential part of the earliest Christian Gospel accounts of the life of Jesus. Also, it is quite possible that even the earliest Buddhist suttas had later editing and additions. But also it is quite certain that the supernormal element did grow with the passage of the years. Here we shall make no attempt to distinguish between earlier and later in any fine degree but notice only some of the currently accepted accounts of the Buddha's life which illustrate the supernormal interpretation.

We may take as an example the story of the Buddha's birth. In its contemporary form, found in popular literature and depicted in pagoda art, we find that the Buddha's mother-to-be was most carefully selected by the devas (gods) after careful consultation with the Buddha-to-be himself, then in the Tusita Heaven. Her character, clan, and kammic history were investigated minutely. When she had been thus certified, the day of birth was carefully chosen. The conception was virgin. In a dream the Buddha's mother saw a white elephant entering into her womb. Sometime later she went apart with her women into a garden and there painlessly and miraculously gave birth to the Buddha-to-be who immediately took some steps and uttered words of wisdom.

There is also that favourite theme of the Temptation of the Buddha-to-be by Mara the evil spirit. Mara's assault (in the hope of turning the meditator aside from his final Enlightenment and the consequent liberation of many mortals from his control) was tremendous in its subtlety, strength, and scope. Even the attendant and sympathetic gods are routed and the meditating Gotama has only the strength of his ten perfections to protect him. These he makes his "sword and shield" against the whirlwinds Mara sends against him, described thus in the scriptures:

> *Straightway the east wind and all the other different winds began to blow; but although these winds could have torn their way through mountain peaks half a league, or two leagues, or three leagues high, or have uprooted forest shrubs and trees, or have reduced to powder and scattered in all directions villages and towns, yet when they reached the Future Buddha, such was the energy of the Great Beings's merit, they lost all power and were not able to cause so much as a fluttering of the edge of his priestly robe.*[1]

In the same manner, the passage continues, continent-flooding rainstorms leave not a drop of water on him, showers of rocks, weapons, live coals, hot ashes, sand, and mud are turned into showers of sweet ointments and flowers. Darkness of storm and night turns into light. And at last when Gotama calls upon the earth to witness to the meritorious deeds by whose power he is about to be a Buddha the earth responds with a confirming roar. An elephant of supernatural size falls upon his knees before Gotama and then turns and puts Mara and his hosts to flight. Whereupon the frightened gods who have been watching all this from "the edge of the world" crowd round once more and with multitudinous earth-creatures hymn the praise of the Enlightened One-to-be. Rejoicing breaks forth at all world levels; flowers bloom, fruits ripen, and the sick are healed instantaneously.

Sometimes supernormal occurrences are reported with regard to the Buddha's daily life on earth. Thus, in the account of his last days in the *Mahāparinibbāna Sutta*, when the Buddha

---

[1] *Buddhism in Translations*, p. 78.

was making his last journey to that little town where he would eventually die, he and his party came to the river Ganges:

> And at that time the river Ganges was brimful and overflowing; and wishing to cross to the opposite bank, some began to seek for boats, some for rafts of wood, whilst some made rafts of basket-work. Then the Exalted One, as instantaneously as a strong man would stretch forth his arm, or draw it back when he had stretched it forth, vanished from this side of the river and stood on the further bank in the company of the brethren.[1]

In Chapter IV of the same Sutta (section 21ff., text ii, 129) it is further related that after a procession of five hundred carts had stirred up a river till it was unfit for drinking, the Buddha super-normally cleared it up in a matter of minutes.

Buddhaghosa, famous commentator of the fifth century A.D., sees the super-normal as the usual or normal occurrence in the Buddha's daily life. In part of his commentary on the *Dīgha-Nikāya* he gives the following description of what occurred when the Buddha went on his daily begging round:

> While, namely, the Lord of the World is entering for alms, gentle winds clear the ground before him; the clouds let fall drops of water to lay the dust in his pathway, and then become a canopy over him; other winds bring flowers and scatter them in his path; elevations of ground depress themselves, and depressions elevate themselves; wherever he places his foot, the ground is even and pleasant to walk upon, lotus flowers receive his tread. No sooner has he set his right foot within the city-gate than the rays of six different colours which issue from his body race hither and thither over the palaces and pagodas, and deck them, as it were, with the yellow sheen of gold, or with the colours of a painting. The elephants, the horses, the birds, and other animals give forth melodious sounds; likewise the tom-toms, lutes, and other musical instruments, and even the ornaments worn by the people give forth sound.
> By these tokens the people would know, "The Blessed One has now entered for alms. . . ."[2]

And finally, according to one version, the Buddha was surrounded by sorrowing devas for twelve leagues about the city where he lay dying, so thickly congregated that there was

---

[1] Chapter I, Section 33 (Text ii, 89), *Dīgha-Nikāya* or *Dialogues of the Buddha* (SBB, Vol. III, p. 94).
[2] *Buddhism in Translations,* p. 92.

"not a spot of ground large enough to stick the point of a hair into that was not pervaded by powerful deities".[1]

No doubt these various versions represent several stages of the growth of the tradition; but they have by now become part and parcel of the popular Theravada tradition; and are endlessly represented in contemporary pagoda paintings. And so out-of-the-ordinary are they that the question as to whether they should be called "miraculous" and "super-human" or, as is preferred in Buddhism, "super-normal", seems academic. Compared to these super-normal occurrences the healing and nature miracles of Jesus recorded in the New Testament seem quite meagre in number and of inconsequential magnitude.

There is another and special class of super-normal powers, promised to all saints in some degree but, of course, possessed by the Buddha pre-eminently, which may be called *Psychic Powers*. These *abhiñña* are usually translated as Higher Spiritual Powers. In present tradition they are six-fold, including 1. a set of Ten Magical Powers, 2. remembrance of one's past existences, 3. clairvoyance (Divine Eye), 4. clairaudience (Divine Ear), 5. penetration of the thought of others' minds and 6. a knowledge of one's approaching Nibbana. The Ten Magical Powers we shall describe first, and consider the other psychic powers under the heading of the Buddha's omniscience.

Thus are the Ten-Magical Powers (*iddhi vidhā*) described in the canon:

Now, O Brothers, the monk enjoys the various Magical Powers, such as being one he becomes manifold, and having become manifold he again becomes one. Without being obstructed he passes through walls and mountains, just as if through air. He walks on water without sinking, just as if on the earth. In the earth he dives and rises up again, just as if in the water. Crosslegged he floats through the air, just a winged bird. With his hand he touches sun and moon. . . . Even up to the Brahma world has he mastery over his own body.[2]

According to the scriptures such powers of appearing and disappearing, of taking one or many forms, and of moving

[1] Ibid., p. 97, from *Mahāparinibbāna Sutta.*
[2] *Majjhima-Nikāya (Middle Length Sayings)*, Sutta 73, Text i, p. 494ff. This is a stereotyped formulation which may be found in several other suttas as well. See *Buddhist Dictionary*, Nayanatiloka, p. 2.

easily through space were commonplace with the gods. The expression found in the above-quoted account about the Buddha's miraculous river-crossing, "as instantaneously as a strong man would stretch forth his arm, or draw it back when he had stretched it forth", appears frequently in descriptions of the gods' journeys from one plane of existence to another. The Buddha, if course, possessed this power too, though he used it sparingly. On one occasion, in order to confute a presumptuous opponent—who could not come to argue with the Buddha because the latter's powers had transfixed him to the spot with terror—the Buddha relates that,

> *Thereupon, Bhaggava, I taught, and incited, and aroused, and gladdened that company with religious discourse. And when I had done so, and had set them at liberty from the great bondage, and had drawn forth 84,000 creatures from the great abyss, I entered on jhana by the method of flame, rose into the air to the height of seven palm trees, projected a flame to the height of another seven palm trees, so that it blazed and glowed; and then I reappeared in the Great Wood, at the Gabled Hall.*[1]

The Buddha is portrayed also as having used the power of gravity-defying movement through space for the benefit of mortal men in trouble, or for the conversion of those whose kammic powers were ripe for it, as we shall note in detail in the next section. And, of course, there are many legends of his having thus visited different parts of the Buddhist world during his lifetime and left tangible evidences of his presence there. North Burma has one "Buddha footprint" presumably dating from such a visit.[2]

---

[1] *Dīgha-Nikāya* or *Dialogues of the Buddha*, PTS edition, Vol. IV, par. 13. (*Patika Sutta*), No. XXIV.

[2] It is also true that popularly the saints are presumed even now to have such supernormal powers. Thus, a contemporary account:

"Thousands of the devout and curious are descending on the tiny hamlet of Tar-Kyar-Leain-su village, Waw Township, attracted by reports that a 73-year-old Sayadaw elder monk has attained the state of 'Zan' (described by Judson's dictionary as 'a certain attainment of state of the mind, which enables the possessor to traverse different worlds, to fly through the air, or go through the earth. . . .').

The Sayadaw is believed to have attained 'Zan' as early as 15 years ago, when he was witnessed walking about 18 inches above the ground by one U Po Chinn and Saw Hla."

Dispatch dated September 14, 1958, from Pegu, in *The Burman*.

The dispatch goes on to say that this had been long forgotten, but just before

3. *The Buddha's Omniscience*

Omniscience is the third great attribute of the Buddhas; and under this heading we shall consider the remaining five Higher Spiritual Powers as found in the Buddha. But we must be certain that we understand the Buddhist usage of the term. We may note again that while the Higher Spiritual Powers are pre-eminently present in the Buddhas, they are not exclusively present there; they are promised by the scriptures to the "average" saint also. And such is also the case with the Buddha's omniscience. To the saint is promised the power of seeing into his own past births, and into the hearts and lives of others. But the Buddha as omniscient possesses these powers, particularly those of seeing others' past births and their essential character, in unusual and even perfect degree. Whether this difference between the Buddha and the saint is one only of degree or in kind, we shall discuss at the end of this section.

We may start with the second of the Higher Psychic Powers, that of knowing one's own past births, i.e. remembering them in a later life. In the scriptures this power is one that can be cultivated and its growth is an indication also of the maturing spiritual powers of the saint. He begins by calling to memory the limited range of his own immediate past, and then extending it until it reaches out to increasingly wider ranges. But, of course, the range of a Buddha, as a perfectly developed psyche, is almost infinite. Countless are the former births that he can recall; and according to the *Jātaka Tales* it is done with the utmost ease at almost any moment.

So far as the Divine Eye (clairvoyance), or the power to recall the births of others is concerned, this would seem to be in some degree limited to the Buddhas in its more extensive and intensive exercise. It is an intrinsic part of the Buddha's power to penetrate into the true nature of another (see below) and integrally related to his power to prescribe for their salvation and come to their aid in crisis. Here also the *Jātaka Tales* portray the Buddha as able to call up from his memory,

the time of the news report an army sentry saw an apparition walking above the water near his post at night, and tried to shoot it with his rifle—which refused to fire. The apparition turned out to be, according to report, the said Sayadaw who went his way unharmed, and got his picture in the paper as a result.

instantly, easily, detailed accounts of the past lives of many of his disciples, friends and even enemies.

Allied to this power of memory of others' past births, is a Buddha's power to penetrate into their inmost thoughts and character. This is considered to be a separate psychic power, and again is to be largely confined to Buddhas though it is promised to all the saints in the scriptures. The formula for this reads as follows:

> *He knows the minds of other beings, of other persons, by penetrating them with his own mind. He knows the greedy mind as greedy and the not greedy one as not greedy; knows the hateful mind as hateful and the not hateful one as not hateful; knows the deluded mind . . . and the not deluded; the cramped and the scattered one . . ., the developed mind and the undeveloped . . ., the surpassable mind and the unsurpassable . . ., the concentrated mind and the unconcentrated one . . ., the freed mind and the unfreed one.*[1]

One further super-normal power is to be noted, the so-called Divine Ear (clairaudience), by which the saint can hear sounds, "both heavenly and human, far and near", according to the *Buddhist Dictionary* definition of Abhiññā. A contemporary Buddhist scholar suggested to the author that this signifies that an arahat can hear all the constitutive notes of a musical composition at once, but he hears them without any sense of attachment, i.e. pain or pleasure. But more in keeping with the above and scriptural description is the interpretation of the Divine Ear, in conjunction with the Divine Eye, as an ability to know what is going on is all the universes and planes of existence at any one moment. When one has these abilities he is able to hear the heavenly music of the higher spheres and to communicate with any beings living therein.

Now if we combine in maximum degree in one mind all these powers to know past births, to see and hear what goes on in all realms, to know the innate character of other beings, and to transport oneself wherever he will, then we can understand how the Buddhist conceives that the Buddha brought men to salvation. According to Buddhaghosa's Commentary on the Dīgha-Nikāya,[2] the Buddha's daily life pattern was as follows:

[1] *Buddhist Dictionary*, Nyanatiloka, p. 3.
[2] *Buddhism in Translations*, H. C. Warren, 1953 edition, pp. 94–5.

During the day he would teach villagers and his monks, till the end of "the first watch of the night". During the second watch of the night the gods of 10,000 world systems would come to him for instruction. The third watch of the night—from 2 a.m. to 6 a.m.—he divided into three parts: one for walking exercise, one for rest, i.e. refreshment in Nibbanic trance, and the third for what we may call "world-scanning". This latter is often compared by modern Burmese Buddhists to a radar-screen view of the world. When a clot of spiritual trouble or need appeared on the screen, the Buddha would focalize his attention on that point until the place and the individual came clearly into view. When such became clearly evident, he super-normally transported himself to that point; or it might be several points at the same time, since a Buddha is capable of multiple appearances simultaneously in different places. Nor, of course, does he operate within an earthly time-scale but, god-like, can do a multitude of things in the twinkling of an eye.

The most famous case of such help is that of the murderous robber Angulimali. Seeing with his radar vision that Angulimali was actually ripe for conversion, despite outward appearances, the Buddha transported himself or his astral likeness to Angulimali in the form of a monk. The robber immediately decided to kill this new victim who stood defenceless but a little distance away from him. But no matter how hard he tried to run toward him in order to attack him, the monk standing perfectly still was always ahead of him, unapproachably separated by a few yards or so. The net result was this robber's conversion into a saint. Here is then the practical use and fruition of the fifth Higher Power, penetration of the thoughts of others, for their own benefit and final salvation.

The final one of the six Higher Spiritual Powers is, in a religious sense, the most important of all; and it is one that saints and Buddhas share equally. Thus:

Through the extinction of all Biases (āsavas, *or fetters or cankers*), *even in this very life he enters into the possession of deliverance of mind, deliverance through wisdom, after having himself understood and realized it.*[1]

[1] *Buddhist Dictionary*, p. 3.

Or, in other words, the state of arahatship is now attained. One who has the above knowledge of his inner purity from all Biases, i.e. who is utterly detached from the desire for existence, and from all its impurities, knows with absolute assurance that he will not return to the realm of existence again in any form but go directly to Nibbana. This the Buddha knew upon his Enlightenment, but at the entreaty of the gods remained in the world to teach other men the way to Nibbana which he himself had just discovered.

Before we turn to a discussion of the power of the Buddha to reveal truth to others, we may again consider what is meant by the term "omniscience" when it is applied, as it frequently is, to the range of the Buddha's knowledge. How absolute is this omniscience? Does the Buddhist mean the same thing as the Christian by this term? If so, what differentiates a Buddha from God?

The answer is difficult because of contrasting strands of thought in the tradition itself. There is that often-quoted instance in which the Buddha likens the little he has told his disciples, when compared to all that he knows, to the few leaves of a tree that a man can hold in his hand when compared to the multitude of leaves in the forest. Mahayanists have, somewhat invidiously, compared the few leaves to the "narrow" Theravada tradition, and the forest of knowledge to their own later and esoteric revelation. Theravadins counter by quoting the Buddha to the effect that he is no "closed-fist" teacher who keeps back any secret teachings, but gives the full truth to all alike.

Yet even in Theravada tradition there is a strong tendency to magnify the extent of the Buddha's knowledge to infinite proportions. Thus from the following passage:

The ultimate beginning of things I know, Bhaggava, and I know not only that, but much more than that,[1]

commentators have sometimes staked out a claim for a kind of omniscience of indefinite infinitude, even though the continuation of the above passage suggests that the knowledge in question applied to the rise and fall of world systems in a general way. And as we have before noted, the popular *Jātaka*

[1] *Dīgha-Nikāya* or *Dialogues of the Buddha*, SBB edition, Vol. IV, *Pakita Suttanta*, No. XXIV, section 14.

Tales magnify both the ease with which the Buddha remembers past events and the infinite range of his memory.

But side by side with this we must set other basic Buddhist convictions, namely that either there are no absolute beginnings of existence, either material or mental, or else they are completely unknowable—presumably even to a Buddha also. Thus we might have to say that a Buddha cannot know all of his or anyone else's past births, because they are infinite in number. And perhaps we should even say that he could not know all the details of all his own past lives, or those of every other being, but only their dominant characteristics. The interpretation of commentators and *Jātaka Tales* may be viewed as later elaborations on a kind of "omniscience" that is often treated in the older scriptures as qualitative penetration of a man's character or of the basic nature of the world, rather than total quantitative inclusion of all existent facts. Thus the Buddha's vision of "things as they are" is an insight into the impermanence, the insubstantiality, and the woe-producing nature of the world, not an omniscient awareness of all its particulars.

Many contemporary Buddhists will say that we must differentiate the Buddha's omniscience from that which the Christian attributes to God in one important respect: The Buddha could will to send his penetrative intelligence toward any fact whatsoever in the world, past or present, and know anything knowable, one item at a time, so to speak. What this implies with regard to knowledge of the future, I do not know; but presumably not a knowledge of absolutely everything therein since the Buddhist believes in an "open" universe whose future is never fully determined. But in any case he did not hold all these particulars in his mind at one time, as God is presumed to do. Thus at any given moment his omniscience was potential rather than actual with regard to all but the item under consideration.

Even considering all these qualifications, however, it may be said that in general and especially in the popular view, Buddha has become omniscient in a theistic sense for all practical purposes. Many would flatly say that he knew "everything". Others suggest that the Buddha had all knowledge of all sorts at his disposal and had he desired, he could have taught mankind all its modern science. Indeed they will point to various parts of his teaching as having referred to, or anticipated, the teaching of modern physics some 2500 years ago. (See above, Chapter IV.) For them every statement which the Buddha made in the Pali Canon—all supposedly his literal word—is therefore absolutely and literally true.

But whatever the degree or kind of omniscience attributed to the Buddha by the contemporary Buddhist, the latter is certain of the supreme importance of the Buddha's omniscence for the Buddhist faith. Some will say that it is the corner-stone of Buddhism itself. And this may be interpreted to mean that all else in Buddhism rests upon the authenticity of the Buddha's Enlightenment, the validity of his insight into the nature of "things as they are" and the efficacy of his consequent prescription for human escape from birth-death. Take this away, and no Buddhist faith or truth of any sort is left. And this turns us to the last of the Buddha's powers, his power to reveal the truth.

4. *The Buddha as Revealer of Truth*

It is often written in sweeping fashion, both by Buddhists and non-Buddhists, that there is no revelation in Buddhism. And in one context, perhaps the fundamental one, this statement is correct. There is no "supernatural" revelation in Buddhism according to the definition of supernatural as meaning an order of being that is intrinsically non-human or more-than-human. In Buddhism there is no God whose metaphysical nature is completely transcendent of man's; there are only gods, who once were and will again be human beings. Nor was that supreme Enlightenment-knowledge that made Gotama a Buddha, the gift of the grace or the coercive manifestation of such a deity. While gods (devas) stood about in wonderment the Supreme Meditator pushed on unaided, save by his own past kamma (i.e. kammic-potential self) and present energy, to the Supreme Knowledge. Still further the Buddhist holds that each ordinary man must also make his own way to salvation by his own will-power and reason, and cannot expect saving faith or sudden revelation to do the work for him. Buddhism, says the Buddhist, is a way of rational self-salvation, not one of irrational salvation by faith in another's truth.

Actually the case is not quite as simple as this. There is the matter of that hidden force in every man, his own kammic Super-Self, from which come mysterious powers for good, and which, in Gotama's case, enabled him to become a Buddha.[1] Thus it may be only a question of terms as to whether this Enlightenment was purely his "own" effort, or represents a work of "grace". But this matter aside, we may say that so far as the Buddha is related to other men, there is a revelation of truth in the full sense of revelation. To this most Buddhists will agree if once the non-Buddhist connotations of the word can be forgotten. It may be put in this fashion, even on strictly Buddhist grounds: *Without the teaching of a Buddha, sentient beings can never come to the knowledge, let alone the attainment, of Nibbana.*

There is one partial exception to this statement: The Pacceka or Small Buddha of whom we have spoken before. He does not need the teaching of a Buddha at this present stage of development to achieve Nibbana. Yet it must be again emphasized that even he is not a true exception. Somewhere in his past he was only an ordinary man who heard the teaching of a Buddha and turned toward the Higher Way. Now at his present level he has progressed beyond the necessity of hearing the truth again, and will gain Nibbana even though born in a Buddhaless epoch. But originally he could not have been converted without such teaching.[2]

Now the original situation of the Pacceka Buddha is that of every ordinary man. He cannot—and this in the absolute sense—attain to the knowledge of the Truth, the saving Truth, without the prior revelation of that Truth by a Buddha. His own "unaided" reason cannot bring him to the knowledge of that truth; it must be there in his tradition, in some book, in

---

[1] This theme is further developed in the author's *In the Hope of Nibbana*, Chapter II.

[2] An interesting speculation: How did the first Buddha gain his Enlightenment with no previous Buddha to provide his initial knowledge of the truth? Here is the Christian dilemma with regard to the uncaused being of God, in Buddhist form. But the Buddhist, contrastingly to the Christian, never pretends to answer it and declares the attempt to answer it fruitless and religiously dangerous. Is this a clue for Christian theology?

someone's mind—where it had been put originally by a Buddha—before he can respond to it. He cannot be saved without the presence of the Dhamma (Teaching) as a given element in his epoch. And we have seen that one of the greatest dangers that can come to a Buddhist is the complete disappearance of the Buddha teaching in all its forms from a world epoch. (See above, p. 171.) Such a world is a "godless", graceless, forsaken one in every sense of the words.

We may note in passing that there is an act of grace involved here. That is: There was no necessity for the Buddha to share his Enlightenment-Knowledge with the rest of mankind. He was indeed disinclined to do so, both because of the difficulty of such sharing and because of his doubt as to whether there were any mortals prepared to receive his revelation. But the gods prevailed upon his compassionate nature and he "graciously" consented to proclaim his subtle truth. And though grace has had little place in Theravada Buddhism in the past—at least in acknowledged form—this act of grace is increasingly emphasized in the contemporary tradition.

In summary we may then say that whatever our verdict about the appropriate use of the category of revelation with regard to the Buddha's own Enlightenment, certainly we must regard his Dhamma as a full-fledged revelation to the rest of the world. For it possesses the following features which would seem to be intrinsic to the meaning of revelation in any context whatsoever: (1) The proclamation of the Dhamma was a fully voluntary gift of the Buddha's grace; (2) Men cannot arrive at the truth of the Dhamma by their unaided reason, but it must have been given to them at some time by a Buddha; (3) The Truth of Nibbana is above reason, not only in the means of its attainment, but in its intrinsic nature. Its quality is perhaps not anti-rational but definitely super-rational; no words or concepts can grasp Nibbana—it must be directly experienced or realized—and even its existence can be revealed only by a Buddha who has himself tasted of its peace.

The Religious Function of the Buddha

Up to this point we have been concerned to outline the basic features of the Buddhist conception of Buddhahood. We may now turn our attention in conclusion to the actual way in which the Buddha-concept appears to function religiously. And again, perhaps tiresomely but necessarily, we must remind ourselves that there is no one way in which this concept functions for all Buddhists. There are differences between what the Buddha "means" to villager, university graduate, Buddhist scholar, layman, monk, and variously orthodox people. To say flatly, "Buddhists think thus and thus about the Buddha" is therefore a wrong approach. The best that we can do is to say: Such and such is the view commonly taught by the vast majority of monks and accepted by the majority of laymen. Individuals and groups may vary considerably in their own ideas from this generally received standard.

In this context we may frame the following general statement of the place of Buddha in Buddhist religious life. The Buddha—and that means Gotama Buddha, though there are, of course, many other Buddhas recognized even in Theravada Buddhism—was the Supreme Teacher of the one true way to salvation in our world epoch. He and he alone has revealed to us that salvation; his word and practice of the way are faithfully recorded in the Pali Canon and preserved and exemplified for us in their purity by the Buddha's order of monks, or Sangha. Yet, though the Buddha is thus worthy of supremest honour, he is not a Supreme Being to whom Buddhists should address prayers or to whom they should give adoration. If they do so, or regard Buddha as more than the great Way-Shower who is now beyond all personal inter-communication in Nibbana, they "are not doing what they have been taught to do" as the Venerable U Thittila phrases it.

Thus the correct way for Buddhists to approach a Buddha image is to think of it only as a symbol of the virtues of the Buddhist good life. Their devotions performed before it should not be thought of as petitions to a God, but as a renewal of their own courage and confidence, and a dedication to that way of life which the Buddha showed to men in the hope of their eventual attainment of Nibbana. Thus the worshipped Buddha should not be personalized even in the mood of worship, but considered abstractly as a once-personalized cluster of spiritual perfections.

And a further word should be said here about the Buddhist use of the word "worship". This word has been taken over rather casually from English, and gives in general an un-Buddhistic connotation to the act and attitude which it attempts to describe. "Veneration", "reverence", or "respect" would actually be more appropriate than "worship", though the latter is continually used. For it must be remembered that a traditionally-minded Burmese Buddhist speaks about "worshipping" his parents, his teacher, a worthy monk or the Sangha as a whole, as well as the Buddha. And he will describe both his form of worship—again the hands-above-head, kneeling-bow—which is given to all these on the appropriate occasion, and his attitude of mind in thus worshipping, as the same in general quality. Perhaps in English, for that greater degree of such reverence present in worship of the Buddha, we ought always to use the term veneration, while for the somewhat lesser variety given to parents and elders we should reserve the term respect.

Such is the theory of "orthodox" Buddhist devotion to the Buddha. For many it is no doubt so. And there are those who disdain all the usual forms of pagoda devotion. But it is too much to expect of human nature that it should remain faithfully within the cold and narrow confines of this rigidly correct attitude toward the Buddha. It overflows them at many points. We have already noted in another chapter how Buddhist religious need fills in the emotional and conceptual need left by the high austerity of "pure" Buddhism with reverence for the devas and nats. Here we may further note that it is also undoubtedly true that the figure of the Buddha himself is warmed and personalized in a corresponding way by the same devotion.

One must say at the very least that the human and personal features of the Buddha's life are treasured by the devout just as dearly as those of Jesus' life are by devoted Christians. His striking parables are on every Buddhist tongue and his recounted deeds have been elaborated and embroidered in loving detail. And though traditionally the Buddha image is not supposed to be a literal portrayal of Buddha's own personal appearance, yet the Burmese raid once launched against Arakan was for the express purpose of capturing the great

Buddha image there because it was reputed to be a genuine likeness of the Buddha himself.[1]

So also there is definitely a devotional flavour about the way in which "the Lord Buddha" is said. I am not speaking here of the term "Lord" which has un-Buddhistic connotations for the Christian. For "Lord", when applied to the Buddha, is not primarily a metaphysical statement but an expression of respect somewhat equivalent to "Master" in Christian language. But the whole phrase, "the Lord Buddha" in the mouth of a devout Buddhist has most definitely a high degree of reverential flavour, very much like that in the voice of a Christian when he speaks of "the Lord Jesus Christ", or "Our Lord". Though somewhat intangible, this quality is unmistakable and has nothing to do with cultural customs. Clearly, whatever its accurate theological content, the phrase has a genuinely worshipful, even adorational, quality in its speaking.[2]

This leads us on to make the point that, orthodoxly restrained as devotion to the Buddha may be, now and then a very deeply devotional quality appears. Thus there was published recently in the weekly Buddhist Supplement of a daily newspaper, and also in a booklet of selections in honour of the 2500th anniversary of the death of the Buddha, celebrated in Rangoon in the years 1954–56, a strongly emotional expression of adoration of the Buddha. Originally it was written by a monk of Ceylon, Widurupola by name, date unknown. It takes the form of the confessions and adorations of a now-penitent believer who is remembering (actually or poetically?) the misdeeds and callous heart that characterized him in many a past existence. The piece is too long for total inclusion. Here we shall quote two passages, one of which is a confession of sin, and the other an expression of adoring worship:

[1] A contemporary writer has this to say about the image: "The resemblance has no doubt faded away with the wickedness of later times, for, unlike most Burmese images, this Paya Gyi has most gross and repulsive features." "Legends of the Great Pagodas in Burma", Venerable U. Kumara, *Light of the Buddha*, Vol. IV, No. 12, December 1958, p. 36.

[2] To be sure this adoration is deplored by some. A meditation master tells his trainees that they must beware of excessive emotional attachment to the Buddha. "The dear old ladies who say, 'Buddha, Buddha! How wonderful the Lord Buddha is! How we love him!' are missing the true Buddhist way", he often says. Such emotion distracts them from the real business at hand, purifying themselves of greed, hatred, and delusion.

Confession:

With a tormented mind, having for long fallen into the blazing fire of hell. . . . I did not remember even once, O Father, to worship your lotus feet, so, O Gotama, Leader of men, deign to forgive this failure of mine.

(He recounts many other evil lives, and even deva births, in all of which he forgot the Buddha.)

Thus while travelling in this wise, from one state of existence to another, in succession, through many ages, countless varieties of evil deeds have been committed by me through body, speech, and mind; so for all these, O Gotama, Destroyer of evils, deign to forgive me and be my guide unto that state of Highest Bliss which is ever-lasting, Immortal, and is the deliverance from all samsaric existence.

Adoration:

Him do I worship, the guide to deathlessness, the Noblest Sage and Peerless One, whose hair resembling dark clouds falls in curls, shining, soft and beautiful, whence is emitted a radiant aura diffused all round the earth. . . .

He whose holy appearance is like unto the immaculate orb of the rising moon; whose works suffused with the essence of compassion are immortal sound to the ear, whose praises are sung in a hundred different ways, nay whose glories fill the entire universe and who is indeed a veritable shrine of sanctity and of delightful auspicious marks. Him do I worship. . . .

Him, with the lotus-bud formed by my hands reverently clasped and raised above the head, do I worship, the entirely Bond-free, Peerless Sage, who, impregnable as a "Diamond-castle", banishes all fear from those who take refuge in Him, and Who delights in guiding the countless fallen multitudes across the ocean of becoming. . . .

Hence, O Sage, whenever I ponder on your spotless virtues, whether by day or by night, indeed at all times, doth my heart in you find delight. . . .[1]

The language and mood of this piece clearly parallels some of the medieval Christian mystical outpourings or modern revivalist devotionals. It is obviously "theistic" and adorational through and through. Does it represent a repressed, or at least seldom-expressed, Buddhist feeling which could be found in the heart of multitudes of pagoda-worshippers of the Buddha images? The answer is probably, yes. But, of course,

---

[1] *Kamalanjali* ("With Folded Hands"), reprinted in *Sangīti*, edited and partly written by Francis Story, European convert to Buddhism.

there will be others who disapprove or qualify. Thus when I tried this piece out on three young men, all university graduates and devout Buddhists, their reactions were as follows:

(1) *The idea of forgivennes is not in accordance with our notion of Kamma. We cannot remit our kammic consequences to others, but must bear the responsibilities by ourselves. Yet the emotion of peace is understandable, for men are creatures of both thinking and emotion.*

(2) *This paragraph is a sort of stimulation. It stimulates my mind to worship Buddha and to remember his attitudes. As a Burman Buddhist my emotions rise up even by the mere reading of this translation. If I could have a chance to read the original in Burmese— my emotion would be stronger than this.*

(3) *I am unhappy to state that almost all of the prayers I have ever seen are composed in unnecessarily emotional terms. Many of them are exaggerated in such a way that the real essence of them challenges the true words of the Buddha. I note that this one was written long after the Buddha's demise. . . .*
Many Buddhists are intoxicated with the practice of worshipping the feet of the Buddha . . . but I wonder how they get the true sense of the virtues of the Buddha at the moment of their recitation which is filled with personalized emotions. . . . On the whole this kind of prayer leads one to the wrong path instead of showing him the right way.

And these responses—the critical but appreciative, and warmly responsive, and the strongly rejecting—no doubt represent a cross section of Buddhist feelings, though on the popular level the second response would certainly be overwhelmingly the largest.

This leads us to the interesting question of whether a Buddhist venerating a Buddha image thinks of the Buddha as being actually present there. We may repeat that according to orthodox teaching, the Buddha is not present. Yet the emotion-filled devotion the worshipper seems to feel toward, or by means of, the image, gives the lie to his strict adherence to orthodoxy. There is clearly something of the "Buddha-presence" which is available here before the image, and not elsewhere. He may be thinking only of a set of perfections, but the odds seem to be against it. Emotion almost surely transforms the past tense of honoured memory into the present

M

tense of petition and adoration. And we must add to this that, despite orthodox teaching to the contrary, a kind of magical efficacy is attributed to the images of the Buddha. Wishes uttered in their vicinity have a chance of being fulfilled that they have nowhere else; the "Buddha-presence" somehow empowers them beyond human power. This seems to be true of almost any image to some degree, but is especially true of some particular ones such as those carried in boat- procession down the Inle Lakes once each year, mentioned above.

To revert to the more spiritual aspect of the Buddha's presence: Can "Buddha" be said to represent a present power, now available for human need? After having discussed the power of the Buddha in his lifetime to "scan" the universes for those souls in need of help (see above, p. 167), I asked a well-educated, middle-aged Buddhist layman whether there was anything comparable to this today, in Buddhist thinking. If someone in spiritual need should send out his S.O.S., would there be a dependable and helpful response to his need? While the precise source of this power was not made clear, the unhesitating answer was, "Yes".

Sometimes this implicit confidence in the present availability of the Buddha's spiritual power breaks out into even more explicit forms. In that near-petitionary form of Buddhist devotions, of "let this be" or "may this come to pass", one particular version fervently desires that the power of the Buddha, who is of "infinite glory, good kamma, and knowledge", may "come down upon the heads of your disciples", "dwell" upon them, "surround and cover them", and establish them in the power of the Buddha's Enlightenment, Teaching, and Nibbana. Those who use this "prayer" are as orthodoxly Buddhist as one can wish, and would steadfastly assert that the Buddha in Nibbana is no god to be prayed to. Yet so intense is their conviction that somehow the power which was in him is still active in the world today, that almost inevitably present-tense, personal-relational language creeps in.

What, then, is the function and potency of the Buddha-concept in practical Buddhist religious life? Allowing for many differences one must say that, whatever the theory, actual practice indicates that the image and memory of the Buddha function as a locus of belief-full devotion very similar to that of a Deity or a Saviour in other faiths. To be sure, the restraint of orthodox conceptions will always tend to inhibit some types of emotional expression with regard to the Buddha himself and channel them into the domain of the devas; and it will continue to be the basic tradition that the higher levels of Buddhist religious practice rise above such emotional attitudes. Yet for the mass of Buddhists the Buddha-figure still represents an ideal personal life, a well-beloved Master-Teacher, a Superman of Supermen far more powerful (save for creation) than any God, and a spiritual potency that is not entirely a matter of the past. Functionally, therefore, or at least for the purposes of religious devotion if not for the categories of theology, the Buddha is a deity or locus of supreme values even in the Theravada tradition.

VI

THE MORE EXCELLENT WAY

The Centrality of Meditation in Buddhism

THE SINGLE MOST IMPORTANT EVENT IN ALL WORLD history in the eyes of Buddhism is the Enlightenment of the Buddha. By this experience the man Gotama was finally and forever freed from the bonds of the birth and death cycle of suffering which had held sentient creatures as miserable prisoners for countless ages. And by this experience he became a Buddha, not only enlightened and liberated himself, but able to show other men the way to that liberation. Thus it is that this Enlightenment is normative for the total Buddhist way of life; for though not all men will become Buddhas, all men must in the end be enlightened with the same quality of enlightenment as the Buddha was, and achieve the same detached serenity of mind as he did, before they can attain salvation.

It is therefore of interest to read a scriptural account of that experience:

> My body is tranquil, impassable, my mind composed, one-pointed. So I, brahman, aloof from pleasures of the senses . . . entered into the first meditation (jhana) . . . the second meditation. . . . I dwelt with equanimity, attentive, clearly conscious. . . . I entered into and abided in the third meditation . . . the fourth meditation.
>
> Thus with the mind composed, quite purified, without blemish, without defilement, grown soft and workable, fixed, immovable, I directed my mind to the knowledge of former habitations [existences]. I remembered . . . one birth, two births . . . a hundred thousand births. This, brahman, was the first knowledge attained by me in the first watch of the night. . . .
>
> I directed my mind to the knowledge of the passing hence and the arising of beings. . . . I comprehend that beings are mean, excellent, comely, ugly, well-going, ill-going, according to the consequences

of their deeds. . . . This, brahman, was the second knowledge
attained by me in the middle watch of the night. . . .
I directed my mind to the knowledge of the destruction of the
cankers. I understood it as it really is: This is anguish, this is the
arising of anguish, this is the stopping of anguish, this is the course
leading to the stopping of anguish. . . .
Knowing this, seeing this, my mind was freed from the canker of
sense pleasures . . . of becoming . . . of ignorance. In freedom the
knowledge came to be: I am freed; and I comprehended: Destroyed
is birth, brought to a close is the Brahma-faring, done is what is to
be done, there is no more of being such and such [i.e. sentient
existence].
This, brahman, was the third knowledge attained by me in the last
watch of the night; ignorance was dispelled, knowledge arose, darkness
was dispelled, light arose even as I abided diligent, ardent, self-
resolute. [1]

Let it be repeated that some of the features of this experience
are necessary to any man's enlightenment, even though this
enlightenment be in some sense of a lesser degree than the
Buddha's Enlightenmenti for not being a Buddha he will not
achieve the height or depth of His psychic powers nor ever be
able to bring others to Nibbana by his knowledge. Yet he, like
the Buddha, must achieve clarity of mind, tranquil detachment of spirit, and come to the knowledge that he individually
is freed from the hold of the last fetters that bind him to sentient
existence. These qualities, inherent in the Buddha-type of
enlightenment even in a meagre degree of approximation, and
described in many a scripture, are essential to the realization
of Nibbana. They are the strait gate through which all
must pass.

And this brings us to the subject matter of this chapter:
meditation, or its scriptural equivalent, mindfulness. For
meditational mindfulness is the narrow way to the strait
gate of enlightenment and liberation. This is implicit in the
account of the Buddha's Enlightenment. After long lives of
good deeds as a Bodhisatta, and after six fruitless years of
austerities according to the Brahmanical pattern of his time,
Gotama achieved his Buddha-making Enlightenment while
he was meditating. But, for that matter, we need not rely alone

[1] *Majjhima-Nikāya*, or *Middle Length Sayings*, Vol. I (PTS edition, 1954),
Bhayabherava Sutta, No. IV, Text i, 21–3.

upon the implications of the Enlightenment to realize the necessity for following the meditative discipline. It is endlessly spoken of in the scriptures in terms of mindfulness, and specific directions given for its practice. As a contemporary writer says, with regard to a specific type of meditation:

> *The Vipassana Meditation is the most sacred gift left us by the greatest of all teachers, the Buddha. . . . He said:*
> *"This is the only way for the purification of beings, for the over-coming of sorrow and lamentation, for the destruction of suffering and grief, for reaching the right path, for the attainment of Nibbana, namely the four foundations of mindfulness!"* [1]

Hence though it may be that meditation produces calmness of mind and has a generally beneficial effect upon the total person; though it may be that the meditative life is in general productive of higher virtues and qualities than the active life; and though it is a good thing always to follow the example of the Buddha—and these statements are made in recommending meditation—the basic reason is simple: Meditation alone leads to the attainment of Nibbana.

This centrality of meditation to the Buddhist way of life may be illustrated in two or three different contexts. We may note, for example, the relation of meditation to morality or *Sīla*. It is true that Sila is a fundamental requisite for the successful practice of meditation. It is always pointed out to the would-be meditator that unless he is a man of good moral character and established in his habits, he will not likely succeed in meditation. (This does not mean that he is already perfect, without sins or failings, but essentially a man of steady disposition and firm spiritual intentions who desires to be even better.) This is true enough. But our point here is that such a one does go on to meditation after he has achieved a reasonable degree of moral self-control; or better, he must add meditation to moral conduct before he can hope for Nibbana.

The same emphasis may be made in another way. It is not by the intellectual knowledge of Buddhist doctrine and history, or by memorization of scripture-texts, or by the

---

[1] "Introduction to a Course of Vipassana Meditation", A. Kell, *Light of the Dhamma*, Vol. III, No. 3, May, 1956, p. 4.

systematic building of Buddhist systems of thought that one comes to know truth in the Buddhist sense. It is by "practice" alone that genuine knowledge or realization of the essential Buddhist truths comes to the individual. And by "practice" the Buddhist means the practice of the meditational discipline. Then it will come to pass that those truths that he does not now understand, or is not now prepared to appropriate to himself, will become clear and available. Thus, by meditation alone can the saving Buddhist truth be truly known to anyone; or, to reverse the statement, only by meditation does Buddhist truth become known in saving fashion.

In this connection we may also note that there is today an especially strong emphasis upon the possibility of achieving the nibbanic quality of peace in this life. There is that well-known passage in which the Buddha expatiates on the short time in which an intensive practice of meditation will produce enlightenment in this life. Shall it take seven years, one year, six months, one month, he asks? He then reduces the term still further.

O Monks, let alone half a month. Should any person practice these four foundations of Mindfulness in this manner for a week, then one of two results may be expected by him: Highest knowledge here and now, or if some remainder of clinging is not present, the state of Non-returning.[1]

Sometimes also Nibbana is described only in terms of freedom from the hold of greed, hatred, and delusion, or else the destruction of the mental and moral defilements. (In this form it is known as *kilesa-parinibbāna*, the utter going out of unskilful or evil personal dispositions.) And this is a condition which it is possible to achieve in this life, if one is an arahat, or highest grade of saint who has achieved the perfection of mindfulness through meditation. And though few would qualify as arahats today, yet many a man may experience something of that nibbanic peace and purity if he persistently and rightly practices the meditational discipline. Such practice brings with it a self-confirming proof of the truths of the faith; as one experiences a growing peace, calm, and detachment he be-

[1] Quoted by Nyanaponkia Mahathera in "Heart of Buddhist Meditation" in *Light of the Dhamma,* Vol. V, No. 4, October, 1958, p. 57.

comes ever more certain in his assurance of the absoluteness of the truths discovered by the Buddha.

We may thus speak of meditation as a kind of Buddhist sacrament—perhaps its supreme sacrament—though in a non-liturgical and non-institutionalized form for the most part. For what is the essence of a sacrament? According to Roman Catholic usage and practice it is two-fold. Theologically considered it is the objective presence of Divine Power in the human world; a sacrament is the tangible form and medium for the entrance of supernatural and transforming spiritual power into the world of time and space. Practically considered, a sacrament is essential to salvation—particularly in the case of baptism and the Eucharist. And are not both these qualities found in the Buddhist meditational discipline, even though in non-theistic context? For, on the practical plane, we have observed that meditation is absolutely essential for the appropriation of the central Buddhist truths and the ultimate attainment of salvation. And it can also be said that the meditational method is a tangible objective process by which the realization of saving truth comes to human beings. Meditation is therefore the Buddhist Eucharist, unconditioned Nibbana-power coming down into conditioned existence. It is with meditation that we enter into the Buddhist Holy of Holies, besides whose holiness mere pagoda-holiness is almost completely negligible.

This leads us to one more question. If meditation is the only way to the higher spiritual attainments and ultimately to Nibbana itself, is there then only one method of meditation that is considered effective? The answer is both yes and no. In a general sense it is yes. For the Buddhist contention is that out of many ways of meditation known to his contemporaries in India, Buddha developed the one and only successful way. Or perhaps we might say that though the Buddha had much in common with the contemporary methods, even utilizing them up to a point, his method carries one beyond other partial salvations to the only full salvation, Nibbana itself. (This is even today a favourite Buddhist way for comparing the truth of Buddhism with that of all other religions.) Thus there is only one general pattern of meditation that can succeed, that found in the Buddha's Middle way. And in the hands of some expositors this may be very narrowly interpreted to mean the absolute essentiality of all the traditional meditational minutiae. But within the limits of the general framework of Buddhist method, great adaptation is possible. There are many subjects for meditation, and several techniques of physical procedure. In one sense indeed Buddhism is quite relativistic and experimental in its methodology of meditation. For the "rightness" of a meditational method in its particular practice can never be set down in a book; it is a matter of a guru, or meditation-master, fitting one or more of the methods to the needs of the individual meditator—and this allows for considerable variation. In the end it is not the orthodoxy of a particular method but the inner result which counts.

It also follows from this relativity of method or exact meditational route that the guidance of a guru or meditation master is almost essential at the beginning of meditation. Left to himself the beginner will more than likely lose his way and succumb to discouragement. And it may be said that the success of a guru's guidance depends upon three factors or abilities possessed by him: His knowledge, i.e. an ability to interpret the orthodox tradition; his intuitive penetration of the disciple's personal character and capacities; his own personal experience in meditative attainment. And perhaps of all these elements the latter is the prime essential. For unless one has himself so practised, how can he guide another? And how can he lead another where he has never been himself?

There is a well-known story of

> *The celebrated scholar Dhammarakkhita Thera . . . who after teaching Tipitaka Culaghaya Thera . . . sat down on a mat at the feet of his pupil and begged of him to give him a topic of meditation. "Why, Sir," cried the pupil, "haven't I studied under you? What can I say that you don't know?" "But my friend," said the teacher, "the path of realization is quite a different thing." Tipitaka Culahaya was a sotapanna at the time. The teacher is reported to have attained arahatship on the kammathana meditation topic given him by his pupil.*[1]

There is a variant on this story, or another similar one, in which the pupil is a mere child in chronological years, but beyond his teacher on the path of meditation. In any case the passage makes two points: meditative realization is quite

---

[1] Walpola Rahula, *History of Buddhism in Ceylon*, Gunasena, Colombo, 1956, 297.

different fron intellectual knowledge; one must be experienced in its practice before he can help another. But there is also another point to be raised. How can a mere sotapanna (first stage of holiness) guide another to arahatship (fourth stage of holiness) on the analogy of one being unable to take another where he has not been himself? Two things may be suggested. One is that the teacher may have encountered gurus of higher attainment at a later time—but this is to add to the story. More convincingly it is this: Given a certain degree of progress, with the key put in one's hand, he may proceed on the higher levels to guide himself. It is not the new device but the new and maturing man that makes the difference. And even were he to have the direct guidance of a Buddha, it is he, the meditator, who must make the effort and know in himself that he has actually arrived at a certain stage of development. Sometimes there are mistakes in one's understanding of his own degree of advancement,[1] but in the end it is a self-won knowledge which is able to share in the Buddha's glad certainty, "I have comprehended: Destroyed is birth, brought to a close is the Brahma-faring, done is what is to be done, there is no more of being such and such (for me)."

The Meditational Routes to Nibbana

We may now turn to a delineation of the way to Nibbana as it is conceived in the Theravada tradition. Its basic statement is found in the Noble Eightfold Path. This series of steps up the ladder of spiritual advancement toward ultimate liberation is usually put in the following form:

1. Right Understanding
2.   ,,   Thought
3.   ,,   Speech

---

[1] According to a Buddhist friend, a Burmese Buddhist man was certain that he was a sotapanna (one who is certain of Nibbana in seven more births at most and will never descend to the hells). During the Japanese occupation of Burma he was offered something to drink by his Japanese hosts at a banquet. Upon tasting some of the beverage he found that it was alcoholic in nature. But because there had been no premonitory quivering in his hand when he reached for the drink, he concluded that he was not a sotapanna. A sotapanna level of attainment should have made him so spiritually alert that he would have known instinctively, or better, by the warning vibrations emanating from the beverage, that he was in danger of violating the Fifth Precept against taking alcohol.

4. Right Bodily Action
5. „ Livelihood.
6. „ Effort
7. „ Mindfulness
8. „ Concentration (or Rapture)

Theravada Buddhism puts its own interpretation upon the above scriptural order. Steps 3 through 5 are put in the domain of Sila or morality. Steps 6 through 8 are classified as belonging to the second stage of the good life, but the first stage of the meditative discipline, Samadhi or concentration. Steps 1 and 2 are considered to be of the order of paññā or that supreme insight-wisdom which brings one to Nibbana. Sometimes it is allowed, in explanation of the above scriptural order, that one may think in a very elementary way of Right Understanding and Right Thought as the first steps in a beginner's intellectual knowledge of Buddhist doctrines. But more often, and somewhat illogically, it is also said that they are put first because they are highest and most important.

But putting the precise order of the steps aside, we may say that in any event the meditational scale of progression is solidly built upon basic Buddhist morality; whatever the intellectual idiosyncrasies of the mediator or his special needs, he must begin here. A minimum for the lay meditator (the monk must conform to all the 227 Vinaya rules of conduct for his Sila basis) is the careful observance of the Five Precepts which teach one to avoid killing of any sort, theft, falsehood, illicit sexual relationships, and drinking of intoxicants or taking of drugs. During actual meditation periods he may be asked to observe the Precepts in absolute fashion: no insect may be killed (though it may be non-violently repelled), no meat eaten, and no sexual intercourse of any sort be indulged in. Still further he may be required to abstain from food after midday (like the monk), from sleeping on soft or high beds, and from any sort of worldly amusement.

It may also be noted here that morality can be given an inner dimension that carries it well up along the scale of development. Non-killing becomes the spirit of harmless, even benevolent, goodwill toward all creatures; avoidance of illicit sexual relationships can be extended to the avoidance of all lustful and sensual thoughts *in toto*. And on the positive side there are meditations upon, and exercises in, loving-kindness, peace, and compassion to be extended ever more widely and inclusively toward one's fellow-beings. In fact the cultivation of some of the higher degrees of mental power is needed to facilitate the universalization of the benevolent attitudes until his own and another's good are identical for the meditator.

This relationship of the "stages" on the way to Nibbana suggests, correctly, that "progress" in meditation is very difficult to estimate—at least according to any external or bookish standard. In particular cases it is accomplished by a combination of one's own self-knowledge and the insight of his guru. But because progress is so many-faceted, the matter is still most difficult to systematize in terms of levels. For one should not think of progress upward toward Nibbana solely in terms of climbing a series of ladder-like steps, i.e. successive and mutually exclusive stages. One cannot say that Sila is first perfected and then left behind when one reaches Samadhi and Paññā stages—even though there is talk of rising above mere morality as one progresses in the meditative life. For even the meditating saint remains moral in his actions. Indeed his saintliness, at least in part, is the perfection of his morality, the turning from mere observance of external standards to the spontaneous exercise of inward virtues.[1] So it is that morality is never left behind. Nor for that matter is the mental one-pointedness of the Samadhi stage ever outgrown but to some extent utilized all along the way. It may be developed either more or less, as we shall see, somewhat according to personal taste. But rather than speaking in terms of dispensing with it we may speak, as also with morality, of needing to spend less time on the basic skills of spiritual living as one progresses along the way. The foundation stones need not be relaid over and over again, to change the figure.

So also the relationship of the "lower" and "higher" spiritual levels is to some extent reversible. That is, progress in the meditational practice tends to strengthen the moral character. All things being equal, the man who meditates will normally be better for so doing, even though his attainments be most moderate. This indeed is the core of the modern emphasis upon lay meditation (see below). It is held that meditative

---

[1] See author's *In the Hope of Nibbana* for further discussion.

periods enrich and better the active periods of a man's life. *If* one meditates he will be a better man in every way, more moral and more efficient. Thus the layman both can and should set apart meditative periods even in the midst of his busy worldly life.

It would perhaps be better to think of spiritual progress as a changing kaleidoscopic vision rather than a ladder. At first the only goods that one *can* envisage, or cares to, are those of a concrete and mundane order—maybe nothing higher than the mere attainment of physical happiness, or rebirth in a physically more fortunate station. But even this desire is not truly evil, for hidden in the desire for happiness and well-being are germs of a higher order of things, the desire for moral goodness and peaceful virtue. If these germinal elements are developed, or, in terms of the vision, if these dim gleams of higher good are cherished and developed by meditation, the vision of what is truly desirable gradually shifts and changes more and more toward the spiritual pole. One becomes firmly attached to virtue and yearns for its perfection. He even yearns for a higher order of goodness above the active mundane virtues of honesty, liberality, mercifulness and the like, for those calm cool heights of detached serenity. And, finally, even this vision dissolves and clarifies until there is only emptiness—or is it formless, timeless Nibbana—which he beholds? Such is progress in meditation.

Yet for all these relativities and inter-relations there is some meaning also in the three-stage order of progression. The kaleidoscopic pictures do change; Sila is less emphasized and meditation is more emphasized; some powers and accomplishments are left behind and others sought for. And here it is that there opens up before us a divergency of ways. One may choose between two alternative meditative ways to Nibbana. To be sure this is not precisely the Buddhist way of putting it; for in orthodox Buddhism there is only One Goal and One Way to that Goal—the Noble Eightfold Path, whose higher attainments are actualized by meditation. But in terms of actual practical emphasis it is also true that contemporary Theravada Buddhism in Burma points out that there is both a minimum or direct route, and a maximum or indirect route to Nibbana. The former is what was classically called the "dry-visioned" way, i.e. without the attainment of the Jhanic Powers or Absorptions; the latter is the way to Nibbana through the Jhanas, and is the classical Buddhist way. But for hard-pressed modern people who have no time for spiritual luxuries, and who now have (see below) some newly discovered or re-discovered methods of quicker attainment of the requisite detachment, the direct route has its great attractions.

We shall turn now to a brief description of each way and a consideration of its relation to the other.

1. *The Traditional Jhanic (Absorption) Route*

The traditional or indirect route shares with the direct route the moral or Sila foundation, of course. (See diagram.) And it shares also the first two steps along the meditational route. There is first the stage of preparatory or *preliminary concentration*. Having fulfilled all the external meditational conditions of solitude and proper seating (see below) the meditator begins to concentrate on some subject or other. He largely ignores the external stimuli but is not entirely insensitive to them. Secondly, he enters into the *access or neighbourhood* meditational condition. (These are all minutely described in Buddhaghosa's *Path of Purification*.) On this level of meditational concentration one is able to cut off nearly all external stimuli successfully.

And it is at this level that the routes part, temporarily and partially at least. For here the meditator is sufficiently concentrated to proceed directly to *Vipassanā*-type meditation—which is the absolutely essential requirement for the attainment of Nibbanic detachment. Or he may go into a deeper stage of concentration, called the ecstatic or attainment concentration, which is that quality of absolute concentration in which he realizes the Jhanic Absorptions.

This latter, of course, is the traditional or classic way to Nibbana. It was the route that the Buddha took in a few moments of time when he ascended from this life to Nibbana (his *parinibbāna*) upon his physical death. For the amount of time taken to ascend the scale of the absorptions is purely relative to the spiritual advancement of the individual mediator. If he is a master, it is momentary. Or again it may take successive lives in which to achieve a new level of concentration. In any case this is the usual way in which the scriptures describe the stages of the way to nibbanic detachment or arahatship.

We may observe at the outset that the Jhanas belong to the second stage of the Eightfold Path. No matter how expert one becomes in the absorptions (Jhanic trances) rising even to the ninth level, he is nonetheless still in the Samadhi or concentration stage, not the Pañña or wisdom level. He is practising at the level of Right Effort, Right Mindfulness, and Right Concentration and must go beyond this level before he has any hope of Nibbana. For no more than the practice of Sila does adeptness in the absorptions bring one to that haven.

What then are Jhanas? The term Jhana (Pali *jhāna*) has been variously translated. Frequently it has been rendered as "ecstasy", or "trance". These terms, however, are strongly objected to by many Theravada Buddhists because they suggest some occult possession by spirits in uncontrollable seizures, or a highly emotional state, or at best the "irrational" mystic trance. From all these Buddhism would differentiate the Jhana by an emphasis upon its clarity, its rationality, its full consciousness, and above all the ability of the meditator to control its length and nature. A jhanic state is essentially concentration of the attention in complete one-pointedness upon one item and one item alone, to the complete exclusion of all else. Therefore the term "musing", which is preferred by some, seems to be too casual and miscellaneous in connotation to serve our purpose. The author prefers the term absorption, also used in Buddhist circles, as indicative of the true nature of the jhanic state. We shall then use either "Jhana" or "jhanic absorptions" or simply "absorptions" from this point on.

We may here note a further characteristic of the Jhana—and this applies to all meditative states in general. The Jhana as the rule is not continuous over a long period of time. To attain the level of the Fourth Jhana, let us say, does not mean to live in that state of awareness (or unawareness) continuously from that point on, but only that one can rise to it at will for a predetermined length of time. He narrows his attention progressively (by methods to be discussed later) until it is one-pointed and completely concentrated. Then, by a kind of shift of mental gears, he enters the jhanic absorption in which he is completely cut off from the world of sense stimulation and ordinary thinking. As he becomes more adept he enters a given state of consciousness, or absorption, at will and for as long as he desires—within limits. But it is not considered desirable (and perhaps not possible) to remain in such states indefinitely. The top-limit in Buddhist tradition is that of the *nirodha-samapatti* condition (that state which is qualitatively nearest actual Nibbana itself) which may be maintained for seven days, after which one must return to normal consciousness to maintain his physical life. But though the state itself passes, he who has once attained a certain level of absorption has permanently advanced to that level of spiritual development which it represents and will be reborn in the corresponding plane of existence.

And what is the nature of the Jhanic consciousness? The Pali scriptures contain an often repeated formula that describes progression up through the four Jhanic Absorptions thus:

Then that Bhikkhu [monk] will be devoid of sensuous pleasures and evil thoughts and abide in the first Jhana which is accompanied by Thought-Conception and Discursive Thinking, is born of Detac h ment, and filled with Rapture and Joy. . . .
Then the Bhikkhu, after calming down and putting away Thought-Conception, and Discursive Thinking, which is Noble and gives one-pointedness of mind, abides in the second Jhana, which is free from Thought Conception and Discursive Thinking born of Concentration, and accompanied by Rapture and Joy. . . .
Then the Bhikkhu, after the fading away of Rapture dwells in equanimity, is mindful and of clear comprehension, and experiences in his person that sense of pleasure which the Noble Ones talk of when they say: "Happy lives the man of equanimity and attentive mind." Thus the Bhikkhu abides in the third Jhana.
Then the Bhikkhu, after giving up pleasure and pain, and through the disappearance of the previous happiness and sadness which he had, enters into a state beyond pleasure and pain, into the fourth Jhana, a state of pure mindfulness brought about by equanimity.[1]

After each of the above passages there is a further formula varying slightly for each of the Jhanas, which goes thus:

---

[1] *Samannaphala Sutta.* Union of Burma Sasana Council edition. This is Sutta or Discourse II in the *Dialogues of the Buddha (Dhīga-Nikāya)*, part I, Vol. II, SBB.

*And his body does he so pervade, drench, penetrate, and suffuse with
("Rapture and Joy born of Detachment" in the First Jhana;
"Rapture and Joy born of Concentration," Second Jhana; "sense
of pleasure, rapture being absent," Third Jhana; "sense of purification of mind, of clarity, of mind," Fourth Jhana) . . . so that there
is no spot in his body not suffused therewith.*

Thus it appears that as one progresses upward through
successive Jhanic Absorptions the emotional accompaniments
become more and more diluted until the Fourth Jhanic
Absorption contains only clearness of mind.[1] This is the key
also for the understanding of the so-called Immaterial Absorptions, which are really further refinements of the Fourth (or
Fifth) Jhanic Absorption. For in these latter there still remain
equanimity and concentration as essential factors, but the
content of consciousness is so refined that not only are all
emotional accompaniments completely lacking but even the
object of attention almost completely disappears. Thus they
are named, in terms of their centre of attention and quality
of awareness,

The Sphere of Infinity of Space;

,,   ,,   ,,   ,,   ,, Consciousness;

,,   ,,   ,, Nothingness;

,,   ,,   ,, Neither Perception nor Non-Perception.

Such, then, is the quality of the Jhanic Absorptions. They
represent the refinement and intensification of the power of
mind concentration (Samadhi) to its ultimate degree in the
highest of the absorptions. With regard to any or all of them
it must be always taken for granted (1) that while the meditator is in such a state of one-pointed concentration, he is
totally unaware of any sense stimuli from without, and (2)

[1] Buddhist tradition has worked this out very carefully. When one enters the
First Jhana it is said that he is free from Sensuous Desire, Ill-Will, Torpor and
Langor, Restlessness and Scruples, Doubts. Present are the following constituent
factors at each stage:

First Jhana: Thought-Conception, Discursive Thinking, Joy, Rapture,
                and Concentration;

Second Jhana: Rapture, Joy and Concentration;

Third Jhana: Joy and Concentration;

Fourth Jhana: Equanimity and Concentration.

In the Abhidhamma and in Burmese Buddhism these are divided into Five
Jhanas, by eliminating only Thought-Conception in going from the First to the
Second Jhana. From this point on the 3rd, 4th, and 5th stages of the Five-fold
rendering correspond to the 2nd, 3rd and 4th stages of the Four-fold.

N

that he can control the length of time he is to spend in the absorption by a previous act of will. This is what distinguishes the Jhanic Absorption from hypnotism, according to Buddhist opinion.

2. *The Route of Bare Essentials (or Dry-Visioned Sainthood)*

There is one inherent limitation or lack in the path of jhanic absorptions, however, and it is crucial. *Jhanic Absorptions by themselves do not lead to Nibbana* (see diagram). Indeed, as we shall note at a later point, they may actually be an obstacle. But in any case this route by itself leads to a dead-end. For Jhanic Absorptions are still only in the Samadhi or mental-concentration stage of development; and no one achieves arahatship and final Nibbana until he passes on into the third stage of Paññā or wisdom-insight. This latter alone can liberate the meditator from those fetters, or purify him from those impurities, that entail his re-embodiment in a new existence which is subject to birth-death again.

We may put it in another way. No matter how far a person may develop his Samadhic powers, he is still mentally impure and is attached in one way or another—emotionally or intellectually—to various states of being. He has some craving either gross or more subtle, for continued existence in this or that condition. So long as this and other attachments remain in any degree whatsoever, the meditator cannot achieve arahatship or liberation. Therefore another discipline or type of meditation must be added. And this is known by the name of Vipassana-meditation. Vipassana (Pali *Vipassanā*) means according to the *Buddhist Dictionary*

> *Insight (which) is the intuitive light flashing forth and exposing the truth of the impermanency, misery, and impersonality of all corporeal and mental phenomena of existence.*[1]

[1] Nyanatiloka, 1956, p. 177.

It may be further noted (see p. 18 of *Dictionary*) that the degrees of sainthood are carefully defined in terms of specific "fetters" which are destroyed. Thus:

(1) *Sotapanna* (Stream-winner) is free from personality-belief, sceptical doubt, and attachment to rule and ritual. He will be reborn at most, seven more times, but never in the nether planes.

(2) *Sakadagamin* (Once-Returner) is more nearly free from Sensuous Craving and Ill-will than in the previous stage. He has only one more birth between him and Nibbana.

Vipassana is therefore a special type of "insight-wisdom" (also the meaning of the more general and inclusive Paññā) specifically directed toward the cutting of all the fetters that bind one to continuing existence. By means of successful Vipassana meditation, often exercised with his own body and mind as subjects, the meditator becomes directly and personally aware of those three great characteristics of all existent phenomena: impermanence, suffering, and insubstantiality. Since it is this awareness alone that destroys the meditator's attachment to existence, whether in gross or subtle form, and readies him for Nibbana ultimately, *so it is also that type of meditation which alone produces this liberating awareness,* i.e. *Vipassana meditation, that is absolutely essential.*

Thus even though the meditator may cultivate the Jhanic Absorptions, he cannot bypass Vipassana meditation if he desires to achieve that nibbanic peace which is born of detachment. Samadhic powers of meditative concentration (and this includes all nine Absorptions), are only incidentally and instrumentally helpful here. If bad past kamma which binds one to existence is to be "burned up" rather than being endured in full-fruited form in some future existence, it is thus that it is done, and only thus. In fact even the Jhanic Absorptions themselves must be made the subject of that same negative consideration in Vipassana meditation that has already been directed toward one's own body-mind. For this is the Buddhist teaching:

> *In order to develop Tranquillity and Insight . . . one first enters into the first absorption. Then after rising from it one regards its contents (feeling, perception, etc.) as impermanent, miserable, etc., and thus one develops Insight.*[1]

The method by which the Jhanic Absorptions are made the subject of Vipassana-type meditation is roughly this: one

(3) *Anāgamin* (Non-Returner) is completely free from all the above five fetters. If he dies at this level, he will be reborn in the Immaterial Spheres and pass thence to Nibbana.

(4) *Arahat* has freed himself from all the lower fetters (above) as well as the five higher fetters, namely craving for existence in both the Fine-Material Spheres and Immaterial Spheres, and also from Conceit, Restlessness, and Ignorance. He will enter Nibbana straightway upon death.

[1] *Buddhist Dictionary*, p. 144. Cf. author's discussion on "burning up" bad Kamma in his *In the Hope of Nibbana.*

"rises up from" the Jhanic Absorption, i.e. he breaks it off, and returns to normal consciousness. Then he ascends to neighbourhood concentration and from thence goes into the Vipassana-type meditation, using as theme the feelings, the recollections, the sense of delight and joy which he had during those Absorptions. With regard to them also, as with his ordinary body-mind states he realizes: These, too, are impermanent, are barely disguised forms of suffering; there is no true reality in them. And thus considering them the meditator avoids being ensnared by their delights and escapes the danger of mistaking them for Nibbana itself, that is for Nibbana-in-this-life and the assurance of full Nibbana to come.

There is one notable fact about Vipassana meditation which must not escape our attention: It requires a relatively minimum degree of meditational skill. One can enter into it from the relatively modest level of neighbourhood concentration. For the higher degrees of psychic skill it substitutes a different type of discipline. (See below.) And this has a considerable appeal today, especially for the would-be lay meditator who may look upon the higher jhanic attainments as beyond him, or as requiring a kind of leisure-time he does not have. He raises the very natural question: Why cultivate the Jhanic Absorptions at all, since the essential business of Nibbana-faring is done in Vipassana meditation? Why not enter this directly, rather than indirectly? Therefore we must next turn to the question of the relation of the two routes to each other.

3. *Relation of the Two Ways of Each Other*

The actual relation of these two ways to each other is complex. If we consider the classical tradition, the standard way to Nibbana appears to be along the route of Jhanic Absorptions. (Or if one chooses he might say that it follows the Double Route of the continuous interrelation of Jhanic Absorptions and Vipassana meditation.) If the shorter or Vipassana route is mentioned at all, it is in terms of the "dry-visioned" saint, i.e., an arahat who knows nothing of the splendour and glory of the Absorptions. While its possibility is recognized, there is always the connotation of inferiority about it—somewhat as a first-class traveller looks upon the third or tourist class traveller. One modern writer, Bhikshu Sangharakohita in his chapter in *Presence du Bouddhisme*, even calls it a-typical.

Be this as it may, one must say that in contemporary Burmese Buddhism the Direct or Vipassana Route has become the preferred or typical one. Its practice has not altogether displaced the other way, but Vipassana is definitely the most prestigious method at the moment. The history of this development, and something of its rationale, are stated in *The Heart of Buddhist Meditation* in these words:

> *As far as the writer's knowledge goes, it was only at the beginning of this century, in Burma, that the Way of Mindfulness, in its singular features, has been sharply outlined again, and practised accordingly. At that time, a Burma monk, U Narada by name, bent on actual realization of the teachings he had learnt, was eagerly searching for a system offering a direct access to the Highest Goal, without encumberance by accessories. Wandering through the country, he met a monk who was reputed to have entered upon those lofty Paths of Sanctitude (ariya-magga) where final achievement of Liberation is assured. When the Venerable U Narada put his question to him, he was asked in return: "Why are you searching outside the Master's word? Has not the Only Way, Satipatthana, been proclaimed by Him?"*
>
> *U Narada took up this indication. . . . The results achieved in his own practice convinced him that he had found what he was searching for: a clear-cut and effective method of training the mind for highest realization.*[1]

Thus began the search for a clear-cut method of direct access to nibbanic peace in this life and Nibbana itself beyond, out of which have grown the present meditational emphases in Burmese Buddhism. The implications of this search, as stated above, are obvious: (1) The way to Nibbana had become obscured somewhat in the long centuries since the Buddha's time, so that few were finding it; (2) there must be in the Buddhist tradition such a simple and direct way. Thus it was a kind of "protestant" searching for primitive simplicity beneath the later accretions of an age-old traditionalized prac-

---

[1] Nyanaponika Thera, a German convert to Buddhism who lives in Ceylon. Published by Buddha Publishing Committee, Colombo, 1953, pp. 8–9. See Sutta No. 22 of the Dhīga-Nikāya *(Dialogues of the Buddha,* and Chapter III, Book III, Vol. V in *Kindred Sayings (Mahā-Vagga Sutta of Samyutta-Nikāya)),* 1956, PTS. edition, for scriptural sources.

tice. And the response, again "protestant" in nature, was completely orthodox: Look in your own scriptures. The result was a new practical experiential emphasis upon a standard scripture well known to all Theravadins. It is a scripture which emphasizes the meditational method of body-mindfulness, breath-mindfulness in particular, as the clearest, simplest, most direct means of achieving liberating detachment. For here within a man himself are the materials for such liberation; using his own body processes and awareness as meditational subjects he may find therein, directly and immediately at hand, the materials for his own salvation.

The appeal of new emphasis—or *re*newed emphasis as U Narada would undoubtedly have insisted—was wide. For one thing it appealed to the layman. For the laity in any religious faith are always dubious about the complications by which the clergy hedge about the path to salvation. Therefore when the ancient way to Nibbana was thus taken out of its traditional context of monkish elaborations, monkish leisure to practice it, and monkish exclusion of the layman from the Higher Way, the layman rejoiced and hastened to appropriate to himself the new opportunity. It was not precisely that the layman had been excluded categorically from such meditation, for the scriptures record some instances of lay arahatship, but that during the years since, he had been made to feel unwelcome therein. Perhaps even the monks themselves had become lost in the complexities of their own tradition! At any rate here was a new door opened to the laymen, or an old door more widely opened. Though they might not become *arahats* in the lay life, perhaps some of the lower levels of saintly attainment might be theirs. And in this new status they would no longer be accounted worthy of striving only for better rebirths.[1] Thus it is that in Burma today there are many laymen who are zealously and hopefully taking up meditation under some form of the direct way. And there is more than a suspicion abroad among them that many monks are dilly-dallying along the way, either through sloth or ignorance.

[1] An interesting contemporary illustration of this: In the *Light of the Buddha*, Vol. I, No. 1, April, 1956, a layman writes an article entitled "My Idea of a Sotapanna", and notes in the course of it that a hundred years ago he would have had his tongue cut out for having suggested the possibility of such an attainment by a layman.

But it would not be quite correct to suggest that we have here mainly or only a Layman's Revolt. For be it noted it was a monk who sought the new simplicity of method. And there is something of his concern that still stirs among the monks today. For is it not recorded in the scriptures that in the days of Gotama Buddha there were many thousands who attained to the higher stages of sainthood? What then is lacking today—even though the world may be worsening and perhaps the level of experience declining (see 99 p.p. above)? Therefore monks too have welcomed this re-discovery of a more efficacious method of meditation.

This desire to make faster progress toward Nibbana is enhanced—though I cannot judge how importantly—by an element in the Buddhist cosmological tradition to which we have referred in a previous chapter. This is the prophecy by the Buddha that his teaching would disappear from this world-epoch within 5000 years. Almost as avidly as Christians of the millennialist persuasion, some Buddhists therefore examine such scriptures and speculate as to the precise chronology of such a disappearance. Are there now only 2500 years left before such catastrophic darkness descends upon the earth, and the hope of salvation is lost to any but Pacceka-Buddhas? If so it behoves the earnest seeker to make more strenuous efforts toward his own salvation, for the time grows short and there is (no doubt) much for him to accomplish.

Such then is the attraction of the Direct Route. But if such be its superior values then why should anyone, short of a Buddha, wish to cultivate the Jhanic Absorptions? (A Buddha cannot be a Buddha, a teacher of others, unless he has become adept in all these Absorptions as well. Or so say Burmese Buddhists.) There are several factors to be noted here that may tend to turn many away from the Direct Route. For one thing the Direct Route is more difficult in a very important sense. It may well be that the mastery of the Jhanic Absorptions seem to require the greater skill and effort, at least of a psychic sort. But on the other hand the Vipassana type of meditation, i.e. that meditation seeking to achieve Vipassana, is more demanding spiritually and morally. For Jhanic Absorptions may even bolster the sense of the ego; it is the self that is thus become adept in attaining to psychic powers of super-normal levels, it is the self that is experiencing joy and rapture. But when one directly faces the complete destruction of all ego-sense within him, and turns the dissolving acids of Vipassana loose upon even his most cherished inward experiences—how much more demanding! How much more sincere, how much more detached must be that meditator who undertakes this more direct but more severe self-discipline! Indeed it is the more severe because it is the more direct and the more simple. And there are many even today who shy away from the most direct versions of the Direct Way because of their difficulty.

But the attraction of the Indirect Route through the Jhanic Absorptions is not merely negative. There are positive elements as well. There is the intrinsically delightful quantity of the Jhanic Absorption itself. Dr Malalasekara has thus described it:

> *They [the absorptions] constitute the first taste of the happiness of Nibbana. It is the joy of having found a possibility of escape from the round of rebirth, suffering and death. The increase of this joy becomes sheer delight, which then gives place to a serene tranquillity, and then to a sense of security and equilibrium, the bliss of well-being (sukha), which is the very opposite of insecurity and unbalanced striving. In that state of tranquillity, not disturbed by likes and dislikes, not made turbid by passions, not hazed by ignorance, like sunlight that penetrates a placid lake of clear water, there arises the supreme insight (paññā).*[1]

In this description, along classical lines, the jhanic states are considered normative and spiritually desirable in that they give the meditator a foretaste of Nibbanic peace itself. It is such occasional and perhaps even fleeting experiences that, as with Christian's glimpses of the Holy City in *Pilgrim's Progress*, encourage the spiritual pilgrim to press on to that glorious goal which he has been told lies at the end of his arduous journey.

Further, it may be said, there are desirable by-products flowing from the Absorptions. They lift one above time-space relativities and concerns, to timeless peace. Thus it is that the

[1] Chapter on Theravada Buddhism in *Philosophy East-West*, University of Hawaii, 1951, p. 194.

meditator returns to his ordinary level of life both spiritually and physically refreshed. Likewise one thus gains a sense of mastery over his spiritual resources, a quality of maturity of depth and control in his spiritual attainments. As he becomes adept in the matter of the Absorptions, he becomes more and more masterful in the manipulation of his own body-mind states and may even achieve those Higher Psychic Powers promised to the saints—though these are not much emphasized in today's world of decadent spiritual powers. And, for that matter, there is no actual antagonism between the two ways to Nibbana. Progress along the route of absorptions does not necessarily hinder progress in the needful Vipassana discipline; it is only that it must be subjected to the latter discipline also. Indeed that state known as *Nirodha-Samāpatti* is open only to those who have followed the Double Discipline of both paths.[1]

There is one further consideration that is of some importance in the Theravada structure of belief and tells heavily in favour of cultivating the Jhanic Absorptions. This is the direct correlation between the attainment of psychic powers and rebirth in to the higher worlds. That is, the attainment of proficiency in a given type of Jhanic Absorption admits the meditator upon death into a corresponding plane of existence. (See Chapter III, and diagram on Meditation.) He may not have become even a sotapanna as yet, let alone an arahat; but his cultivation of psychic powers will admit him to one of the higher planes upon rebirth. And when he finally descends again from one of these to the human plane, most frequently his new human existence will be more pleasant and fortunate than his former human embodiment. And even though some of the jhanic progress may not have been fully converted into nibbanic progress, nonetheless it is commonly held that even

[1] This is the nearest to Nibbana that one may come in this life. This is a stage (see *Buddhist Dictionary*, p. 101) in which "bodily, verbal, and mental functions have been suspended and come to a standstill, but life is not exhausted, the vital heat not extinguished, and the faculties not destroyed." To all outward appearances the meditator in this state is dead. It may last 7 or 8 days. What the attractiveness of this state consists in is not clear; presumably it is its similarity to Nibbana. In any case only one who has mastered the total number of absorptions and also become an arahat or anagamin can "enjoy" this state. It is not within the power of the dry-visioned saint, even though he can and does go on to Nibbana itself.

this better rebirth somehow represents progress along the way to final salvation.[1]

Thus, in the end, the two ways are essentially one, but with differences in emphasis and in heights and depths between them. Of the two, the Direct Route represents the embodiment of the absolutely necessary minimum. The Indirect Route represents a possible enrichment of its meagerness, the joy of the saintly life added to its bare discipline; but it contains both dangers and temptations not found in the shorter way. Perhaps, ideally, the best way is the classical combination of the two ways in which the jhanic powers are cultivated deliberately yet subjected also to the Vipassanic discipline all along the way. The saint who follows this combined pattern would be the full-orbed embodiment of the Buddhist meditational ideal, a man of supremely detached equanimity (Vipassana result) and also a man of supra-mundane psychic powers (jhanic result); and in this combination of attainments he would approach as nearly as possible to the stature of the Buddha.

Meditation Method in General

Having now sketched out the basic theory of meditation we shall turn to a discussion of the actual meditation methods themselves. This in turn can be little more than a sketch because of the wide variety of meditational techniques that various meditation masters use in accordance with Buddhist flexibility in spiritual matters. And, as is well known, there are some forty subjects of meditation recognized in the orthodox tradition. What I shall attempt here will be primarily the discussion of a few of the more general features of all meditational procedures and brief account of one particular method with which I had some slight personal experience.

A basic factor in all Buddhist meditation is the *guru*, or medi-

[1] This "somehow" suggests vagueness about the how of this double progress—which is correct. One is urged to *try* for Nibbana; if he does *not* attain it, he is encouraged to believe that nevertheless his unsuccessful efforts will produce a better rebirth, as a kind of consolation prize. And even this, it is assumed, will bring one somewhat nearer Nibbana—perhaps because the fortunately born have more capacity, hope, and opportunity for spiritual development than the wretched.

tation master. He is considered to be essential for the beginner. To be sure there are now a number of do-it-yourself manuals, especially for the non-Buddhist and foreigner.[1] But even in such manuals it is usually stated that meditation is best done under personal direction. Otherwise the beginner becomes discouraged and loses his way; or, on the other hand, he gets inflated ideas of his own progress, which are as harmful as discouragement.

A basic requirement for the successful guidance of a meditator by his guru is that he place himself completely in the hands of his guide. He may decide to choose another master after a time, but for the period of his meditational practice he must regard his present guru as a patient regards his chosen doctor. He will not question his interpretation of the Buddhist tradition, nor his system of meditational method, nor his diagnosis of the meditator's spiritual condition, nor his prescription for his betterment. This means in practice a non-questioning docility on the part of the meditator that many a Westerner finds it difficult to accept.

Such docility, however, has a deeper significance for the Buddhist than a mere operational harmony between master and pupil. It roots in the Buddhist conception of the proper way to approach truth—by means of realization or practice rather than by conceptual theory. If one has questions about the truth of the basic tradition itself, or the possibility of enlightenment, let him put these aside for the time being and commit himself provisionally to the Way. If he has thought to penetrate to the truth of personal liberation by the power of scholarly learning or intellectual analysis, let him give up his intellectual pride and "become as a little child". Let him now practice under the direction of his master; let him humbly and unquestioningly seek to appropriate the truth in his own person. Questions may follow later—if they still remain after practice; but let the meditator remember that saving truth is absorbed, not analytically known.

But if the disciple is to commit himself completely and confidently into the hands of his master, then that master likewise has a large responsibility toward his disciple. The latter's

[1] For example, *Buddhist Meditation*, G. Constance Lounsberry, Luzac, 1950; *Anapana Sati*, Cassius Pereira, Island Hermitage, Ceylon, 1943.

spiritual progress and ultimate destiny are now in his hands. The guru's basic function is to interpret the meditational tradition and discipline to his disciple, and to mediate them to the latter's personal need so that he may find in them the solution to his own problems and the key to his own spiritual progress—which key must be put into his own hands for self-direction when he has reached his teacher's level.[1]

Not only does the guru undertake to provide proper guidance in meditative techniques; he undertakes to control any psychical disturbance that the meditational discipline may produce. Whatever he may get his disciple into, he must be able to get him out of. If he cannot, then he is an incompetent.[2] In the East, where spirit-possession is still a very real category of experience—as real as it was to the people of the New Testament world—this power may be interpreted as the casting out of evil spirits and protection of the victim from their power. The guru must be able to radiate such a force of beneficent power that it fully overcomes and banishes the evil influences. For here, too, as in the New Testament, such spirits often depart only after a painful crisis experience.[3]

It may be noted that the meditation-master in Burma is traditionally a monk. For the meditation discipline is his ancient heritage; he is presumed to be the most constant and adept meditator in the Buddhist world. Yet, as we have seen, the mere tradition of meditation is not sufficient to produce the master, but only the personal practice of the discipline.

[1] It should be observed that for some time a beginning meditator is not able to judge his own progress. He must take the word of his guru as to the progress which he is making.

[2] This represents something of a problem at the present time in Burma, where there are so many meditation centres. Some meditators become so disturbed that they must be taken to mental treatment centres, or so I was told—this probably because some are guiding meditation who cannot control its products. How frequent or widespread this phenomenon is, I cannot say.

[3] For example: In one case a meditator was possessed of a "dragon spirit", though this was not at first evident. But during one period of meditation the meditator began to vomit, became convulsed, frothed at the mouth and, without use of hands, he wriggled forward on his belly toward the guru. Coming at last to rest his head against the guru, he fell asleep; when he woke after an hour he asked for water and after drinking it was completely recovered. Another instance was that of a meditator of Chinese heritage who was periodically taken with spasmodic tremblings of a violent and prolonged nature. He was cured when his guru cast out the "devil-god" that possessed him, which the meditator "saw" when it departed from him.

Therefore there are only a relatively few monks who can actually guide meditators—those who have practised it for many years and themselves attained to some marked spiritual advancement.

A second general prescription for meditational method is the proper posture. The classic Buddhist statement on this matter is as follows:

Monks, under this rule, a monk . . . sits down cross-legged, holding the body straight.[1]

This, of course, is the position made famous by the traditional Buddha images in which the crossed legs are locked firmly into each other as a solid base from which the trunk of the body rises like a straight column. The head too is held straight, or only a little forward-inclined, with the eyes half-closed and the hands resting relaxedly in the lap. While this is the basic position for meditation, the lying, the walking, and the standing positions are also recognized variants.

There is in the background of Buddhist meditational techniques the whole yoga philosophy of physical and mental relationships in which it is maintained that certain types of insight are possible only as a result of certain types of bodily position. The latter may even almost automatically produce the former. However, Buddhism does not take the whole of this philosophy seriously. It inherits the classic positions from Yoga but uses them only as the most practical, and perhaps the best positions in general, for the meditational practice. As such they represent a physical posture that can be maintained (by the Easterner) for long periods of time without change and which offer the minimum of sense-stimulation, and hence distraction, to the meditator.

One other physical requisite for the meditator is a measure of solitude. When the monk wishes to sit cross-legged he also presumably "goes to a forest or the foot of a tree or a lonely place". But since lonely forest glades are not in full supply for every meditator and besides possess some disadvantages, huts, caves, and cells or private rooms may be substituted. The actual physical character of the place indeed makes no essential difference. The main purpose is to enable the meditator to

---

[1] *Samyutta-Nikāya* or *Kindred Sayings*, Vol. V, Book X, Chapter 1.

achieve a non-distractive situation. Presumably the expert may finally be able to maintain his high level of meditative mindfulness even when riding in a car, walking on a street, or sitting in a railway station; but for most some physical seclusion, in which loud noises and intense lights or varied visual stimuli are cut off, is essential. Ideally perhaps a completely sound proof, sight-proof cell might be best—and some of the ancient meditative caves or cells used by monks almost fulfilled this prescription.

We may finally speak of the meditation subject. In this respect there is considerable variety in meditational practice. Here we shall note only the general classification of the traditional forty subjects which are as follows:

(1) The ten kasinas or devices representing form and colour. They are often merely geometric circles, or coloured circles or even holes that are at a stipulated distance from the meditator's eyes and gazed upon until a luminous after-image appears even with the eyes closed. Further practice enables one to produce such an image at will, without dependence upon the physical stimulation, and to "expand" it until it fills the whole consciousness as pure colour, form, or space. These devices are still employed in Burma.

(2) The ten *Ashubas* or meditations on the human corpse in the various stages of its decomposition. These are sometimes called the graveyard or cemetery meditations.

(3) Ten thematic subjects such as the Buddha, the Dhamma, the Order of monks, morality, liberality, the glorious devas, peace, death, and in particular the two on the body and on breathing which have been made the centre of an almost complete meditation system much in vogue today. (See below.)

(4) The four *Divine Abidings* of lovingkindness (*mettā*), compassion (*karuna*), altruistic joy (*mudita*), and equanimity (*upekkha*).

(5) The subjects of "repulsiveness of food" and "analysis of the elements" that constitute all material being.

(6) The Four Formless meditations, corresponding to the four highest absorptions already mentioned. (p. 193 above.)

The general purpose of choosing such subjects or themes of meditation is three-fold: (1) To help the meditator fasten his attention upon some one subject, preferably an emotionally neutral one, so that he learns the art of one-pointedness of mind. This subject may be physical or ideational. (2) To help him "inwardize" his attention by depriving it of all specific outward stimuli. Thus even when external objects are chosen as meditational subjects, they are generalized or expanded eventually to a nearly characterless continuum; (3) To help the meditator overcome his own personal and individualistic weaknesses and to balance his meditative development.

To a large extent the nature of the meditational subject is indifferent provided that it accomplishes its purpose of fastening and controlling the attention. The guru will use his judgment as to which is best suited to the individual meditator. Some traditional lines are of course drawn. Certain types of meditation subjects are considered best fitted for certain temperaments. (See diagram of Meditational Subjects.) Lounsberry suggests (from tradition or personal experience?) that "the Space meditation should be preceded by the meditation on Compassion"; and that the proper preparation for the Absorption of Infinite Consciousness is a meditation upon mudita, or Sympathy with the Joy of Others.[1] It is further opined by the same author that the graveyard meditations are not suited to Westerners in general. In any case there should be no emotional attachment to a particular type of meditative subject or object. When one has served its proper purpose it should be left behind and the meditator should move on to the next stage, never forgetting that the great end-goal of all meditation is that liberating wisdom which is beyond all meditation states or subjects. Indeed, in the higher levels many of the 40 traditional subjects are to be left behind; they are essentially beginner's aids, though they may be of continued use in their more subtle forms.

The Breath- and Body-Mindfulness Method

One of the meditational subjects most highly recommended in the Buddhist scriptures is that of the body—body-awareness or body-mindfulness as we may call the corresponding

[1] Op. cit., pp. 61, 62.

method. Or more accurately it is a body-process-awareness, which is useful at almost all stages of meditative progress. We read thus in the *Samyutta-Nikāya*:

> *Monks, he who would rightly use the words "Ariyan way of life, the best of ways, the Tathagata's way of life" would rightly do so in calling by this name the intent concentration on in-breathing and out-breathing, . . .*
>
> *As for those monks who are learners, who have not won their goal, who dwell aspiring for the unsurpassed security from bondage—for such the intent concentration of in-breathing and out-breathing, if cultivated and made much of, conduces to the destruction of the asavas. Moreover, Monks, for those monks who are arahants [Pali arhat], in whom the asavas are destroyed, who have lived the life, done the task, lifted the burden, won their highest good, worn out the fetters of becoming, who by perfect knowledge have become free—for such also the intent concentration on in-breathing and out-breathing, if cultivated and made much of, conduces both to pleasant living and to mindful composure even in this very life.*[1]

It is difficult to imagine a more comprehensive indorsement of any one meditational subject or method than this. (And many in Burma today look upon its rediscovery, or at least re-emphasis, as of prime importance; perhaps it may be called the Buddha's preferred meditative method!) It is good for both beginner and for Nibbana-ready saint, and all others in between. And indeed in another passage in the same work it seems to be suggested that body-mindfulness—of which breath-mindfulness is one variety—is the only successful meditational method, at least in the beginning. We read:

> *This monks, is the sole way . . . to Nibbana, to wit: The four stations of mindfulness. What are the four?*
>
> *(1) Herein a monk dwells, as regards body, contemplating body (as transient) by having restrained the dejection of the world arising from coveting.*
>
> *(2) He dwells, as regards feelings . . .*   *(repeat refrain.)*
>
> *(3) He dwells, as regards mind . . .*   *„   „*
>
> *(4) He dwells, as regards mind-states . . .*   *„   „   .*[2]

---

[1] *Kindred Sayings*, PTS edition, Vol. V, Book X, Chapter II, section i. *Asavas* is translated cankers, fetters, hindrances, and so on, meaning in general those impurities of mind and disposition which must be destroyed before Nibbana is attainable.

[2] Ibid., Book III, Chapter I, section i (*Mahāvagga* division, *Ambapali* section).

Even this progression to feelings, mind, and mind states is the spiritualized intensification of body awareness, for they are "within" one's own body so to speak.

This method of body-mindfulness, particularly as localized in the breathing rhythm, forms the core of the meditation method used in many of Burma's meditation centres today. And why should it be considered so fruitful, perhaps the best of all methods? Not merely because it has been highly recommended by the Buddha, though that is one reason. It is rather that body-mindfulness methods in general seem to be those best fitted for the most vivid and the most immediate realization of those great liberating truths of anicca, dukkha, and anatta—the impermanence, unsatisfactoriness, and emptiness of all existence and existence states. And as we have noted it is only when one has been completely convinced of these truths, or better yet, experienced them in himself, that he is ready for that serene detachment from all desire which is the essence of nibbanic liberation.

What better place, then, to realize such truths than in one's own being? He may indeed contemplate the passing of civilizations, the rise and fall of universes, the decay of beauty, the death and decomposition of bodies. But where else can he sense all this so vividly and so convincingly as within his own very being? It is in his body-mind that the lusts and appetites and preferences that bind him in love or hate to continued existence are to be found. It is here in his own person that he most intimately and compellingly feels both the desire for continued life and the touch of disease and death. And it is here, if anywhere at all, that the meditator can begin to exercise some measure of that self-control which, when perfected, will finally liberate him from the suffering of birth-death.

The breath-process in particular seems in turn to be the focal centre or heart of the whole body-mind being. Breathing, or the breath-apparatus, seems to represent a cross-roads at which the physical and spiritual (or mental) meet and mingle. Our breath is our life; and at the nostril the "inner" and "outer" worlds of which man is a composite, come together. Therefore the most vital and central part of this our personal being, one which is always with us and tied up directly with our continued existence, is this breathing process itself. What more inevitable or better focus for body-awareness than the breath awareness; and at what point is the breathing process more intimately and sensitively perceptible than at the point where breath enters the body, that is, the nostril and upper-lip area?

It was with a variety of body-mindfulness meditative method that began with fastening the attention on the upper-lip breathing-point that the author's brief experience lay.[1] Or perhaps it would be truer to say that it began in orthodox Buddhist fashion with due attention paid to Sila or morality. Since meditation at this particular centre could be undertaken only after a personal interview and a recommendation by some common friend, it was assured that the would-be meditator was a decently moral man. And at the beginning of the period he pledged himself to observe in complete measure the Five Precepts' prohibition of killing any living being, of lying, of stealing, of drinking intoxicants, and of sexual intercourse of any sort for the duration of the period.

This pledge being taken, and after some preliminary instruction from the guru, the meditator began his private meditations in the cell assigned to him. Seating himself in meditative posture—though some flexibility in this matter was allowed the Westerner—he began by attempting to fasten his complete attention upon the in-breath out-breath rhythm at a point on the upper lip immediately below the nostril. For long periods of time, up to a total of ten hours per day, he concentrated on this and this alone.

The purpose of this has been generally indicated above. It is necessary that a meditator withdraw his attention from external stimuli, or even his own varied thoughts, and achieve one-pointedness of concentration by some means or other. The nose-lip area forms an admirable focus for such concentration. As an immediate part of the meditator himself, it makes other or external devices unnecessary. And because it

---

[1] Only a short summary of this experience is given here since it has been described in detail in an article in the *Journal of Religion*, 41, 1961, entitled *An Experience in Buddhist Meditation*, and in a privately printed pamphlet from the International Meditation Centre at Rangoon added to the book as an appendix. This centre is perhaps unique in that its chief meditation guide or guru, is a layman, U Ba Khin, and that it makes provision for non-Buddhist foreigners.

contains the element of physical sensation, it provides a tangible centre upon which the fledgling meditator may one-point his attention without losing it in a vacuum of meditational abstractness. Still further the sensation-element may be progressively decreased as the meditator progresses, i.e. the breathing may become lighter and lighter.

Sometime during this period of the cultivation of Samadhi, i.e. power of concentrating, the meditator has other sensations. He sees "visions" before his closed eyes, often in the form of lights of various sorts. These are considered to be signs of meditational progress, but are not to be taken too seriously. And if they become distractive, they are to be brushed aside. For the main goal at this stage is the achievement of purity and intensity of concentration, until the breath-lip awareness fills the total consciousness to the exclusion of all other content.

This stage of training lasted until the meditation master was convinced—as a result of several brief reports to him each day by the meditator—that the meditator had achieved a sufficient level of one-pointedness of mind to enable him to turn with some profit to the Vipassana meditation. He was by no means deeply developed in Samadhi; roughly he had attained to the level of Neighbourhood Concentration. (See diagram on Meditative Routes.) But since the essence of Vipassana meditation is not the achievement of the deep trance-state of the Jhanic Absorption but the loosing of the bonds of attachment to self and to selfish life, the meditator was now considered ready to make the transition to the second stage of his training.

In recognition of the basic purpose of Vipassana-type meditation, each meditator affirmed his sincere desire to achieve nibbanic peace within and was then given preliminary directions by the guru for his individual efforts. Such power of attentive concentration as he had attained was now to be turned upon parts of his body other than the lip-breath area. The meditator was told that he would know when his efforts were successful by feeling physical sensations of prickling movement or glowing heat, even to a painful degree, in the body as a whole, or in those particular parts upon which he narrowly concentrated his attention. The specific procedure was to begin with lip-breath awareness and, when concentration there was complete, to shift its focus to some other part of the body, preferably the top of the head, and then extend the area of the resulting burning-prickling sensations to the rest of the body, if he were able.

And what is the significance of such symptoms? It is two-fold. In one context they are considered to be purificatory. The guru—quite in keeping with the Buddhist tradition of the intimate relation of body-mind states—interpreted the burnings as indications of impurities, stresses, disease-producing strain, or perhaps even of evil spirits within the individual. Or better, the burning sensations are the result of the purificatory force of the meditator's concentrated attention encountering these impurities within himself. Probingly he must bring each hard lump of impurity, or sore area of tension, into the focus of his meditative concentration and there burn it up, no matter how painful the sensations become. Gradually he must seek to concentrate attention within the heart-chest area for here is the centre of the human being; here the tensions and impurities have their deepest seat. It is at this stage of meditation that some of the crisis-experiences (see note above) occur. But, whether mild or severe, it is only by the purificatory fire of concentrative meditation that final detachment and liberation will be won.

It is in this connection that the basic themes of impermanence, suffering, and insubstantiality (anicca, dukkha, anatta) are introduced. For they are the great slayers of all conceit, lust, hatred, greed, and attachment to self and life. When these three "concepts" become instead personal "realizations" within the deepest core of one's being, then he is setting his foot solidly and certainly upon the highway to nibbanic Peace. And this, indeed, is precisely the central purpose of Vipassana-type meditation: to bring the great basic (and negative) concepts of impermanence, suffering, and insubstantiality from the realm of mere intellectual idea into the fullness of personally experienced truth-reality. The body-burning sensations serve as direct evidential proof of the reality of these central Buddhist truths—their second significance for the meditator.

To put it in other words: Physical science, says the Buddhist, teaches us that there is no solid matter or substance in anything. All sensible realities are made up of an infinitely rapid flux of atomic combustions, in which constantly changing energy assumes ever new and ever impermanent forms. One such form is the human body-mind being. Therefore when the meditator experiences body-burning he becomes directly aware within himself of this atomic combustive flux *en masse*; he feels its heat in himself and becomes personally and vividly aware that he too is a part of this passing show of empty restlessness. Indeed he must go on from body-burnings to realize the same truths of insubstantiality and impermanence with regard to his feelings, mind-states and own personal consciousness, as well as his body. When this has been done, at least the seed of detachment from existence has been sown within.

This, then, to change the figure, is the key to liberation that meditation places in the hands of the meditator: He may so meditate upon the elements of his life, even of his own being, that he ever increasingly and ever more vividly realizes that all of everything, himself included, is completely impermanent, full of suffering and without true reality. Thus will his attachment to self and self's works be destroyed; thus will the world of sentient experience appear to him as it truly is; thus will a longing for the utter peace of Nibbana grow ever stronger within him. And the energetic and continuing use of meditation will surely bring him to his Goal in the end.

One passing word is needed in concluding this section, Is the goal of meditation purely negative? Does it produce only the emptiness of detachment? This is one facet of the whole question of the relation of positive and negative in Buddhism, discussed in an earlier chapter.[1] Here it may be said only that while there seems to be an increasing negativity of concept as one progresses in meditation, in terms of feeling there is increasing positivity. There arc to be sure those periods of desolation when the new "emptiness" seems to destroy the old feelings and ideas without remainder. But—and this is perhaps a notable feature of the new meditation—there is also a generally increasing peacefulness and balance of mind, and even flashes of intuitive perception of that highest goal, Nib-

[1] See also author's *In the Hope of Nibbana*, Chapter III.

bana itself. As the negation wears away the false positives of sentient life, the True Positive of the Only Real appears in its glory.[1]

Summary Evaluation

How then shall one assess the importance and value of the meditative method? As to its current popularity there can be no doubt. And we have noted some of the reasons for such popularity above: The Buddhist sense of the waning of this Dhamma epoch; the appeal of the new and simplified forms of Bare-Attention and Body-Mindfulness meditation; the conviction that meditation furnishes an empirical verification of essential Buddhist truths as well as differentiating Buddhism completely from other religions; and a desire to appropriate the by-products of meditation, found in tranquillity of mind and health of body. Does this popularity mean that the new vigour of meditational practice represents also a basic revival of Buddhism itself? In the nature of things no confident predictions can be made but we may attempt a few tentative conjectures and observations.

That a genuine revival of genuine meditation practice would mean a revitalizing of Buddhism, there can be no doubt. Theravada Buddhism has tended to a kind of bare scholasticism of dogmatic affirmation and an established ecclesiasticism of formal and exclusive character. Buddhism as an inwardly vital experience has thus been shut away from the rank and file of Buddhists, for the most part. Meditation has been almost the exclusive privilege of the monk in his monastery, and its discipline has been deemed too hard for the layman in general. Thus the multitudes have turned to pagoda and nat worship and the externalities of religious observances as their type of Buddhism in part at least because no other sort was available. Here at least some warmth and tangibility of experience could be found.

---

[1] Technically it is true that only the arahat "sees" Nibbana itself. But practically it is true that those who meditate live in the hope (and sometimes experience) of feeling the Nibbana dhatu (nibbanic element or quality) within their consciousness. And as elsewhere noted, one of the new emphases in contemporary Buddhism is upon the present possibility of achieving some measure of Nibbanic peace at almost every level of experience—or at least its reasonable facsimile.

It cannot be said, of course, that meditation automatically lessens the hold of the pagoda externalities; nor that all the "new" meditators are laymen. But it can be said that vital meditative practice tends to undercut the nat-pagoda type of religious practice; and that if increasing numbers of laymen take up serious and extensive meditational training, so too the spirituality of Buddhism may well run deeper and stronger. And it may be added as a matter of fact, that the present emphasis upon the technically simpler methods of meditation has encouraged laymen to meditate in increasing numbers. And, further, it may here be recalled that at least the International Meditation Centre in Rangoon is completely governed and guided by laymen. Thus increased meditational activity, and hence a much more significant religious role, is characteristic of the contemporary Buddhist layman. One might even say, perhaps extremely, that meditation will be the means of freeing Buddhism from its dominance by the Sangha.

This very popularity of meditation leads to some problems and questions, however. May it not be that Theravada Buddhism, particularly in Burma, expects too much from meditation and is tempted to seek in it a complete panacea for all its ills, religious and moral, individual and social? And in this context of supreme expectation, may not the character of the meditational discipline itself be changed and distorted? Such seem legitimate questions in the light of some of the following factors.

It is often urged, for example, that meditation will provide or substitute for the answers to intellectual questions about Buddhist doctrines. If one finds certain doctrines unbelievable, or raises logical difficulties with regard to them, he is recommended to meditation which it is said will either answer them, i.e. convince him of the truth of Buddhist doctrine, or lift him above interest in such questions. It is in practice that one learns truth; truth is gained by realization, not analysis.

This viewpoint is not unique to Buddhism, though some exponents of the meditational avenue to truth seem to suggest that it is. One remembers the statement attributed to Jesus in John's Gospel (7:17). "If any man will do his [God's] will, he shall know of the doctrine whether it be of God, or whether I speak of myself." Here, too, the doing of truth (in the religious sense of practice) leads to a first-hand conviction of its certainty. Or, one may remember the pattern of the mystery cult: Only the initiate could profess to know anything of the truth of cultic doctrine. Indeed any man of genuine religious faith says at some point or other: "After all arguments are heard and all possible reasonableness of my doctrine demonstrated, there remains one final and ultimate test of its truth. That is its practice." And it may also be that a new type of inter-religious exchange will result in which less attention is paid to doctrinal disagreements and more sympathy is felt for experiential likeness and common denominators. There is some evidence for this in view of considerable numbers of persons of non-Buddhist background who are primarily interested in Buddhist meditation, rather than in Buddhist doctrines.

This means, of course, that some provisional commitment of faith is required for the following up of such a line of proof, even of the truth of the Noble Eight-fold Path. One must tentatively accept the intellectual statement implied by such a way of life at least enough to think that it is worth his while to follow it up by practice. Nor will a completely cold-blooded casual experiment in a "proof process" such as praying or meditation, produce genuine results. One of the requisites for a meditator is "sincerity", i.e. some partial belief that perhaps this way has some truth in it, a half-convincement as it were.

This, of course, raises a problem, as old as religion itself: How can one balance the necessity for making a partial faith-commitment with a completely objective pursuit of the truth? This question cannot be dealt with here except to note its relevance to the claim made for Buddhist meditation: that it is a completely objective, scientific method of certifying the truth of Buddhist doctrine. The best that one can say (as he must say also in corresponding terms with regard to other religious faiths) is that if one is intellectually convinced of the truth of anicca-dukka-anatta previously to meditation, then meditative experience will confirm him more deeply in that faith. It will seem to provide empirical confirmation of those doctrines and will probably also seem to guarantee the truth of all the remaining structure of doctrine and tradition. But also it must be said that this is scarcely the kind of proof that will

convince the unbelieving, or other-believing, who find insuperable difficulties in Buddhist doctrines. Nor, for that
matter, will it solve all the internal intellectual problems
within the Buddhist doctrinal structure; nor will it adapt those
doctrines to the understanding of the contemporary non-
Buddhist world. These matters must be dealt with in their own
appropriate intellectual terms.

This must be emphasized because some Western converts to
Buddhism have hoped to take to the West the meditational
methodology as a purely neutral, non-Buddhistic, non-
religious pattern of mind-culture and thus save the mind, if
not the soul, of the West. All such inter-cultural bridges are of
interest and value. But this particular attempt should cast off
the pretence to neutrality and openly announce its Buddhist
quality. The very method itself assumes a certain view of the
self and the proper goal of its endeavours and development,
and implies distinctive metaphysical views, all of which are
Buddhistic. As such it may well make a contribution to the
religious life of the West. But as a pseudo-neutral technique it
will be sailing under false colours and produce only an
insignificant crop of possibly interesting psychic and physical
by-products.

Another usually implicit, but sometimes explicit, claim is
that meditational discipline will solve all the personal and
social problems in the world. Or, perhaps better, that the
meditating individual will be able to solve all these problems.
He will have a quality of mind-balance, a renewal of energy,
and an ability to concentrate one-pointedly on the business at
hand that will make of him a superior business-man, execu-
tive, government servant, or whatever else he may set his
mind to.[1] Or, to put it in more properly moral and religious
terms: If the individual achieves pureness of mind and detached peace within, then he can and will transmit this
pureness and peace to the world about him. Hence, if everyone would engage in proper meditation, all the problems of
the world would be solved.

No one can deny the measure of truth that there is in such
statements. This, too, is a strand in the belief of every major

[1] For a fuller discussion of the relation of meditation to social problems see
author's *In the Hope of Nibbana*, Chapter VII.

religion: Make the individual man good, and you make the world good. Or, in different form: The only way in which I can be sure to change the world for the better is to change myself for the better. Certainly there is no public integrity without private integrity; the former grows in the soil of the latter. Yet specific social principles, ethical standards, and technical competence have their place too, and no amount of meditational purity will, *ipso facto*, supply them. Indeed such narrowly individualized virtue might even seem to draw a man away from the view that such worldly matters are of prime importance. But in any case the danger seems to be that the modern enthusiast may think to find in the meditation centre the answer to all his nation's problems, and dangerously undervalue the other factors in social progress.

There is finally the question as to whether meditation-practice may not come to be chiefly valued in terms of its by-products. They are many. There are the direct major physical healings which meditation seems to produce in some cases,[1] and such related but minor advantages as overcoming sea-sickness by meditational techniques. There are also the indirect benefits of the balanced mind, the emotional equanimity, and the power of one-pointed concentration, that are believed to be transferable to any materials whatsoever. Many are seeking these benefits today, particularly in a time when Buddhism is trying to prove to itself and the world at large that it has a gospel for the mundane as well as the super-mundane realms, and to throw off the onus of other-worldly pessimism. Even the government seems convinced of the practical utility of meditation, since it supports meditation centres, grants leave for meditation purposes in some cases, and utilizes the services of notable meditators for teaching its personnel.

Whether this will corrupt the basic Buddhist character of meditation in the end, remains to be seen. Certainly the danger is there. For valuable as the by-products may be, and much as

[1] At the International Centre I met one individual who had been cured of a heart-condition of near-fatal proportions some five years before. Both diagnosis and cure were backed up by competent medical testimony. There were other individuals who reported the cure of migraine headaches, acute nervous and digestive disorders, asthma, and one case of an external cancerous growth. This is quite in line with the Buddhist psychosomatic belief that mind states produce like body-states.

they may indicate some quality of experiential validity in meditational discipline, the cultivation of meditation for the sake of its by-products is to distort its basic purpose and ultimately to destroy its value. Buddhist meditation is classically conceived to be a total religious discipline of the person, partially for the achievement of detachment, serenity, and benevolence of spirit in this life, but primarily for the ultimate attainment of release from this life in Nibbana. Such side effects as there may be are mere incidentals. And this would still seem to be its proper and religious mission. But when and if it comes to be valued only for its practical benefits, then it will have become only a species of mentalistic gadgetry, attractive to the Westerner (or Easterner for that matter) who wishes to cure his ulcers and get a better job, but who has no real interest in his own spiritual salvation.

MEDITATION SUBJECTS

Type of Person (to whom suited)	Subject and Themes	Absorptions (Jhānas) Attainable by respective type of meditation
I		
Devotional	Buddha, Dhamma, Sangha, Sila, Benevolence, Devas	Neighbourhood Concentration
Intellectual	Calmness or Peace, Death	,,
Passionate or Sensual	Body Constituents	,,
Dull and Unstable	Respiration	,,
II		
Intellectual	Repulsiveness of Food, Analysis of Four Material Elements	,,
III		
Passionate or Sensual	Corpse or Cemetery Meditations	1st Absorption
IV		
Angry (Choleric or irritable)	Illimitables (Metta, Karuna, Mudita, and Upekkha)	1st Four Absorptions
V		
	Kasinas	
All types	1. Earth, air, fire, water	All Absorptions
All types	2. Hole or gap, and light	,,
Angry type	3. White, yellow, red, blue	,,
VI		
All types after they reach Fifth Absorption level	*Formless (arūpa) objects* Infinity of Space, Infinity of Consciousness, Nothingness, Neither Perception nor Non-Perception	Four highest (formless) Absorptions

Note: These subjects are presumably psychologically fitted to each type. Thus meditation on a corpse cools the fever of lust and sensuality; breath-concentration gives both the unstable and dull (opposite types) training in attention; meditation on death takes away the speculative, imaginative fear of it; etc.

Explanatory Notes on
THE MEDITATIONAL ROUTES TO NIBBANA

1. *Nirodha-Samāpatti* (attainment of extinction) represents the near maximum possible degree of the suspension of ordinary mental-physical activity; it is a state of trance, death-like in appearance. It is possible only for those who have mastered the absorptions. It may be returned from to ordinary consciousness, must be subjected to *Vipassanā* "analysis", and does not *per se* conduce to the attainment of Nibbana. Also possible only to arahats.

2. *Arahatship*, or Nibbanic peace-in-this life, is the final state or le vel o spiritual attainment from which one "enters" Nibbana directly upon the death of the present physical organism. It is attainable by either route.

3. The series numbers B-1, B-2, etc. indicate only that the thus numbered states belong to the *Samādhi* (or B) level of attainment.

4. The *Samādhi* level is that of proficiency in mental concentration, or one-pointedness of mind. Its value is primarily instrumental, as preparing one for the kind of mental discipline necessary to the achievement of all *Paññā*-level attainments. *Paññā* is usually translated as "wisdom" or "insight".

5. All *Samādhi* states are temporary, though their length may be controlled by the meditator. From them one returns to ordinary consciousness. Their memory (or possibly content?) must submitted to the *Vipassanā*-type meditative discipline which is defined as "intuitive light flashing forth and exposing the truth of the impermanence, misery, and impersonality of all corporeal and mental phenomena of existence". (*Buddhist Dictionary*, Nyanatiloka, p. 177.) Only by realizing that even such pleasant and illuminated states of consciousness are *not* Nibbanic attainment, can one finally arrive at true Nibbana (or arahatship).

6. The *Sīla* level of living includes the observation of the Five Precepts and the cultivation of moral character. Genuinely good moral character is both pre-requisite and continuing basis for all further meditative attainments. The meditator continues to be a moral individual but devotes his meditative attention to super- or other-than-moralistic states of mind.

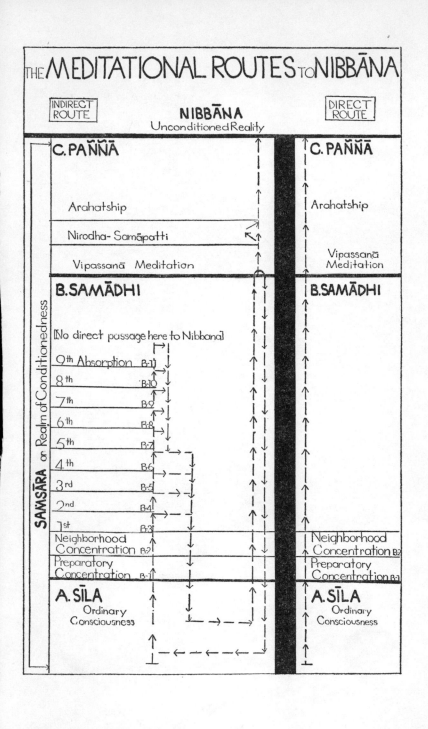

THE MEDITATIONAL ROUTES TO NIBBĀNA

INDIRECT ROUTE

NIBBĀNA
Unconditioned Reality

DIRECT ROUTE

C. PAÑÑĀ

Arahatship

Nirodha- Samāpatti

Vipassanā Meditation

B. SAMĀDHI

[No direct passage here to Nibbana]

9th Absorption B-11
8th B-10
7th B-9
6th B-8
5th B-7
4th B-6
3rd B-5
2nd B-4
1st B-3
Neighborhood Concentration B-2
Preparatory Concentration B-1

A. SĪLA
Ordinary Consciousness

SAMSĀRA or Realm of Conditionedness

C. PAÑÑĀ

Arahatship

Vipassanā Meditation

B. SAMĀDHI

Neighborhood Concentration B-2
Preparatory Concentration B-1

A. SĪLA
Ordinary Consciousness

APPENDIX

AN EXPERIENCE IN BUDDHIST MEDITATION

IF THERE is any one phrase that a foreigner studying Buddhism in Burma hears more than another it is: "But you can't understand Buddhism without *practicing* it." This does not quite mean that one must become a Buddhist to understand anything about Buddhism; or exactly that if one practices Buddhist moral virtues in his daily life, he will know whereof he speaks. "Practice" means the practice of meditation, which is held both to be the central discipline of the true Buddhist path and to provide the supreme, firsthand proof of the truth of Buddhism.

I

There are some two or three hundred meditation centers in Burma at the present to which layman or monk may resort—many of them government supported. Most of them are conducted by monks, since meditation is their professional calling, but a very few are run by laymen. Of these the International Meditation Center in a Rangoon suburb is the outstanding one. It is conducted by U Ba Khin, Accountant General of Burma, retired. Here a ten-day course in Buddhist meditation is held each month, with special regard to the foreigner. So here it was that my wife and I came for our experience in meditation.

The present center was built in 1952, though the *Gurugyi* (goo-roo-jee), or head teacher, U Ba Khin, had been using a room in his governmental office for such purposes for some years before. It is a pagoda-like structure about 30 feet high, built on a little knoll in Golden Valley. The exterior is octagonal at the base, with a double door leading from each of the eight surfaces into a meditation cell which is in the shape of a truncated triangle, wide end out, small end in, radial to the central and circular shrine room. The base of the triangle is about 9 feet, the sides about 7 feet, and the truncated tip about 3 feet or just wide enough for a single door into the shrine room. This latter is a step up from the cell (or cave) floor and is about 12 feet in diameter. (One of the 8 cells is occupied by a small Buddha image; another serves as entrance for the Gurugyi to the shrine room.) At a lower level on the hillside, but concentric to the dome, is an arc of 17 additional cells soon to be connected with the shrine room by a telecommunications system.

The purpose of this arrangement is obvious. The shrine room is the headquarters of the Gurugyi. Here he may sit and meditate in silent fellowship with those in the adjoining cells, be available to them in case of need for counsel, and look in on them through the adjoining doors at his discretion. My wife and I were each favored with a private meditation cell, though there were two meditators in some of the others. Even thus, privacy in the Western sense was not complete, since the sound of coughs, sneezes, and body movements, as well as the Gurugyi's counseling, carried into all the other cells through the shrineroom doors. However, in time, one learned to disregard most of this.

The sole purpose of the center is "promoting the practice of Buddhist Meditation according to the teachings of the Lord Buddha." It is open to any "who are really anxious to experience the Nibbanic Peace Within." Though Buddhist in teaching and conception, no effort is made to coerce the non-religious or other religious into a Buddhist profession. As a mark of its tolerance, the Jew or Christian may say "Amen," the Moslem *"Alm,"* and the Hindu *"Aum"* to the in-breath, out-breath rhythm of the *samādhi* practice.

There has been criticism of the center, particularly by the monks and the more conservative laity. This is in part because a layman presumes to "give the *Dhamma*," or Buddha-teaching, to disciples. It is also in part because of the seeming promise of quick results in spiritual attainment implicit in the ten-day course. It is true that in some of the literature emanating from the center there *are* suggestions that some candidates are encouraged to believe that they have reached a *Sotāpanna* or Stream-Winner stage, i.e., a stage of advancement from which they can never be reborn on the lower-than-human planes of existence. Yet in our time there, after we were assured that we had reached sufficient one-pointedness of attention (*samādhi*) to go on to a higher stage of meditation, no further claims were made as to our specific attainments. It was indicated that we had made only a beginning in the true method of meditation which, if continued and perfected, would bring us to Nibbanic peace.

The Gurugyi believes that many Buddhists (monks and laity alike) are dawdling along at the business of gaining *Nibbāna*. Through ignorance of true meditative methodology or because of sloth, they are making slow progress. Hence with typical lay impatience at traditional doctrinal complexities, he proposes to cut the Gordian knot and pierce through to Nibbanic peace, even here and now, by the fastest method possible. Though there are forty traditional meditation subjects in Buddhism, and many methods in Burma, U Ba Khin believes that immediate intensive concentration on breath-flow at the upper lip is the key to the most rapid attainment of the necessary one-pointedness of mind. At least two honored sayadaws (senior monks) after hearing his version of "giving the *Dhamma*" and feeling his vibrations, i.e., his spiritual quality, have given him their blessing.

The center and its work are entirely supported by voluntary contributions. No campaign is made for its support, though the Gurugyi is always willing to speak with enthusiasm of the work he carries on; and, quite unusual in Burmese Buddhism, no public credit is ever given in any way for gifts, except a business-like receipt to the individual donor. There is a devoted following of those who have experienced the benefits of meditation at the center, both physical and psychic; among them are many prominent Burmese and not a few foreigners.

II

The center is actually the projection of the personal life and faith of its founder, U Ba Khin, who is its director and Gurugyi also. He is now a vigorous man, just over sixty, who in addition to the center work—where he spends all his out-of-office hours during the courses—holds two major government responsibilities.

By any standards, U Ba Khin is a remarkable man. A man of limited education and orphaned at an early age, yet he worked his way up to the Accountant-Generalship. He is the father of a family of eight. As a person, he is a fascinating combination of worldly wisdom and ingenuousness, inner quiet and outward good humor, efficiency and gentleness, relaxedness and full self-control. The sacred and the comic are not mutually exclusive in his version of Buddhism; and hearing him relate the canonical Buddha stories, with contemporary asides and frequent salvoes of throaty "heh, heh, heh's," is a memorable experience.

The program of the center grew out of his own personal experience of inner peace and physical healing gained through meditation. Some fourteen years ago he was afflicted with a cancerous growth on the bone and in the flesh immediately below his right eye. In the course of some years of meditational discipline, sandwiched in between his working hours, he cured himself completely. To him the moral was obvious: a calm, pure spirit produces a healthy body and furthers efficiency in one's work. Because of his ability to achieve both detachment and one-pointed attention, he believes that his intuitional and productive powers are so increased that he functions far more effectively as a government servant than most men. Whether he is a kind of genius who makes his "system" work or whether he represents an important new type in Burmese Buddhism—the lay teacher who combines meditation and active work in a successful synthesis—is not yet clear in my mind.

III

The daily schedule at the center is intended to produce the maximum amount of profitable meditation. To this end it is strenuous but flexible, designed like a revival meeting to achieve a spiritual crisis and break-through in those who are ready for it. The pattern is as follows:

Meditation	4:30– 6:30 A.M.
Rest and breakfast	6:30– 7:30 A.M.
Meditation	7:30–10:30 A.M.
Rest and lunch	10:30 A.M.–12:30 P.M.
Meditation	12:30– 5:00 P.M.
Rest	5:00– 6:00 P.M.
Talk by Gurugyi	6:00– 7:00 P.M.
Meditation	7:00– 9:00 P.M.

As Westerners, unused to meditational methods, we were given special consideration, since U Ba Khin believes that actual meditation, not a set pattern for it, is the essential. We each had a separate meditation cave and a private room with bath at opposite ends of the center compound. We ate our meals together in my wife's room, and we were allowed a light meal in the late afternoon, a privilege not given to our Burmese fellow-meditators. Likewise, we could experiment with meditational postures till we found those that allowed the maximum amount of comfort compatible with meditation. I finally settled on three alternative methods: (1) seated flat on a cushion, back against the wall, legs out straight in front on the floor, slightly separated, and hands in lap; (2) seated in an acute-angle corner, feet together and drawn up near the buttocks, legs (bent) spreading out on either side till they rested against the walls, clasped hands resting on the cushion near the feet; (3) semireclining in a deck (lawn) chair. I tried to keep each position at least half-an-hour at a time.

The whole pattern might be described as concentration without tension. The Western method of attention, said the Gurugyi, is concentration with tension on outward things; the Eastern is inner concentration within a context of relaxation, or as expressed in a canonical text, meditation "with zestful ease." (Hence we were allowed to exercise discretion.) Aching muscles do not necessarily conduce to good meditation; they may indeed distract. If a position becomes intolerable or if his mind becomes dull or the meditator becomes sleepy, he should change position, lie down to rest, sleep a little, or take a walk for five minutes. Only the person himself can hold himself to the meditative process— not a given position or pattern.

We were urged to find the "middle way" of Buddhism between a sharp tight tension of mind and sloth. Gently but firmly, relaxedly but persistently, the meditator must focus his attention on the given subject till outside noises, wandering thoughts, and all other distractions sink into the background and one-pointedness of mind is at one's command.

Three levels of attainment are recognized in Buddhism. *Sīla,* or external morality of the basic sort, is the first. On the first day we were all required to promise observation of the Five Precepts during our stay at the center: no killing of any living beings (mosquito nets and repellents) were allowed; no lying, no stealing; no sexual intercourse; no drinking of intoxicants. In addition, the Burmese meditators ate no afternoon meal and slept on mats rather than beds.

Sīla thus being taken care of, we turned to the next stage called *samādhi,* or concentration. The goal here was to achieve one-pointedness of mind. And our Gurugyi's method—one of the orthodox methods—is to concentrate the attention on the upper lip below the nostrils with only the thought "in-breath, out-breath" allowed. This thought, plus the thread of the physical awareness of breathing, is to be the total content of consciousness. As one pulls a bull with a ring in his nose, so he keeps steadily pulling his attention closer and closer to its object. U Ba Khin thinks that this is the logical point for meditative discipline to begin, where "inner" and "outer" worlds meet; he believes concentration here produces results much faster than the grosser methods.

For three days and a half of meditation time this was our sole occupation: to focus our attention on our breathing at the upper lip just below the nostrils. I found it best to close my eyes to avoid the eye-distraction even of the bare unlighted cave, and I avoided using the deck chair during early morning or night periods lest I sleep. If his attention wanders to the outside noises, other parts of his body, or miscellaneous thoughts, the meditator must turn his attention again and again to the given area. If his attention flags for the moment, he may begin to breathe rather vigorously and rapidly to renew the necessary central thread of physical sensation for anchoring

the attention again. So it was that repeatedly one might hear a fellow meditator, like a little pump, breathing himself back to one-pointedness of mind.

When the Gurugyi judges that his meditator has gained sufficient concentrative power—this through conversations with him—he is then turned toward the next stage, *Paññā* or wisdom. This third and highest stage is not gained at once; there are many degrees of it, but the highest degree of this highest state is the kind of insight which finally produces enlightenment; it is such a knowledge of reality as destroys all desire, save for *Nibbāna,* and finally produces *Nibbāna* itself.

Many meditation masters take a long time to introduce their meditators to this stage, or better, to that kind of meditation which produces *Paññā,* namely, *Vipassanā* (*vee-pah'-sah-nah*); but U Ba Khin believes that, as soon as the meditator achieves a reasonable degree of one-pointedness, he should go on to *Vipassanā* meditation on the body, mindfulness of the changes in the body.

The starting point in *Vipassanā* meditation is to turn the now one-pointed attention to various parts of the body in order to discover its "true nature," i.e., that it is only a flux of split-second atomic-level combustions. This, the nature of all reality including the body, has been but recently "discovered" by science; but the Buddha, says the Buddhist, discovered this long ago by introspective attention, calling the smallest particles in the physical plane "*kalāpas.*" Of course one does not observe the individual atoms at play within himself, but he does directly experience, as in a laboratory, the atomic combustion en masse. By a dual consciousness of *heat* in the body, part feeling and part thought, though mostly the former, he experiences for himself that combustion of atoms or, to put it differently, the impermanent nature (*anicca*) (*ah-neé-chah*)[1] of that body. A little later, after this body-burning consciousness is established in the mind, one comes to include the mind itself in the impermanence-awareness realizing that his attention, thoughts, and awareness themselves come and go. This is the second great truth which one is to realize by *Vipassanā*, namely, *anattā* (*ahn-ah't-tah*), the non-entity of self. And as a final truth, inseparably bound up with *anicca* and *anattā*, there is *dukkha* (*doh'-khah*) or suffering awareness. Indeed, how can one resist *dukkha*-feeling when he feels the pulsing, burning awareness of his own body-mind! And how can he fail to be detached from it, in Nibbanic peace! . . . Such is the goal of *Vipassanā*.

To achieve this kind of meditation, we were instructed to begin with the breath-lip awareness and, when attention was fully gained there, to shift the focus to the fontanelle, which, as the coming-together point of the skull bones on the top of the head, is the "most sensitive point" in the human body. As a result of successful concentration here one begins to feel pricklings, stingings, itchings, or burnings. By widening his attention he is to "push" or "widen" this tingling area over the crown, then down the sides of the head, and finally down through the whole body. The goal is to gain such a body-awareness that a person can focus his attention on any one point in the body in such a way that separate physical sensation springs up there at will—evidenced by burning or prickling. As he grows in power to do this, he tries more and more to center his body-awareness in the heart-chest region, which is the core of man's psychophysical being, according to Buddhism, and the last refuge of those impurities he is now seeking to "destroy."

The burning, prickling feelings which come at this stage serve a double purpose: as already noted, they make the meditator vividly, personally aware of *anicca*, that great slayer of all conceit and I-ness; and second, the appreciation of *anicca* in relation to the burning sensation leads to the actual destruction of one's impurities, i.e., the bad results of evil deeds done in past lives. Therefore, as the tender of a refuse-burning operation, the meditator keeps poking the fire (by meditative attention on various parts of the body) until even the hard, wet, heavy lumps are burned. My head was apparently such; it never properly burned!

What were we expected to do in ten days' time? That depended upon us. By the fourth day we were told that we had sufficient one-pointedness of mind to pass on to the next stage. From there on we were only urged to keep on till perhaps some crisis was reached, i.e., the burning became almost unbearable; and by continued burning to consume the further impurities as far as possible. Presumably one *might* accomplish something here, once and for all, like Christian sanctification; for, according to Buddhist teaching, one may by meditation, even as a layman, achieve the Stream-Winner stage (*sotāpanna*), after which he will never be reborn again in subhuman planes of existence. Thereafter, meditation periods serve the purpose of washing away the impurities which collect in one because of his contact with unholy men and mundane affairs; but the Great Divide has been crossed. However, no such actual statement was made about any of us.

IV

A brief summary of my actual experiences during the ten days will now be attempted, with accompanying interpretations given them by the Gurugyi. But first a word needs be said about my personal approach to the discipline, and ensuing complications.

A basic question which I confronted from the very beginning was that of personal perspective. In what way should I approach the meditative practice? To some extent I felt that I had been pushed into the experiment by the constant insistence: "Don't try to understand or talk *about* our Buddhism until you have practiced it. Then you won't need to ask some of your questions; they will either be answered or seem unimportant." Further: Should I think of it merely as a cold-blooded experiment in religious research for the sake of future writing? This would violate the basic requirement of "sincerity" of search for Nibbanic peace on the part of the candidate. For, while Buddhism reiterates that it cordially invites investigation, it does not consider that mere casual experiment brings any notable results. One must be at least precommitted to a serious personal effort. Yet, to be honest, I did not feel myself to be precisely a desolate, storm-tossed soul desperately seeking light, come to meditation as a last resort.

The compromise attitude which I tried to maintain consistently throughout the course was that of seeking to penetrate the Buddhist meditation experience from the "inside," both to achieve understanding of it and to see whether it offered me anything personally. I was interested to see whether it seemed to be a spiritual methodology which could be adapted in the West without benefit of specific Buddhist beliefs and commitments. To this extent I tried steadily and "religiously" to follow the Gurugyi's directions, to carry them out in the Buddhist manner as nearly as possible, without directly translating them into Christian experiential terms or equivalents. It may be that the consequent lack of a completely single-minded spiritual quest limited my success; at several points I was strongly tempted to declare the whole business impossible on these terms and found that my feelings about the experience fluctuated considerably.

A further difficulty was that of conflicting viewpoints and terms. Here was a visceral approach, characteristic of the East, in which the best knowledge is in part feeling; decisions intuitional rather than logical; and truth to be approached experientially rather than intellectually. But I came as a Western, cerebral man. Hence it was that throughout the ten days, sometimes more and sometimes less, I found myself struggling with interpretations both of the method and of my experiences rather than experiencing simply and instinc-

tively. Even in the midst of meditation when I was supposedly feeling-knowing the burning flux of *anicca* in my own body, I found my attention wandering to questions about the meaning of *anicca*, whether this experience really proved its truth, whether it were a mere conditioned sensation, and so forth.

I could not help realizing what a world apart the Gurugyi and I were in conceptual terms, whenever he gave his lectures or interpreted my experience to me in his counseling. *He* spoke of casting out the evil spirits of Chinese devil-gods and Hindu deities by the power of the realization of *anicca;* of the storage of one's past good deeds or evil deeds in some one of the thirty-one planes of existence, and of possible rebirth there; of sensing "atomic combustion" in the burning sensations in one's body; of localizing one's bad kamma in some part of his body and there burning it up by focalized meditation. *I* thought in terms of neuroses, psychoses, split personalities, and psychosomatic tensions. The thirty-one planes were not a reality to me, or rebirth into one of them. Though I experienced lights and burnings (see below), to me they were not direct experiences of atomic combustion or absolute proof of *anicca-anattā-dukkha*. I always had need of the Gurugyi to tell me *what* my experience signified; and it seemed that I must needs tack the label *"anicca"* rather artificially on certain feelings rather than finding its realization immediately therein.

V

The experience itself I will deal with in terms of four periods by first describing each stage and then giving its interpretation by the Gurugyi, U Ba Khin.

First Period: three and one-half days. The first day or two was a time of acute physical discomfort in which I sought to find the proper position. Likewise there was great difficulty in holding the attention closely to the breath-lip focus. External noises in particular (bird calls, bells, coughs, voices) troubled me. Gradually they receded into the far-off background; if not actually unheard, they ceased to be distractive. Questions about the meaning of the method and my experience continually disturbed my concentration, however.

And there were various specific occurrences. In the afternoon of the second day I had, for some minutes, a strongly felt sense of being above and beyond the stream of breaths, thoughts, and bodily pulsings going on within "me." There was a delightful sense of detached freedom, a sense of living only in the "here-nowness" of those moments, without past or future. Likewise—one of the most interesting features of the whole meditation period— there gradually came a new sense of the relativity of time. Time seemed to be infinitely spacious; a moment lasted forever, and three hours was an infinity—yet strangely it passed quite rapidly too. Only when I was quite tired, as at night, or for some reason could not concentrate, did time seem to drag.

There were physical sensations as well. During the latter half of the second day there appeared a sensation which continued off and on throughout the ten days, though less in the latter few. This was the sensation of a flashing light, pulsing at the rate of 2 or 3 to the second. It was rather like continuous "heat lightning" on the horizon—a general flickering illumination rather than one bright spot. At first the intervals were short—up to four or five seconds in duration, and appearing on the right side. Later on the light came from the left and then all over my eye range as well. This occurred with my eyes fully but not tightly closed. It usually stopped, momentarily at least, if I opened them, though sometimes a slight eye-twitching sensation remained. At other times there were not discernible eye-twitchings at all.

The other sensation was that of a distinctly marked off area of physical awareness around the nose. It was not on the upper lip in orthodox position, but like a set of parentheses it inclosed the end of my nose, extending roughly from the bridge area to the upper lip on either side. In moments of success I was aware of only this area in which breathing was going on; it was the total content of my consciousness.

Interpretation.—The Gurugyi said that though one concentrates on the upper lip, just beneath the nostril, different people experience varying areas of awareness. Such awareness is a sign of some success in achieving *samādhi*, or one-pointedness of mind. Likewise the flickering light which I saw was the result of a mind which was perfectly controlled and evenly balanced for at least the moment. But undue attention must not be given to lights, even though they are signs of progress, for they will divert one from his true focal center.

Second Period: one and one-half days.— During this period we were introduced to *Vipassanā* meditation. The initial period began with instruction as to the purpose of *Vipassanā* (see above) and a dedication to seek Nirvanic peace within. It was carried on for four and one-half hours, with the Gurugyi sometimes comediting with us.

The attempt to begin with the fontanelle area in the head was not very successful in my case. Only a few times was I able to arouse minor pricklings in my scalp area; only once or twice to stroke them down (by attention) to the rest of the body. More successful was my concentration on the feet, which came to feel glowingly warm after a few minutes of steady concentration on them. Later on I was able to extend this sense of glowing warmth up to the chest area, though this usually resulted in a stuporous, near-sleep sense. At this point I would change the area of concentration.

These symptoms came to be more or less under my control during the next day or two. Several times I found myself, after a preliminary period of half an hour, being able to "move" the sense of glowing warmth or sometimes prickling, up and down the body almost at will, even up to the face, though the head on the whole remained refractory. Sometimes the warmth seemed to be a kind of total awareness of an area from the inside of the arches of the feet clear up to the nasal region all along the "front" of my body.

It should be noted that this sense of warmth did not seem to result in heating of the skin. When I put my finger on a "glowing" part, the finger was the warmer of the two. This was always the case, though once or twice later I broke into a sweat.

On the fifth day I was able to induce a sense of pressure, similar to that produced by a pencil pressing, eraser-end down, on the crown of my head at a specific point. It was slightly painful, surrounded by some mild pricklings, and lasting for fifteen minutes or so. My sense of terminological conflict still continued.

Interpretation.—The warmth I felt was not physical, said Gurugyi, but was insight-knowledge of atomic flux en masse. Thus I was having direct personal experience of impermanence in myself as a small part of the total flux of nature. This sense of impermanence was the great liberating truth discovered by the Buddha in his meditation.

Attention is not to be given *primarily* to the burnings and prickling themselves; they only serve to locate the attention and indicate success. It must rather be given to *anicca* (impermanence) made evident in the burnings. Imaginary burnings need not be worried about, for the real sort spreads and remains unmistakably. A question about their being "mere" physical effects was discounted.

Third Period: sixth day.—The mood of this day was different from those before, though the instructions had not much changed. (We were to continue concentrating on body-awareness, trying to center it increasingly in the chest area; likewise to keep in mind that even awareness itself is impermanent. We must not fear or restrain the burning, for burning indicates purification.) The better mood came because I had finally shelved the vocabulary conflict, or at least de-emotionalized it. I would forget terminological differences and

keep my attention on the business at hand.

In the morning of the day, I had a passing, but distinct, impression for some minutes of a kind of repulsiveness about the throbbing, pulsing, grasping kind of awareness which makes up ordinary consciousness and life-interest; and of the attractiveness of a pure, cool, impersonal consciousness above and beyond it.

In the afternoon of this day I experienced a kind of climax or crisis-experience (with a somewhat similar though different experience on the ninth day). I had centered my concentration on the chest area, from which sensations of glowing warmth spread all the way down the inside of the legs to the arch of each foot—though the outer edge of the foot remained distinctly cool.

After 45 minutes or so I changed to the deck chair. At first I felt the coolness of the air on my back, in contrast to the warmth of my "front"; but soon the sense of glowing warmth spread through the whole thoracic area from front to back. Concomitantly there came the need to breathe deeply and rapidly, as though gasping for air. After a time the heavy breathing and sense of warmth gradually subsided, leaving behind it a sense of quietness and "cleanness."

During the experience itself there was a tremendous sense of importance or significance about it, perhaps also something of a kind of impersonal consciousness breaking through the ordinary self-awareness. But later in the afternoon, indeed within a half-hour, though the memory of the experience remained, it was impossible to feel its importance. Its quality of significance seemed utterly unreal, the experience itself almost trivial.

Explanation.—The Gurugyi did not seem to find this experience as climactic as I had. However, it did seem to him evidence that my impurities were being burned away by the inward realization of *anicca;* and that the burning was centered in the chest-heart area was an encouraging sign. He predicted that as impurity-burning went on, the warmth in various parts of the body would become less in degree. Likewise, since I reported that the flashing-light phenomenon still continued to some extent, he counseled me to open my eyes or get up and change position to dissipate it. That represented the *samādhi* stage and would *now* only distract me.

Final Period: four days.—During this period our attention was to be directed still to the task of burning out our impurities, through body awareness, with increasing attention given to the flux of mind-states also. Finding these directions somewhat vague, I concentrated on various parts of my body, with more and more attention to the chest area. Increasingly during these days I was able to do this, with some help from the heart throb.

There was still a continuing sense of body glow subsequent to concentration on a particular part of the body, especially the feet and legs; but, as predicted, this tended to lessen. In general, there was a greater sense of relaxation and peace.

On the afternoon of the ninth day there was a variant of the experience of the sixth day. It made itself felt as a sense of almost suffocation, or at least the almost involuntary progression into deep and rapid breathing at perhaps twice the ordinary rate. This continued for fifteen or twenty minutes. The pulse beat seemed normal, however. Along with the heavy breathing went a sensation of rhythmic swaying to the left (and back) and a slight dizziness, particularly when I held my breath for a half-minute or so. There was also an accompanying sense of vibrations in the chest area, at the rate of three or four per pulse beat.

Gradually the symptoms subsided, perhaps helped out by some deliberate effort to reduce them. Again, as on the sixth day, at the height of the experience it seemed significant, this time as a mood of overflowing benevolence or love to all persons. But again, as before, the whole mood and "reality" of the experience seemed unreal a half-hour later.

The rest of the period was anticlimactic, being interrupted by some other events on the final afternoon; and on the last evening I had such fatigue-twitchings in my legs (for the first time) that I was scarcely able to sit still. In general, however, and particularly in the early morning session just before we left on the eleventh day, there was a pervasive sense of peace and relaxation.

Interpretation.—For various reasons my opportunity to talk to Gurugyi was limited toward the end of the course. He said that the continuing sense of body-glow indicated the continuing burning of impurities. Perhaps my feet tended to remain warmest because impurities often flow out through the feet. It was generally encouraging that I was able to concentrate my attention primarily in the heart-chest area, that center of man's life for both good and ill.

VI

The final evaluation of this experience is difficult except in terms closely related to my own personal viewpoint; therefore perhaps the result is not universally valid with regard either to Buddhist meditation in general or to Westerners who attempt it in particular.

With regard to the psychosomatic therapy which goes on at the center, there is no doubt. One of our party with a catarrhal sniff was not, indeed, cured, as had been hoped. But we did actually talk to a Hindu who, because of a blood pressure of 240 and a serious heart condition (showed by an X-ray), had been given only three months to live five years ago. A meditation course at that time had cured him, and today he is in vigorous good health, permanently grateful to the Gurugyi who "pulled me out of the grave." (He is now an expert in jhanic trances, up to five hours in length.) Nor have I any reason to doubt the reality of other reported cures of asthma, chronic migraine headaches, spasmodic tremblings, a jaw twisted out of shape by muscular tensions, and so on. However important and impressive these cures seem, they are considered to be only by-products of the main business of meditation.

In this same connection it might be said that the East, whatever its terms—devil-possession or impurities—appreciates the fact of the psychic nature of many ills better than the West. It may seem to the West that the East *over*appreciates the psychic, in fact, and too generally excludes the physical aspect of illness and physical means for its cure. Yet there is no doubt that meditation as practiced in the East is able to release much inner tension, perhaps even for the Westerner.

The parallels between Buddhist and Christian religious experience, particularly Christian mystic experience, are interesting. The Christian mystics too, perhaps having learned it originally from the East, emphasize a one-pointedness of mind as essential to genuine religious insight—though with them such insight implies direct knowledge of Deity, rather than *anicca* and *Nibbāna*. So likewise the Buddhist emphasis upon "emptying" the self of its illusory pretensions to permanence and importance and using the resulting sense of impermanence to burn away impurities and stand alone before the unconditioned peace of *Nibbāna*, may find its analogue in the Christian war against the self and the Christian mystic's effort to penetrate beyond the namable, or conditioned, aspects of God into the unconditioned Godhead. The "old man" equals the "deluded self"; and the Christian "new man" is not unlike the one who is nearing "enlightenment" or the knowledge of "things as they are." And the resulting sense of "calm and cool," i.e., experience of Nibbanic peace in this life, is comparable to a Christian's "deadness" to the world and self-will. My wife especially felt this sense of experiential similarity which goes much deeper than differing terminologies.

This leads me to a suggestion which the Buddhist apologetic would find unwelcome, but which seems at least partially valid to me. Should not the great trio of concepts, *anicca-anattā-dukkha* (impermanence, nonentity of self, dissatisfaction) be taken *experientially* rather than conceptually? Is not this their *main* significance? For *dukkha* this is indeed natural, since it is experiential rather than conceptual. But may not *anicca* be considered as the conceptual extension of the feeling one gets from body-burning consciousness? and *anattā* an implication of the *fluctuating* and *dim* self-awareness present when consciousness is reduced to a barest minimum of content? So likewise *Nibbāna* is the ultimate projection of the calm, coolness which ensues upon such experiences; it is the delight of the voided mind living in sheer here-nowness. Is it not when these experiential elements are hypostatized and hardened into dogmas concerning the metaphysical nature of reality and the self that they become difficult of comprehension and acceptance by a non-Buddhist, and perhaps less than fully fruitful, religiously speaking, to the Buddhist himself?

Perhaps, however, this is a hen-egg situation: Can one have such an experience without such intellectual beliefs even though the center makes an implicit claim that it has a method which proves itself, regardless of one's faith or lack of it? Also, I was urged by Buddhist friends, as noted, to find in meditation answers to my intellectual questionings. And some Western converts to Buddhism see in meditation a completely neutral and "scientific" method of insight which can be transported meaningfully to the West.

It seems to me at this point that there are only two ways in which to make Buddhist meditation of maximum experiential value; and that both of these negate the presupposition that there is a neutral methodology which guarantees per se an experience of spiritual significance and brings to solution the intellectual difficulties attending Buddhist doctrine. One is to translate the Buddhist experience into the terms and emotional equivalents of one's *own* faith. (This my wife did and ironically was considered to have been more successful than I, who attempted such experience solely in terms of the method itself!) But then this is not precisely a Buddhist experience which results; nor even a neutral one.

On the other hand, one may approach meditation as a believing Buddhist to whom *anicca, anattā, dukkha, Nibbāna* are meaningful and feelingful terms. (For I became aware that the higher reaches of "knowledge" are for Buddhists a kind of *feeling*.) As realities already believed in, these terms become authentic and direct experiences of truth, when tied by the meditational method to certain sensations and feelings which the method is bound to produce. Because the doctrine is previously held true intellectually, it is certified by the ensuing experience achieved in its context.

This situation explains my personal difficulty. Not that it was profitless. Quite the contrary. Such aloneness with one's self, whatever realities there be, is always of immense value personally; the likeness to some Christian experience is genuine; and I gained some insight perhaps into the interior Buddhist experience. Yet I was caught between the two possibly successful approaches, incapable of either. The path of finding Christian equivalents as I went along, I tried to avoid as a genuine researcher in Buddhist method. Yet, not being a Buddhist intellectually, the *anicca-anattā-dukkha* methodology of spiritual purification was not natural to me; it never became an organic feeling-knowing experience for me as it does for the Buddhist. And certain psychophysical results, which the method almost automatically produces, did not therefore produce in me a deep feeling of religious reality. Hence, unless Westerners translate the Buddhist meditational technique into equivalent and meaningful terms in their own religious experience, or else become Buddhists, such a method is, at most, likely to produce a few psychosomatic effects, interesting in themselves and of instrumental value but of no great religious significance.

NOTE

1. The Buddhist order is *anicca-dukkha-anattā*, since it is considered that the realization that existence is suffering comes after that of impermanence but before the full realization of the insubstantiality of the self, the last and highest stage.

INDEX